KING SOLOMON
THE
MAGUS

"In this splendid compendium, Claude Lecouteux brings together stories, folktales, lore, and legends associated with the Biblical King Solomon. King of ancient Israel, he founded castles and cities as well as a palace of glass and his most famous Temple in Jerusalem. Solomon's legacy spread across the Middle East into Europe, Africa, and beyond. Reputed author of one thousand and five books of poems, psalms, and songs and three thousand parables, he also interacted with animals, whose languages he understood. Solomon was one of the great historical practitioners of magic. Solomon's seal and ring gave him power over various kinds of spirits. All his possessions—his net, his throne, and his chalice among them—were infused with magical power. Claude Lecouteux's masterly reconstruction of the wondrous world of King Solomon from ancient documents is by far the most comprehensive survey yet published of the many different aspects of this ancient and influential monarch."

NIGEL PENNICK, AUTHOR OF
THE ANCESTRAL POWER OF AMULETS, TALISMANS, AND MASCOTS AND *ELEMENTAL MAGIC*

"Lecouteux's in-depth study and presentation of the legend and importance of the image of King Solomon in the magical mythology fills an important role in our understanding of the history of the practice of magic in both Europe and Asia. Solomon was ascribed some of the most important magical grimoires and symbols and signs bearing his name that may be found from Arabia all the way into the realm of the Far North in Iceland."

STEPHEN E. FLOWERS, PH.D., AUTHOR OF
ICELANDIC MAGIC AND *ORIGINAL MAGIC*

KING SOLOMON
THE
MAGUS

Master of the Djinns and
Occult Traditions of East and West

CLAUDE LECOUTEUX

Translated by Jon E. Graham

Inner Traditions
Rochester, Vermont

Inner Traditions
One Park Street
Rochester, Vermont 05767
www.InnerTraditions.com

Originally published in French under the title *Histoire légendaire du roi Salomon*
by Éditions Imago, 7 rue Suger, 75006 Paris
First U.S. edition published in 2022 by Inner Traditions

Cataloging-in-Publication Data for this title is available from the Library of Congress

ISBN 978-1-64411-243-4 (print)
ISBN 978-1-64411-244-1 (ebook)

Printed and bound in India by Replika Press Pvt. Ltd.

10 9 8 7 6 5 4 3 2 1

Text design and layout by Debbie Glogover
This book was typeset in Garamond Premier Pro with American Brewery,
ITC Goudy Sans Std, Source Sans Pro and Gill Sans MT Pro used as display typefaces

Contents

PART TWO

THE MAGICIAN

PART THREE

SOLOMON
IN FOLKLORE

Acknowledgments

Thanks to Julien Véronèse (Orleans) for so kindly sending me his articles, and Ronald Grambo (Kongsvinger, Norway) who shared his observations about my manuscript, without which my research would not have been so fruitful. Emanuela Timotin (Bucharest) and Ion Talo (Cluj-Napoca) helped me discover the Romanian traditions concerning King Solomon; may they find here the expression of my gratitude. And I will not forget to thank my French publishers, Marie-Jeanne and Thierry Auzas.

The Legend of King Solomon

Few sovereigns have left such a deep imprint in legends and folktales as King Solomon. A historical figure who built the Temple of Jerusalem and founded cities and fortresses, the son of David was God's chosen prophet who had dominion over demons and owned many magical objects. This king, known for his wisdom, was the subject of a thousand stories and has found a place in the pantheon of men who left their mark on history. The Hebrews called him Schlomo; the Arabs, Sulayman; the Greeks and Romans, Salomo—a family name that carries the notion of peace for his reign, and he was, according to all the traditions, quite peaceful. His memory has traveled through the centuries and can be found among the Arabs and Persians, as well as in the work of the church father Origen. His name can also be found among the Bulgarians, the Byzantines, the Russians, the Ukranians, the Egyptian Copts, the Egyptians, and the Ethiopians.

The primary sources of his legend are the books of Kings of the Bible, as well as Flavius Josephus, the Qu'ran, and the Talmud. Over the course of time, these elements have been embellished, developed, and enriched with outside contributions, and, little by little, came together to form the history of a monarch whose notoriety is equaled only by that of Alexander the Great—both kings serving as model monarchs for rulers throughout history. Furthermore, we can find certain episodes from the

1

life of the Macedonian conqueror in the Solomonic history, for example, his descent to the bottom of the sea and his flight into the heavens.

The legend of the son of David has been the subject of countless studies, such as that of René Basset, who investigated the traces he left in Arabic literature, followed by the research of Pierre Saintyves. Eugène Hins collected the Ukrainian traditions; Lidia Shishmanova, those of Bulgaria; Vuk Stefanovic those of Serbia; and Isabel Florence Hapgood those of Russia. The echoes of his legend resound as far as Indonesia and Mongolia.

Novelists were also inspired by this figure. As examples, I can mention Henry Rider Haggard with *King Solomon's Mines* (1885), Romain Gary's *L'angoisse du roi Salomon* (*King Solomon,* 1979), and José Rodriguez Dos Santos's *A Chave de Salomäo* (*The Key of Solomon,* 2014).

Scriptwriters and producers followed on their heels: King Vidor offered us *Solomon and the Queen of Sheba* (1958), Jack Lee Thompson, *Quartermain and King Solomon's Mines* (1993), and Iranian filmmaker Shahriar Bahrani, *The Kingdom of Solomon* in 2009.

In turn, graphic novels took on this subject: Catherine Zarcate gave us *The Dream of Solomon,* Eric Heuvel and Martin Lodewijk, *King Solomon's Treasure,* and Vassaux and Facon, *The Pillars of Solomon* (1991).

Video games were also not immune to the appeal of this subject, and among them we have *Baphomet's Knights: The Guardians of the Temple* (2006) and *Hidden Expedition: The Crown of Solomon* (2014).

So just what could be the reason for this persistent infatuation with the son of David? Could it be his power over the genies and demons, referred to as djinns, divs, and peri,* thanks to a ring the angel Gabriel gave him? This object is at the heart of his legend; it is what gives this king a supernatural, or even what we could call a wizardly, power. It draws its power from the carving of a divine name in the shape of a pentalpha that forms the name of YAHVE. This ring is an emblem of elec-

---

*Djinn (*ğinn,* singular *ğinnī.*): A kind of spirit or demon from the Muslim tradition. In English, the word "genie" refers to the same being. Div: A demon from Persian beliefs that is often confused with a ghoul or genie. Peri: A female spirit of Persian mythology that corresponds to a European fairy.

tion justifying royal duties and provides a mediating role between the godhead and human beings. Without it, there would be no Solomonic gestures, no enslavement of the demons and genies, which the stories of Aladdin and the fisherman from *The Thousand and One Nights* bring onto the stage.

And that is not all! Ruling over the winds and the animals, understanding the language of the birds, and owning an assortment of marvelous objects and weapons, Solomon was regarded from very early on as a magician responsible for a vast array of magic works.[1] A number of scholars in the medieval West, for example, Michael Scott and Roger Bacon, drew up a list of them. But today the *Clavicles* (the "little keys"), copies of which can easily be found in occult bookstores, still enjoy the widest renown.

Solomon's legend did not develop out of whole cloth; it is based on pre-Islamic beliefs and Indian and Persian tales. For example, today we know that the prototype for Solomon's throne is that of Vikramaditya, the mythical sovereign of Ujjain, India, who, like Solomon, was renowned for his wisdom.

We have barely inventoried everything that the son of David was able to accomplish. The number of buildings he constructed is impressive, and quite often these edifices became the support for new etiological legends to explain their components. Solomon, like Alexander the Great, was also an explorer who sprang into the heavens and descended to the bottom of the sea.

Folktales were engendered by his legend, not only in Europe, but in the Maghreb and Indonesia as well. Solomon's presence can be found as far away as Malaysia where, in the seventeenth century, Bukhari of Johore discovered several anecdotes about him.[2] In Ukraine, for example, several stories revolve around Solomon's mother, a mother who has no hesitation when it comes to trying to slay her son. Other tales illustrate the wisdom of the son of David but also his lust. These stories give us a kaleidoscope whose images enchant and astound us in turn and sometimes make us smile. The readers will judge for themselves.

This great king thereby appears not only as a historical figure, but also one of folk traditions, and his celebrity is not confined to the Bible,

Talmud, or Qu'ran. A figure who mirrors the dreams of humanity, Solomon has left a deep impression in our minds. The attempt to trace his story requires a great deal of work in sourcing the texts, scrutinizing them, and, most importantly, cross-checking all the accounts. We must gather all the widely scattered material together and learn to discern the variables and the constants, with the latter giving us the guiding thread to his legend. In short, we need to base our investigation on the clues in our possession.

My plan is to reconstruct his legend using the largest number of documents possible while classifying and, if necessary, annotating each of them. Each text is followed by its source, and if that is lacking, bibliographical references. I have also sought to enrich this study with illustrations from ancient books and manuscripts in order to show how our ancestors depicted those they looked upon as legends.

PART ONE

THE KING

ONE

The Source Texts

1. THE BIBLE

The first book of Kings in the Bible gives us some of the fundamental elements of the legend of Solomon, some of which also appear in the Qu'ran.

> Solomon's wisdom grew until it surpassed that of the ancients and of all the sages of Egypt. He wed the daughter of the Pharaoh and brought her to David's city while he completed building his palace and the Temple of the Lord first, and then the wall he erected to surround Jerusalem. He completed these buildings in seven years time, employing seventy thousand men to transport the materials and eighty thousand to cut the stone in the mountains. Solomon had the great basin known as the Brazen Sea and its supports made, as well as the large pools, the pillars, and the fountain of the forecourt.[1]

> Solomon was first to open the principalities of Lebanon; he built Tadmor (Palmyra) in the desert. The midday meal of Solomon (in his court) consisted of "thirty measures of flour, sixty measures of meal, ten fatted calves, twenty oxen from the pasture, one hundred sheep, and, in addition, deer, gazelles, roebucks, and the best fowl from the fields."[2] He was leader of all the land from Raphi to this side of the Euphrates, and of all the kings below the river, and peace ruled everywhere in his lands.

2. FLAVIUS JOSEPHUS

The historian Yosef ben Matityahu HaCohen, better known under the name of Flavius Josephus (37/38–100), devoted a lengthy text to Solomon from the time he acquired his wisdom to the preparatory work for building the Temple.[3] For more clarity, I have broken up the text with subheadings.

> After strengthening his grip on the throne and chastising his enemies, Solomon married the daughter of the Pharaoh, King of the Egyptians (Φαραώθου τοῦ τῶν Αἰγυπτίων βασιλέως), he built the walls of Jerusalem much larger and stronger than before and, thenceforward governed in an atmosphere of deep peace without his youth preventing him in any way from dealing justice, observing the laws, and remembering all his father on his deathbed had advised him to do. To the contrary, he discharged all his duties with perfectly precise judgment equal to that of aged men who have reached the full maturity of reason. He made the decision to go to Hebron and sacrifice to God on the bronze altar built there by Moses, and he offered a thousand burnt offerings. This act testified to his great reverence for God.

We shall skip over the story of Solomon's dream for the moment and revisit it later.

The Judgment of Solomon

During this time, a thorny problem was laid before him, one that he was hard pressed to solve. I deem it wise to explain the facts of the case so that readers may know how difficult it was, and when they find themselves in similar circumstances, they may be inspired by the king's example so that they may more easily judge the questions submitted to them. Two women, who were harlots by trade, came before him. One of them claiming to be the victim of an injustice spoke first: "I dwell, O king," she said, "in the same room as this woman, where it came to pass that we both gave birth on the same day to a male child. Two days later, this woman having smothered her child by lying atop him while she was sleeping, took mine from my breast and lay the corpse of her own child in my arms while I slumbered. In the morning when I wished to give the breast to my child, I did not find him anywhere. I saw that the corpse of her son was lying next to me, for I recognized him after a careful observation. I thereupon requested the return of my son and when I was unable to obtain him, I came to seek shelter of your protection, Lord. Because we were alone and she realized that there were none who could contradict her, she grew confident and denies this with all her force."

Once she had spoken, the king asked the other woman what she had to say in reply. The other woman denied that she had done what she was accused of and maintained that it was her child who lived and that it was the son of her adversary who was dead. Because no one there could offer a judgment and the entire court could not see the answer to this riddle, the king came up with an idea on his own. He had both the living and the dead child brought forth and ordered one of his personal guards to draw his sword and cut the bodies of the two children in half so each mother could have a half of the living child and a half of the dead one.

Hereupon all those gathered there laughed at the king under their breath for being such a child. But at the same time, the true mother of the living child cried out that he should not perform this deed but deliver the living child to the other woman as if it were truly hers. All she asked was that the child be allowed to live and that she be allowed to see it although the other woman was deemed to be its mother. The other woman, on the contrary, was fully ready to see the child cut in half and, moreover, desired to see her rival's torment. The king, realizing that the words of each woman had revealed their true feelings, ordered that the child be given to the one who had screamed as being the true mother and condemned the other as a wicked liar who, not content with the killing of her own child, wished to see the death of her companion's. The people saw this as a great demonstration and striking display of the king's wisdom and grandeur, and from this day, began to heed his words as if he were filled with the spirit of God.

The Table of Solomon

The king had other rulers who governed the land of the Syrians and the people of the foreign races that stretched from the Euphrates to Egypt, and they were charged with the duty of collecting taxes from these people. These rulers also made a daily contribution to the king's table and his meal of thirty cori* of fine flour and sixty of meal, as well as ten fatted oxen and twenty from the pastures, and one hundred fat lambs. In addition to these were the game taken by hunters, which is to say the harts and buffalos and the fowl and the fish, brought to the king every day by foreigners.

Solomon's Horses

Solomon had such a great number of chariots that forty thousand stalls were required for the horses that pulled them. Moreover, he had twelve thousand horsemen, half of whom were stationed near the king in Jerusalem, and the other half were scattered throughout the royal villages. The same official entrusted with the king's expenditures also provided for the horses' needs and saw that they went to wherever the king happened to be.†4

Solomon's Wisdom

The judgment and wisdom given to Solomon by God were so great that they outstripped those of the ancients and were comparable to those of the Egyptians, who were said to be the most intelligent in all the world, proving to be not only their equal but even superior to theirs. Solomon excelled and surpassed in wisdom those who were regarded most highly among the Hebrews for their shrewd insights, by whom I mean the sons of Hemaon: Athan(os), Herman(os), Chalcos, and Dardanos.

Solomon's Literary Works

Solomon also wrote one thousand and five books of poems and songs and three thousand books of parables and comparisons. He created a

---

*A cori is an Ancient Greek unit of volume that equals approximately 51.84 litres.

†His horses, stolen during an expedition against Damascus and Nisibis (Mesopotamia), were so fast that they left Persepolis (Persia) in the morning and reached Sana in the evening and reviewed the djinns in Rey.

parable about every tree, from the hyssop to the cedar, and also about the beasts of burden and all the animals of earth, water, and air. He overlooked nothing, indeed, of natural history, and left no area unexplored. He could expound on them all and showed a perfect knowledge of all their properties. God also granted Solomon the art of fighting demons for the benefit and health of men.

3. SOLOMON IN
THE THOUSAND AND ONE NIGHTS

The Thousand and One Nights reaped a vast harvest from the field of Arabic and Persian legends, so it comes as no surprise that the stories make some mention of Solomon. Here we see again the djinns, of course, as well as the power of the son of David's ring, his carpet, his magic mirror,*[5] his castles, his throne, his tomb, and even one of his proverbs.

In "The Tale of the Fisherman and the Djinn," the copper lamp imprisoning a genie has been sealed by Solomon's Seal. In "The Story of Aladdin" (Ala ed-Din), the marid† that appears to the hero "resembles one of those that appeared before Solomon," and in "The Story of the Peasant Abdullah and the Merman Abdullah," when the peasant sees the merman, he thinks "that he is one of the demons that Lord Solomon customarily imprisoned in copper vessels and cast into the sea."[6]

Solomon's table and other possessions fell into the hands of the Umayyad strategist Tariq ibn Ziyad (died 720):

> It was of emerald, or so it was said, and golden vessels and plates made of chrysolith [peridot] were placed upon it. There was also a Book of Psalms written in Greek letters on gold pages embellished with precious stones, a book made of gold and silver on the useful properties of plants and stones, minerals, talismans, and alchemy [. . .], a large and wondrous circular mirror made for Solomon from

---

*A Romanian tale presents Solomon as the inventor and seller of mirrors.
†A rebel genie.

a blend of metals, the son of David and whosoever that could, when looking into it, would see the seven climates of the world."[7]

The Caliph Harun al-Rashid owned this table.[8]

The Thousand and One Nights mentions a castle, guarded by apes, in which Solomon had the habit of staying once a year for amusement. In a different story, another castle is guarded by Sheik Nasr, the king of the birds, to whom Solomon had taught the language of the birds, establishing him as Master of the Birds.[9]

The "Story of the Slave Tawaddud" gives this riddle: "Name me a man reciting his prayer while neither on the earth or in the sky. It is Solomon praying on his carpet carried aloft by the wind."[10]

The "Story of Bulukiya and Affan" is told in its entirety in "The Story of the Serpent Queen," in which Solomon's carpet is kept in a room of a palace.[11]

"The Seventh Voyage of Sinbad" mentions the tomb of Solomon that is located beyond the land of the genies,[12] while the tale of the first voyage quotes this proverb by the son of David: "Three things are better than three other things: the day of one's death is better than the day of one's birth, a live dog is better than a dead lion, and the grave is better than poverty."[13]

In "The Story of the Mermaid Djullanar," King Shariman asks this woman: "How can you move through the water without getting wet?" She answers: "We travel in the the sea like you walk on solid ground, and this is thanks to the power of the magic names carved on Solomon's ring."[14] Three other passages from *The Thousand and One Nights* mention an incantation "by that which is carved on the ring of Solomon."[15] It is used, for example, to calm the anger of the person with whom one is speaking.

I would also like to note a comical detail, which is a metaphor used when speaking of a woman: "Her mouth looks like Solomon's Seal."[16]

Solomon and the Animals

While the previous chapter examined the main source texts, this chapter collects folktales from around the world to illustrate that King Solomon's special relationship with animals is central to his legend. Among the many clues that suggest Solomon possessed the features of a shaman, we should look at his privileged relationships with animals. He was the master of animals and understood their language. We will examine that which prompted me to form this hypothesis in Part Three.

1. THE SWALLOW AND THE SNAKE (CIRCASSIA)

Once a very, very long time ago, Solomon, the son of David, ruled over all things. This powerful king understood the language of mortals, the roaring of wild beasts in the forest, the cries of the four-legged beasts, the chirping of birds,* the buzzing of insects, and also what the trees of the deep forests and the tiny flowers of the paths were saying.

Solomon had assigned to every creature the food it needed to live; to some he gave the flesh of weaker animals, to others the grass of the fields or the fruit that ripened in the groves.

The son of David told the serpent: "You shall get your sustenance

---

*The language of the birds, *manṭiq al-ṭayr.*

from the blood of humans," and the snake, hidden in the brush, lay in wait for a man to pass on whom it would hurl itself to feed on his blood. The unfortunate humans grumbled so loudly that even the powerful monarch could hear it. Solomon asked the man: "What are you complaining about?"

"Lord, if the serpent lives on our blood, the human race will disappear!"

"Go, I shall think on your request," the son of David responded.

The great Solomon thought on the matter for a long time and then alerted all the animals of creation. He commanded them to gather in the center of an immense field. The lion, the tiger, the wolf, the horse, the elephant, the eagle, the vulture, and thousands of other animals came running at the king's command. "I have called you all together to hear your complaints. Speak."

The man walked up to the throne, bowed to the king, and said: "Lord, I ask that the snake choose the blood of another animal to be his food."

"And why is that?"

"Because I am the first of all beings."

The other animals began to grumble: some roared, others growled, yelped, barked, shrieked, or howled. "Silence!" Solomon ordered. "May the crane fly, the smallest of all animals, from this day seek to discover what blood is the most delectable in all of creation. Whatever blood that may be, even if it is that of humankind, I swear to give it to the serpent. On this day, one year hence, we shall gather here again to hear the crane fly's report."

The animals parted and over the next year the crane fly visited all of them to taste their blood. When the crane fly was returning to King Solomon's assembly, he met the swallow: "Hello, swallow," it said.

"Welcome to you, too, crane fly friend. Where are you flying so quickly?"

"The assembly of all the animals."

"That's right. I forgot the mission that our powerful sovereign charged you with. So, which blood was the most delicious?"

"It was the blood of humans."

"The blood of . . ."

"I said it was the blood of humans!" repeated the crane fly, who thought the bird had not heard him.

But this was nothing but a ruse. As soon as the crane fly opened its mouth to repeat what it had said, the swallow hurled itself on the insect and ripped out its tongue. The crane fly continued on its way, furious, still followed by the swallow, until they finally reached Solomon's assembly. "So," the son of David asked, "did you taste the blood of every animal?" The insect nodded to show that it had accomplished its mission. "Whose was the most delectable blood?" Solomon asked the fly. This was quite awkward for the crane fly, who had lost its ability to speak since the swallow had torn out its tongue. "Ksss! Ksss! Ksssss!" it said.

"What did you say?"

"Ksss! Ksss! Ksssss!" the crane fly repeated in desperation.

Solomon was quite discomfited when the swallow showed up in front of him.

"Lord," it said, "the crane fly suddenly became mute. But while traveling with it, it shared the results of its quest with me."

"Speak!" Solomon commanded.

"The frog is the animal whose blood has the most exquisite taste. That is what the crane fly told me. Isn't that true, crane fly friend?"

"Ksss! Ksss! Ksssss!" the insect muttered.

"Very well," said Solomon, "from this day hence, the snake shall feed on the blood of the frog. Humans shall live in peace." And the king gave leave to all the animals to depart.

The swallow always liked humans. And they never showed themselves ungrateful. Whenever they waged war fiercely with all the other birds, they granted the swallow a place at the threshold of their houses, and they viewed its presence in the home as a sign of good fortune.[1]

2. SOLOMON AND THE ANTS (ARABIA)

This legend echoes the eighteenth verse of the twenty-seventh surah of the Qu'ran. "The Ants" (An-Naml), which says:

When they came to the Valley of the Ants, an ant said: "O ants! Go into your homes lest Solomon and his troops crush you [beneath their feet] without realizing it."

While building one of his palaces, Solomon made a journey to Damascus in order to visit that city whose territory is irrigated by the four rivers that emerge from the earthly paradise. The djinn, on whose back he was making this journey, flew there in a straight line over the Valley of the Ants, which is surrounded by mountains so steep and precipices so sharp that no man before Solomon had ever been able to see it. The king was astounded when he saw beneath him a crowd of ants as large as wolves whose eyes and feet were green in color.

The queen of the ants, who, for her part, had never seen a human, was also gripped by a powerful emotion when she caught sight of Solomon, and she yelled to her subjects: "Return to your caves as quick as you can!" But God commanded her to gather all her people together to pay homage to Solomon, the lord of all the animals. When the king had come within three miles, he could hear the words of God as well as those of the queen. He descended and saw the valley completely covered with ants for as far as his eyes could see, and he said to the queen: "Why are you scared of me when you have so many troops that they could conquer the entire world?"

"I fear nothing but God," the queen replied, "for if any danger whatsoever threatens my subjects, at my first sign, seventy times as many as those you see gathered here will appear."

"Why did you order the ants to retreat when I was passing over this valley?"

"Because I was scared that they would follow you with their eyes and thereby end up forgetting their Creator for a moment."

"Have you no recommendation to make to me before I make my departure?"

"I shall give you but one piece of advice, which is to never allow your ring to come off your hand before you have said: 'In the name of God filled with mercy.'"

"Lord," shouted Solomon, "your empire is greater than mine!" and he took his leave of the queen of ants.[2]

3. THE KING OF THE ANTS (ARABIA)

One day when Solomon was passing through the countryside, he encountered the king of the ants, who he picked up and placed in his hand. The king shouted to his entire band: "Ants, move away lest the throne of the prophet king crush you!" After asking the ant many questions, Solomon asked him if he acknowledged his greatness. The ant king replied: "No, I am greater than you because you have only a material throne and your hand is my throne."[3]

4. SOLOMON AND THE GRIFFIN (BERBER)

One day our lord Solomon was arguing with the genies. He told them: "a girl has been born in Djabersa, and in Djaberka a boy.* This boy and girl are destined to meet." The griffin† told the genies, "Despite the will of the divine power, I will not allow them to get together." The son of the king of Djaberka came to Solomon's home, but scarcely had he arrived when he fell ill. The griffin abducted the daughter of the king of Djabersa and carried her off to a fig tree at the edge of the sea. The wind pushed the prince who had set sail, and he told his companions: "Bring me to shore." He went to this fig tree and lay down beneath it. The young girl cast leaves on him. He opened his eyes and she started speaking to him. "Except for the griffin, I am alone here with my mother. Where do you come from?"

"From Djaberka."

"Why," she went on, "didn't the Lord create other human beings besides me, my mother, and our lord Solomon?"

He answered her: "God has created every kind of human and country."

"Go," she told him. "Get a horse and bring it here. When you do, slit its throat. Also, bring enough camphor to dry the hide as you hang from the top of the mast."

---

*Djabersa and Djaberka are situated at the Eastern and Western ends of the earth.
†A griffin is a beast with the head and wings of an eagle and the body of a lion.

The griffin returned and the princess began weeping while she asked him: "Why don't you ever bring me to the home of our lord Solomon?"

"Tomorrow I shall take you there."

She told the king's son: "Hide yourself now inside the horse's hide." He hid himself as she instructed. The next day, the griffin picked her up along with the horse carcass and they left the place. When they came to the palace of King Solomon, the king spoke to the griffin: "I told you that the young woman and the young man would be brought together." Filled with shame, the griffin immediately fled to an island.[4]

5. SOLOMON AND THE HOOPOE (A)
(NORTH AFRICA)

It is said the hoopoe one day told Solomon: "I would like to invite you to be my guest."

"Only me?"

"No, you and your entire army, on this island and on this day."

Solomon made his way there with all his troops. The hoopoe picked up a grasshopper, strangled it, threw it into the sea, and said: "Eat, prophet of God, the person who does not have meat will partake of broth." This made Solomon laugh, which he and his army did for an entire year.[5]

6. SOLOMON AND THE HOOPOE (B)
(BERBER)

Consider the hoopoe: when its behavior is honest and its heart is pure, its piercing gaze can penetrate the very depths of the Earth and see what is concealed from the eyes of other creatures there. It can see the water that flows as you would be able to see it through a crystal and, guided by the excellence of its taste and its veracity, be able to say: "Here is fresh water and that there is bitter." The bird then went on to say: "I can boast of possessing in my small body that which Solomon has never owned, he to whom God granted a kingdom such as no one has ever seen. I am speaking of the science that God has assigned to me, a science that neither Solomon nor any of his people have been endowed. I followed this great monarch everywhere, whether he was walking slowly or hastened his step, and everywhere I pointed out to him those places where water lay underground. But one day I suddenly vanished and during my absence he lost his power. Addressing his courtiers and the people of his retinue, Solomon said: 'I do not see the hoopoe. Has he departed from me? If that is the case, I will cause him to suffer violent torment, and perhaps sacrifice him as vengeance, unless he gives me a legitimate excuse.' Then wishing the full extent of his authority to be felt, he repeated his words: 'I will punish him—no, I will slay him!' But fate told him: 'I will lead him to you and I will guide him myself.'

"When I next came out of Sheba, charged with a commission for this powerful king, I told him: 'I know of that which you know not.' This increased his wrath toward me, and he shouted out: 'You whose small body contains so much malice, not satisfied with arousing my anger and removing yourself far from my presence, now you claim to be wiser than me.' 'Mercy, O Solomon,' I replied. 'I acknowledge that you have asked for an empire such that no sovereign will ever again have its like, but you must also admit that you have not asked for a science that no one else can attain. I have brought you from Sheba news of which all the wise know nothing.'

"'O hoopoe,' he then responded, 'one may entrust the secrets of kings to someone who knows how to behave prudently, so carry my letter.' I hastened to do so and hastened to bring back the answer. He then heaped me with his favors, placed me in the ranks of those he called friends, and I took a place among the guardians of the curtain that covered his door whereas before I scarcely dared approach it. To honor me he then sat a crown upon my head, and this ornament goes far in embellishing me. After that, all mention of my execution was removed and verses that feature praise of me were read." [6]

7. THE BAT (ASIA MINOR)

Solomon, son of David, king of men and beasts, one day gathered together all the birds of the Earth. "Each one of you shall give me a feather," he ordered. "I am old, and I need a soft bed in which to rest my body that has been weakened by the weight of the years." All the birds of the sky, the eagle and the vulture, the mourning dove and the black-bird, the quail and the partridge, each brought him one feather. The bat said: "What good is one feather for the bed of the son of David?" It then tore off all its feathers and brought them to the sovereign. "May you be blessed above all others," Solomon declared. Then he gave it some thought and realized that in the centuries to come, the bat would be the laughingstock of all the other birds. The king told him: "Fly only at night, birds and men will not notice you in the darkness." It is since that time that the bat has been a night bird.[7]

8. THE VULTURE (SYRIA)

While Solomon was sitting on his enchanted throne that would take him wherever he wished, the sun burned his neck. He asked several vul-tures that were flying in his proximity to shade him with their wings, but they curtly refused. Instead, the hoopoes offered their services. Solomon cursed the willful vultures to have the feathers stripped from their necks and heads. He gave his thanks to the hoopoes to whom he extended his favor. The king of the hoopoes may well have asked for something for himself, but his wife convinced him to ask for golden crowns, and therefore since that time, the hoopoes' heads are crowned.[8]

9. THE WREN (GEORGIA)

All the birds gathered one day and petitioned Solomon with the request to choose one among them to be the tsar. He acquiesced and ordered them to come before him in the early morning. The first to arrive would be named tsar. In the morning Solomon arose and saw a miniscule bird appear. He thought it would be impossible to name this bird tsar of all the birds and told it: "Fetch me a staff that is neither straight nor curved." The wren set off in search of such an object and is still looking for it today, which is why people call it *gobe-mdzvrala*. Solomon chose the peacock to be tsar.[9]

10. THE DOLPHINS (EAST AFRICA)

In the beginning there were no dolphins. There came a time when the prophet Solomon, a powerful sovereign, ruled over all that lived on the earth: men, demons, animals, and winds. This power was housed in his ring. One day when Solomon was lost in thought, a demon stole his ring and wore it until one day it fell off into the sea. This is the reason that we now have dolphins. When God witnessed this theft, he sent the dolphins in search of this ring. They dove through the waves looking for it, but it had already been found again. They continue looking for it and will not stop until the Day of the Last Judgment.[10]

THREE

Solomon's Constructions

Tradition has attributed the paternity of many buildings to Solomon. One such, the Castle of Qaryah in central Arabia, was built from a single stone. Solomon built Sana'a, Ghomdan, and Silh'in for his wife, the queen of Yemen, as well as the castles Sirouah and Qachib for Bilquis, the Queen of Sheba, and the mosque of Persepolis (Istakhr).[1] He is also responsible for the construction of a labyrinth, a drawing of which can be found in a manuscript of the Saint Mark Library in Venice, as well as in another manuscript in the Ambrosian Library of Milan.[2] He had the walls of Jersualem built and he fortified Hezar, Megedden, Gazer, the two Bethorons, Balaat, and Palmyra.

On his orders, the djinn built the city of Lodda (Lyddus), Djairoun near Damascus, Tadmur (Palmyra), and Zanderward in Iraq. They dug a canal for him near Baghdad, but their most famous construction remains the Temple of Jerusalem, which I shall speak more about later.[3] Around 1325–1330 BCE, the great traveler Ibn Battuta spoke of a mosque in Hebron and added: "It is said that Solomon ordered genies to build this edifice."[4]

Wahb ibn Munabbih (654–730) expands the list of these works:

In Sakhr he ordered the construction of a glass city whose walls would not be able to conceal anything from him. The djinn built him one that was the length and width of the camp of Sulayman. In the city, he built a palace for each of the tribes that was a thousand ells in width and length. In these palaces there were dwelling places, houses, and galleries for the men and women, a thousand square ell meeting hall for scholars and judges, then, for Sulayman, a large and glorious palace that was five thousand square ells, which he covered with the widest variety of gems and glass.[5]

I would like to note in passing that this city and palace are oddly reminiscent of the island of the Crystal Castle that several Arab authors mention in the legend of Alexander the Great, as well as a Czech chapbook that has a wealth of exotic elements.[6]

Solomon was also responsible for the digging of the well in Linah in the Nedjed. Yaqut ibn Abdullah al-Rumi al-Hamawi also known as Yaqut al-Rumi (1179–1229), a Syrian encyclopedist and geographer, retells this legend:

After leaving Jerusalem to go to Yemen, Sulayman stopped in Linah, a beautiful land whose inhabitants were always thirsty due to the scarcity of water. A demon that was lingering by Sulayman's bedside began laughing. "Why are you laughing," the king asked him.

"I laugh at the sight of people who live above a huge expanse of water suffering from thirst."

Sulayman then gave orders for the djinn to strike the ground with their staffs until they reached the water.[7]

In 1547, Guilielmus of Pastrengo recorded that Solomon founded Asor and Baleth in Syria, Thermoth in the desert, and Palmyra and Mageddon.[8] There is even a tradition that claims the Alhambra in Granada was like Solomon's palace built of crystal and that it was supposed to have been built by genies on his orders.[9]

1. THE TEMPLE OF JERSUSALEM

The description of Solomon's Temple can be found in the first book of Kings (1 Kings 6–7) and in the second book of Chronicles (3–4), where it is said, "Never could the sound of hammers, picks, or any iron tool be heard in the temple during its construction." This was the launching pad for a legend that was presented in various forms.

On returning to Jerusalem, Solomon heard the terrible racket that the djinns were making with their hammers while working to build his temple. The din was so loud that none of the city's inhabitants were able to converse together. He ordered the genies to halt their task and asked them if any among them knew a means to shape metal without making so much noise. One of the djinns then told him: "There is no one except for the powerful Sakhr who knows this method. But up to now he has managed to avoid submitting to your authority."

"Is it impossible to make our way to him?" the king asked.

"Sakhr is stronger than all of us put together," the djinn replied, "and he exceeds us both in speed and vigor. I know that he comes every month to get a drink from a fountain located in the country of Hidjr;* perhaps you shall find a way, O wise King, to make him yield to your scepter."

Solomon ordered a band of djinns to remove all the water that was in the fountain and replace it with wine. He then told them to remain hidden nearby and watch what Sakhr did. Several weeks later, Solomon was on the terrace of his palace when he saw a djinn coming toward him faster than the wind. He had raced from the land of Hidjr and Solomon asked him if he bore any news about Sakhr. The djinn answered: "Sakhr is drunk and stretched out next to the fountain. We have bound him with chains that are as thick as the pillars of your temple, but he will break them as easily as if they were a single hair from the head of a young girl once he has slept off his wine."[10]

Solomon had the djinn transport him immediately to the fountain, which he reached in less than an hour. He arrived in the nick

*Hidjr, al-Hidjr now Madain Saleh, was an ancient Nabatean city including Petra in contemporary Jordan.

of time as Sakhr had just opened his eyes, but his hands and feet were still bound. This made it possible for Solomon to place his ring on the djinn's neck. Sakhr let out a shout that caused the entire land to shake, but Solomon told him: "Have no fear, powerful djinn. I will free you as soon as you have told me a way that the hardest metals can be pierced without making any noise."

"I have no idea about this thing you want," Sakhr replied, "but the crow can give you reliable advice about this. Take the eggs you find in a crow's nest and cover them with a crystal bowl. You will see what the mother does to pierce through the crystal."

Solomon followed Sakhr's advice. When it saw that it was unable to break or cut through the crystal slab, the bird flew away, then returned several hours carrying a stone that is called Samur in its beak. The crystal split in half as soon as this stone came into contact with it. "Where did you take this stone from?" Solomon asked the crow.

"From a mountain that is far in the west," the bird replied.

The king ordered several djinns to follow the crow and bring back several stones of the same kind. He then freed Sakhr just as he promised he would. The djinn let out a joyful shout that sounded to Solomon like a snicker. Once the djinns had returned with the Samur stones,* Solomon had them return him to Jerusalem. He then distributed the stones to the workers in the temple who from that time on could perform their work without making the slightest noise.[11]

The story of Sakhr is found in the *Kitab al-Mandal al-Sulaymani,* which was written for exorcists and physicians so they would be able to diagnose the type and origin of their patient's ills. There are a number of interesting variations of the tale in this book.

---

*The Samur, known as Shamir in the Jewish tradition, is, according to the stories, a green crystal or a worm.

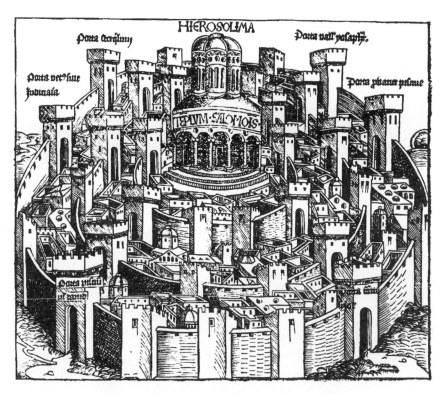

Fig. 2.1. The Temple of Solomon, an engraving from
Hartmann Schedel's *Liber chronicarum* (Nuremberg), 1493

2. TADMUR (PALMYRA)

Sulayman ibn Dawud (Solomon, son of David) loved a Nazraniyeh*
named Sitt Bilquis and married her. This Christian lady wished to have
a house between Damascus and Iraq where the desert air was good,
but it proved impossible to find a house matching this description.
Then Solomon, who was the king of the birds of the air as well as a
king of men, sent a request to the birds to tell him where this place
that Bilquis desired was located. All the birds came at his call, except
for a *nissr* (eagle) who did not come, and Solomon asked them if they
knew of a spot where the air was good between Damascus and Iraq.

---

*An Arabic term for a Christian woman, which literally means "woman from Nazareth."

They answered that no such place was known to any of them. Solomon counted them to make sure that all of them were there, and he noted the eagle's absence. So, he sent someone to fetch the eagle, and when he was brought before Solomon, the king asked him why he had disobeyed his first request. The *nissr* answered that he was taking care of his father, an old eagle who was so old that he had lost all his feathers and could no longer fly or feed himself when his son wasn't there. Solomon asked the *nissr* if he knew of the place that Bilquis needed. The *nissr* answered that his father should know its location because he knew all parts of the world having lived for four thousand years.

Solomon ordered that the *nissr's* father be brought before him in a cage as he could no longer fly. But when the attempt was made to transport the eagle, he was so heavy that no one was able to lift him. Then Solomon ordered the bird to rub an ointment all over his body so that he would become young again. This was done and feathers grew back on the bird's body as well as on his wings. The eagle could now fly to Solomon and alit in front of his throne. Solomon asked him the location of this place that Bilquis desired in the desert between Damascus and Iraq where the air was so good. The eagle replied, "That would be Tudmur,[12] the city that lies in the depths of the sands," and he told him its exact location. Solomon then commanded the djinns to remove the sand and once they had done this, Tudmur* lived again with its beautiful ruins and columns.

Yet the city's water had been imprisoned inside a cave that lay within the neighboring hills. It was captured by a serpent, twenty times as long as twice the length of a man's arm, who blocked the entrance of the cavern. Solomon commanded the serpent to leave, but the snake replied that he was scared. Solomon therefore promised not to slay him. But as soon as he had emerged halfway out of his cave, and they knew it was halfway because of a black mark that he bore on his body indicating half of his total length, Solomon placed his seal on the mark and the serpent died. The djinns then pulled the rest of the snake out of the cave so the water would flow. However, the venom of the serpent had

---

*According to ibn Khordabeh, Bilquis would have lived in Qachib.

poisoned it and the people could not drink it. Solomon then took some sulfur (*kubrit*) and tossed it into the cavern, and the water became fresh and good to drink. Sulfur can still be found in the water today.[13]

3. SOLOMON'S BATHS

Purification rites appear frequently in the Scriptures. For example, in Exodus 30:17–29, God asks Moses to manufacture a basin for ablutions.[14] In Jewish communities we find the *mikveh* (מקוה), a ritual bath, and the hammams of the Arabs are reminiscent of the Roman thermal baths.

> The heat that reigns in the Qala'ah of the Blessed Rachid, in the province of Oran, is caused by a hell created near this town by Solomon who imprisoned rebel djinns inside it. The high temperatures of the thermal waters of Hammam Emmesia in the same province come from baths built underground by the son of David and heated by deaf mute djinns. Because of their handicap, no one was able to inform them about Solomon's death, so they continue their work without any interruption.
>
> King Solomon, who was eminently wise and far-seeing, had steam baths built in every corner of the earthen globe we live on for the health and cleanliness of the human body. The only beings he placed there to serve as servants to heat the water, bathe the guests, and serve as bath boys, were genies. But in order that these employees could neither hear nor repeat what was said and done in these countless establishments of hygiene, he saw to it that these genies were blind, deaf, and dumb. Why did he take this precaution? It was most likely due to the fact that things occurred in the baths of King Solomon that should remain eternally enshrouded in mystery. Discretion was obviously one of this sovereign's virtues! But Solomon died one day, just like any common mortal, and when attempts were made to communicate to these bath boys that their master was no longer in this world, they were unsuccessful. Consequently, the disabled genies continued to heat the baths as if nothing had happened,

Fig. 2.2. Arab baths of Granada

and even now, at the present hour, they continue to heat it with their customary enthusiasm. This is why in certain parts of Algeria we find hot water springs where those who have not been initiated into their secrets cannot understand what keeps them heated this way.[15]

Kaschefi Hassan ben Ali, also known as Waez-el-Heraoui, a native of Herat, mentions the baths of Tiberias that were created by Solomon. There were twelve springs, each of which possessed a healing virtue. Another etiological legend is told about the Bath of the Cursed: the sacrilegious and robbers were swallowed up by this pool and transformed into sulfurous blocks that were displayed on the top of the Hammam Meskoutine.

Additionally, Jerusalem had a pool of five porticos[16] near the Temple gate that bore the name "Sheep Gate." An anonymous pilgrim from Bordeaux who visited the city in 333–334 reported that its water was a reddish color and that it was also the site of the crypt where Solomon tortured demons:

In Jerusalem there are two large pools in the side of the temple, one to the right and one to the left, that were built by King Solomon. A little further into the city, there were twin pools with five porticos that are named Bethesda in which people who have been suffering from long lasting illnesses are cured. These pools hold water that turns red when it is disturbed. There is also a crypt in which he tortured demons.[17]

4. THE CITY OF COPPER OR BRASS

Told by numerous authors, Masudi (died 956) and Yaqut (1179–1229) for example, the story of the mysterious city of copper or brass has many variants. In his *History of Kings and Peoples*, Tabari (838–923) tells us:

Solomon gathered peris and ifrits* together, as well as men, and asked them to build him a monument from molten brass[18] that would endure until Judgment Day. They deliberated together and all came to the same conclusion. They advised Solomon: "With this molten brass we must build you a great city that will be twelve miles long by twelve miles wide. This brass must be carried to the place chosen in an area where men never pass, for otherwise they will employ ruse and cunning to destroy the construction. This city must be made into the storehouse for all the treasures and books that you have in your possession."

It is said that there is a city named Andalus beyond a vast desert whose beginning and end is known to no creature. Men never go by this place and no creature ever reaches it. Solomon commanded the ifrits to transport the fountain of molten brass to a place twenty days' journey beyond Andalus. In this place they built a vast city. The ifrits made an underground gate to it, and they crafted a talisman to prevent anyone from finding the road that led there. There were no humans who could go to this place because in this desert there was no food nor drink, no water nor grass, and no one knew where the city was located.

---

*Ifrits are djinns who rebelled against Solomon.

Tabari next gave an abridged version of the Solomonic legend (chapter 13, 45–48), a legend that was much more explicit in the work of Abu Hamid al Gharnati (1168–1080):

> Tale of the City of Copper, built by the djinns for Solomon, son of David in the deserts of Al-Andalus in the Maghreb al-Aqsa, not far from the Sea of Darkness (Bahr al-zulumat).
>
> Lahqal ibn Ziyad says that Abd al-Malik heard the story told of the City of Copper that was located in el-Andalus. He wrote to his governor in Maghreb: "I have learned the story of the City of Copper constructed by the djinns for Solomon, son of David. Go see it and describe for me its wonders so that you will have seen with your own eyes. Reply to me quickly if God so wills it." When the governor of Maghreb received Abd al-Malik's letter, he set off with a huge army and a substantial amount of equipment and foodstuffs—enough for some time—and guides able to lead them to this city. Musa ibn Nusayr pursued a most uncommon route for forty days until coming upon a vast land with lots of water, springs, trees, wild animals, birds, herbs, and flowers. The wall of the City of Copper looked to them like something that had not been crafted by human hands. It frightened them. Then the emir Musa ibn Nusayr divided his army into two parts and installed them at each side of the city wall. They sent a general leading one thousand horsemen to travel around the city in search of a gate to see if they might encounter any living soul.
>
> The general left and was gone for six days. On the seventh day, he returned with his men and reported that it had taken him six days to complete the circuit around the city without seeing another living soul or finding even the smallest gate. Musa ibn Nusayr then said: "What should we do to learn what is inside this city?" The engineers (*muhandisun*) replied: "Give the order to dig beneath the foundations, perhaps you will be able to enter into the city." So, they dug beneath the foundation of the city wall until they reached a layer of water. The copper foundations were buried so deeply that the excavators were stopped by the water. They then realized that they would never be able to get through the foundations. The engineers

then suggested to the emir: "Have a building erected near one of the corner towers that will allow us to overlook the city." He gave the order, and they began to cut stones and prepare plaster and quick-lime. Next to the corner tower they raised a building that was three hundred cubits tall, until they reached the point where they could no longer add another single stone nor any plaster or quicklime. They were still short by two hundred cubits.

Musa ibn Nusayr then ordered them to build with wood and add it to the existing stone construction. By this method, they were able to add another one hundred seventy cubits. Then Musa ibn Nusayr summoned a herald to announce to the men: "I shall reward any-one who can climb to the top of the city wall with his blood money price." Immediately, a valiant soldier stepped forward from his fel-lows and claimed the reward. The emir ordered it to be given to him. He took it and left it with Musa to hold it, telling him: "If I come through this alive, I will take this as my wages, but if I die, it shall go to my heirs as inheritance." He then climbed up to the top of the city wall, and once he could see what was on the other side, he began to laugh, clapped his hands, and jumped down into the city. An immense din arose punctuated by terrible screams. This terri-fied them all greatly. These screams lasted for three days and three nights before stopping. The emir's men called to their companion but got no response.

Once they had lost all hope, Musa summoned another herald to announce: "The emir will bestow one thousand dinars to whoever climbs to the top of the wall." Another bold man stepped forward at once and said: "I will climb to the top." The emir ordered that he be given his one thousand dinars at once. He took them and made the same arrangements as his predecessor. The emir gave him this advice: "Don't do what your companion did, tell us what you see and do not go down to the others and abandon your compan-ions." He promised his companions that he would do just that, but when he reached the top of the wall, he started to laugh and clap his hands, then jumped to the other side. The entire army began yelling at him: "Don't do it!" But he didn't listen and vanished. Again, they heard terrible screams that were even louder than the first time and they feared for their very lives.

Musa ibn Nusayr then said: "If we leave here without learning anything of this city, what can I write in response to the prince of the faithful?" He went on to say: "Whoever will climb to the top, I shall give him two times his value in blood money." A third man stepped up and said: "I'll climb up but tie a sturdy rope around my waist and hold the other end. If I try to leap to the other side, you can stop me." They did just this; the man then scaled the wall to the top and once he got there began laughing and clapping his hands. He then began to hurl himself into the city. They hung on to the rope, but the man pulled so hard in the other direction that it tore his body in two. The lower half of his thighs and legs fell on one side and the other half fell into the depths of the city. The screams and racket doubled in intensity from the previous times.

The emir despaired of ever learning anything more about this city and told his men that it must be the abode of djinns who captured all those who tried to climb down to it from the wall. He then gave the order for his army to depart.[19]

In *Seif el-Tidjan* (*Sword of the Crowns*),[20] an Arab romance, this city had a triple enceinte formed by three crenelated marble walls. Each crenellation held a large talismanic figure with two eyes and ears equipped with little bells. There was no gate into this city. The first warrior climbed to the top of the wall with the aid of a ladder, clapped his hands, burst out laughing, looked back at his companions, then threw himself inside the walls. Several others did likewise and perished.

Banner of the State summoned one of his henchmen, had ropes bound around his body, and then told him to scale the wall. As soon as the man reached the top, he looked back, clapped his hands, burst out laughing, and made ready to leap headlong into the city. They then pulled on the ropes that bound him, and he fell outside, with his head lopped from his body. No one could doubt anymore that the place was inhabited by djinns. . . .

Why did this city draw these men into its midst and cause them to laugh fatally? Thanks to other authors, we have learned the origin of this laughter and the cause of the disappearances of the soldiers sent to explore the city. In his *Abridgement of the Book of Countries,* the tenth century historian and geographer Ibn al-Faqih al Hamadani, mentions the city of Baht (Madinat al-Baht) that stands in a desert and remains inaccessible because a river of sand bars all passage. It only stops flowing on Saturdays.[21] It so happens that the *baht* or *bahit* is a stone that causes laughter and draws men to it. In a lapidary attributed to Aristotle, this stone is called "elbehecte." It has the color of golden marcasite and is found in a place never touched by daylight (*ubi nunquam est dies*). It attracts flesh "like a magnet and it is said that a man subject to that attraction will start to laugh." In his *Chronicle,* Sheik Shams al-Din al-Ansari al-Dimashqi (1256–1327) describes this mineral as follows: "Whoever comes close to it will feel drawn by a force of love and enchantment; when coming close to it, he will become attached to the stone and remain ceaselessly joyful and happy until he dies." He places this gem in the Mountains of the Moon, behind the sources of the Nile.[22] The legend of the City of Brass is similarly given new life by the author of *The Thousand and One Nights.*[23]

The legend of this city whose stones provoke lethal laughter has its echo in the West. Around 1290, the Viennese physician Heinrich von Neustadt claimed that the city was located on an island and that it had a sparkling polished wall around it with no gates or windows. A sailor leaped to the parapet from the top of a mast. He burst out laughing and vanished. A second sailor clapped his hands, laughed, and hurled himself down on the other side of the wall. Ten others did the same thing. An eleventh sailor had a rope tied around his waist, and when he tried to leap from the wall into the city, he was pulled back despite his screams and wails of sorrow. Once he was back on the boat, he was blind and mute and soon died. Witnesses say that this island must be some kind of paradise ("*das mag wol sein ein paradeiz*").[24]

This last sentence opens some new perspectives on the development of the legend of the City of Brass. The great Persian writer Nezami or

Gandjavi (ca. 1140–1209) connects the legend of the laughter-causing stone to Alexander the Great and an earthly paradise:

> After crossing through a large sandy desert, Alexander reached the ocean at the very edge of the world—the place where the sun sets. Wise men advised strongly against sailing it because of its many perils. He entered a desert full of shining stones that caused an irresistible fatal laughter. His men gathered them up wearing blindfolds. When he reached an oasis, Alexander built a castle with these stones. Nizami notes that many travelers have perished there. When they scale the wall after not finding a door that leads into the city, the stone slays them.
>
> After a six-month journey in the desert, Alexander decided he wished to see the sources of the Nile. He came upon a steep, green mountain, the color of glass.* None of the men he sent to scout its summit returned. Finally, he designated a man and his son to attempt the task. The first would scale the mountain and write what he saw on a note, then toss it to his son. The boy returned alone with the note that described a veritable paradise with gardens, fountains, and roses. The father ended his note saying: "Who would have the courage to tear himself away from heaven to go back into the desert? I am staying here."[25]

An oddity of legends and their transmission, we also find the principal motifs of the legend of the City of Brass in a letter from the Archbishop of Novogorod, Vasili (1331–1352), to the Archbishop of Tver:

> Moiszlav of Novogorod and his son Jacob found paradise. They set off with three boats, but one sank and the other two eventually landed by some tall mountains. On one mountain they saw Deesis—the Redeemer between Mary and Joseph—haloed in light [. . .] On the mountain they heard shouts of joy and playful voices.

---

*A reference to mythic glass mountains whose green color symbolized the other world.

They ordered one of their companions to climb up to see where this light and these voices were coming from. Once on the mountain, the man began clapping his hands and started to laugh; he then headed in the direction of the voices. Stupefied, they ordered a second man to climb up and come back to tell them what he saw on the top of the mountain. But their companion did the same as the first man. He raced away and did not come back. Gripped by fright, they sent a third man with a rope tied around his ankle. He, too, began clapping his hands and forgetting that he was tied, tried to flee, but they held him tight, and he fell to the ground dead. They quickly departed and never again had the opportunity to set eyes upon such a wonder (Deesis) and hear such shouts of joy.[26]

We can see that the legend of the City of Copper or Brass, or Baht, was extremely widespread in the Arabic countries such that an encyclopedist (Qazwini), a geographer (Ibn al-Faqih), and a historian (Mas'udi, *The Meadows of Gold*) were among those who passed it on. In the medieval West, the manuscripts of Leyden and Montpellier (Latin) and Munich (Hebrew) offer confirmation of a stone that attracts, causes laughter, and kills. The legend was attached to Alexander the Great and the Mountains of the Moon where the Nile originates (Nezami), then an island (Heinrich von Neustadt), and eventually crops up again in one of Vasili's letters.

Fig. 4.1. The Dream of Solomon, son of King David,
together with the interpretation of the dreams of the prophet Daniel:
recollected with extraordinary precision, whole and without error.

FOUR

The Judgments
of Solomon

1. HOW HE ACQUIRED HIS WISDOM

In 1 Kings 3:1-15[1], Solomon speaks with God in a dream:

And the king went to Gibeon to sacrifice there. . . . In Gibeon the
Lord appeared to Solomon in a dream by night and God said, "Ask
what I shall give thee." Solomon replied: "Give therefore thy servant an understanding heart to judge thy people that I may discern
between good and bad." And God said unto him, "Because thou
hast asked this thing, and hast not asked for thyself long life; neither hast asked riches for thyself, nor hast asked the life of thine
enemies; but hast asked for thyself understanding to discern judgment; Behold, I have done according to thy words: lo, I have given
thee a wise and an understanding heart; so that there was none like
thee before thee, neither after thee shall any arise like unto thee.
And I have also given thee that which thou hast not asked, both
riches, and honor: so that there shall not be any among the kings
like unto thee all thy days. And if thou wilt walk in my ways, to keep
my statutes and my commandments, as thy father David did walk,
then I will lengthen thy days."

The historian Flavius Josephus's study of Solomon, which we explored in chapter one, did not overlook the dream:

For as he was asleep that very night, God appeared to him, and commanded him to ask of him some gifts which he was ready to give him, as a reward for his piety. So, Solomon asked of God what was most excellent, and of the greatest worth in itself; what God would bestow with the greatest joy; and what it was most profitable for man to receive. For he did not desire to have bestowed upon him either gold, or silver, or any other riches; as a man and a youth might naturally have done, for these are the things that generally are esteemed by most men, as alone of the greatest worth, and the best gifts of God. But, said he, "Give me, O Lord, a sound mind, and a good understanding; whereby I may speak and judge the people according to truth and righteousness." With these petitions God was well pleased and promised to give him all those things that he had not mentioned in his option: riches, glory, victory over his enemies, and, in the first place, understanding and wisdom, and this in such a degree, as no other mortal man, neither kings nor ordinary persons ever had. He also promised to preserve the Kingdom to his posterity for a very long time if he continued righteous, and obedient to him, and imitated his father in those things wherein he excelled. When Solomon heard this from God, he presently leaped out of his bed, and when he had worshipped him, he returned to Jerusalem, and after he had offered great sacrifices before the tabernacle, he feasted all his own family.

It was this extraordinary wisdom that immortalized Solomon so notably in the tales and legends of various countries. For example, in Romania, Sabina Ispas has noted seven texts that refer to it.[2]

2. THE TEN QUESTIONS

The angel Gabriel spoke to David: "The one of your ten children who can answer these questions will be your successor after your death. Genies, men, demons, birds, and the entire universe will be under his domination." David then gathered his children together and told them: "O my children, know that Gabriel brought me these pages on behalf of God. They contain ten questions. Whoever answers them correctly will be, as said by God, a prophet with the character of an apostle." David then began to read these questions in his children's presence. None of them could reply except for Solomon who got up and said: "O my father, I will answer these questions with the might of God." David was filled with joy and read him one of these questions asking him: "Tell me what is the smallest thing that exists? What is the largest, what is the bitterest, what is the sweetest, what is the most shameful, what is the best, what is the nearest, what is the most far away, what is it that causes the greatest grief, and what is it that is the most pleasant?" Solomon answered: "That is quite easy, Father. Now the smallest thing is found in the human body—it is the soul. The largest thing is doubt, the most bitter thing is poverty, the sweetest thing is wealth, the most shameful thing to be found among the children of Adam is lack of belief; the most evil thing to be found among Adam's children is a wicked woman; the thing that is closest to Adam's children is the other world, and the thing that is most far away is this world because it has passed on. The thing that causes the children of Adam the greatest grief is the soul that parts from the body, and the most pleasant thing for them is the soul that is in the body."

"You have spoken the full truth," said David.

Now this ring with four faces that had been brought down from Heaven became the seal of Solomon. The following was written on one of these faces: "The empire is God's." On the second face it was written: "excellence is God's." On the third side it read: "Supreme authority is God's." On the fourth: "Omnipotence is God's."[3]

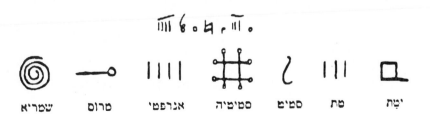

Fig. 4.2. The engravings on Solomon's seal according to various sources

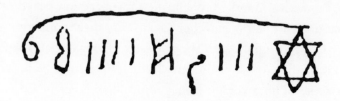

Fig. 4.3.

The Sun of Wisdom by Ahmad ibn ʿAlī al-Būnī, (*Shams al-ma ʿarif al-Kubra*) reproduces another form of this seal (shown in figure 4.3).

Ahmad ibn ʿAlī al-Būnī explains the signs, going from right to left, this way:

> Three rods in a row follow a seal; above them is a line that looks like a raised arrow. A blind and truncated mim, then a ladder toward what is hoped for but cannot be attained by a ladder, and four lines similar to the phalanx. There is then an H bisected followed by an upside down wāw, like the hose of a suction cap fitting without a suction cap. O you who bear the name that has none like it, with these figures you shall avert all calamities and remain safe and sound.[4]

The interpretation of the symbols proposed here is as follows: the *mim* represents Islam; the ladder, the upward quest for the most sublime name of God (the ladder of science); the four vertical lines are the four letters of the Tetragrammaton;* and the last two signs are the alpha and omega. It should be noted that this seal will dispel all danger.

Liana Saif has analyzed the information provided by the Sheikh al-Buni, author of *The Sun of Wisdom and the Secret of Gnosis* (*Sams alma ʿarif wa-lata if alwarif*), a longer version of the book mentioned earlier, on the correspondence between the seven characters forming the

---

*The Tetragrammaton is the four-letter transliteration of the Hebrew name for God, YHWH.

supreme name of God with the letters, planets, character, and so forth, that she diagrammed as follows:"[5]

Letter	Planet	Character	Day	Spirit	Minister	Divine Name	Goal
F	Sun	Y	Sunday	Ruqya il	Mudhab	Fard	Silent gods
Ğ	Moon	ĩĩ	Monday	Gibril	Murra	Gabhar	Harmony
Š	Mars	ℓ	Tuesday	Sims ail	Al-Ahmar	Sahid	Victory, discord, hot disease, hemorrhage

James A. Montgomery, for his part, collected a body of Aramaic charms in which we find the recurring phrase: "Enchanted and Sealed by Solomon's Seal."[6] Another more extensive phrase says: "With the wand of Moses, the pectoral of Aaron, the seal of Solomon, the shield of David, and the miter of the High Priest, I execute this charm."[7]

Let's look at a typical example:

By the seal of Aaron, son of Zand, and by the seal of King Solomon, son of David, thanks to whom were sealed the Oppressors and the Latbê, all evil will be enchanted and sealed within the body of Mihr-homizd b. M., in his house, in his wife and his sons, in his livestock and properties. And we have sealed with the seal of El Shaddai and of Abraxas, the powerful lord, and the high seal with which were sealed heaven, earth, and all the demons, and the stinking knots, and the Latbê who battle against him. And this seal stands against evil and constraint so that they gain no entry."

The Oppressors are a category of demon, and the knots represent the magical power of binding. El Shaddai (אל שדי) is one of the names of God. Abraxas is a divine and cosmic name that appears in magic papyri of ancient Greece and on countless amulets.[8]

3. DAVID AND SOLOMON

When King David still ruled, he often placed his son Solomon on his throne so that he could learn how to form his own judgments. In his conversations with the great men of the world on the subject of earthly matters, he often spoke of the other world and what became of a person after death.

"Happy is he who leaves after him children that pray to God for him and perform expiatory sacrifices for their parents so that they may go to Heaven!" said King David. "For here no man can become a saint even if he so desires."

All these old men believed King David's words, but they did not please his son Solomon at all. He wished to speak of it to his father, but he was ashamed and put off from one day to the next his desire to show him that if an individual does not work for his salvation during his lifetime, he will have nothing to hope for from his children when it came to entering paradise.

"Father," Solomon finally said to King David on a day he found him in good humor, "I ask that you grant me something, but first I will tell you what it is."

"I would give you my kingdom, my son, if you asked it of me, and I would not go back on my word, for that is how much I love you, as you should know full well."

"I thus desire, Father, that you yield me your throne for three days so that I may rule a short while. After that, I will have no regrets if I were to die."

"I grant you this, my son Solomon, not for three days but for thirty."

Solomon stood up, kissed his father's hand, and sat on the throne to rule. Several days went by and one evening Solomon sent forty men, each holding a lantern, to go to King David. He commanded that the king be led through the darkness by two people, followed by the men with the forty lanterns a few steps behind. They would be just far enough behind him so that their light would not reach King David and he would not be able to see where he was walking. Solomon instructed that if the king asked for the men with the lanterns to light the way before him, they should pretend not to hear him, and his two guides should lead him quite briskly. Whether there was mud in his path or not, they should lead his father to him by the quickest way possible.

The men sent by Solomon did all that he had ordered. They brought David into the great hall before Solomon. "Why are you so filthy with mud Father? Servants!" yelled Solomon. "Bring water quickly and clean my father! How did you manage to get so dirty with mud, Father, with the forty lanterns I sent to light your way?"

"Eh? May the good Lord punish your light bearers! They mocked me. They walked twenty steps behind. How could I see well enough not to get dirty, my son?"

"Ah! You could not see anything when the lantern bearers walked behind you? It's true, when they walked behind you, you were unable to see anything, and you got dirty. This is what it is all about, my dear father. When a man dies, the alms that his children give after his death are like the lanterns that were just following you. What you have given with your own hand is what you shall find again before God, and the bed you make in this world is the one in which you shall lie in the next."

"You have taught me a wonderful lesson, my son," said King David. "May all those who hear it benefit. Everyone should repent while he lives and not wait for death as I once said."

4. SOLOMON'S WISDOM

David noted one day that his tribunal looked poorly on his son Solomon's interference in their discussions, although these judges were forced to acknowledge that his opinion was always the best. He challenged them to test his son on all the teachings and laws of Moses, in the presence of all the great men of the kingdom, adding: "If you are certain that he knows them perfectly and does not form any judgment that is contrary to the law, even when his opinion on the wielding of the law differs from yours or mine, it is not to be scorned. God grants wisdom to whomsoever he wishes."

The jurists were clearly convinced of his erudition but hoped to catch him off guard with cunning questions and thereby increase their own renown. They therefore made arrangments for a public examination, but their hopes were cruelly dashed. Before they had the last word on any question posed to Solomon, he would come back with the correct response. He was so quick that many of the people present were almost certain that he and the judges were in cahoots and that David had organized this examination in order to designate his son as his worthy successor, but Solomon quashed this assumption. He stood up and addressed the judges: "You have worn yourselves out with nitpicking. Allow me to ask you some simple questions whose answers require no study and will come simply from the mind and reason. Tell me: what is whole and what is nothing?" Solomon remained silent for a long time and when the judge to whom he had asked this question showed he was incapable of answering it, Solomon said: "God is the whole, the creator. The world, the creation, is nothing. The believer is something and the hypocrite is less than nothing."

Turning toward the second judge he asked, "What is the majority and what is the minority? Who is the sweetest and who is the most bitter?" As this judge was unable to come up with an answer, Solomon told him: "The sweetest things to have are a virtuous wife, children that remain good, and good revenue; the most bitter things are an immoral wife, spoiled children, and poverty."

To end, he turned toward the last judge: "What is the most beautiful thing and what is the ugliest thing? What thing is most certain and what is most uncertain?" As the judge remained mute, Solomon explained: "The ugliest thing is a believer who loses his faith and the most beautiful is a sinner who converts. Death is the most certain of all things, and the Last Judgment, life, and the fate of the soul after resurrection are the most uncertain. You see," Solomon went on, "that the oldest and the most erudite are not always the wisest. True wisdom does not come from age or learned books, only from God the Most Wise."[9]

5. THE JUDGMENTS OF SOLOMON

The historian and Byzantine theologian Michael Glycas said in the twelfth century that Solomon had handed down three thousand judgments,[10] but we have only found those that follow.

One of the most impactful of Solomon's judgments was that of the two women who both claimed one child, as told in chapter 1 (see pages 7–8). It is depicted on a central column and on a stained glass in the cathedral of Strasbourg, framed by the two famous statues of the *Synagogue* and the *Church*. It was also the subject of works by great painters, for example Nicolas Poussin.

Fig. 4.4. Strasbourg Cathedral

Fig. 4.5. Stained glass from Strasbourg Cathedral

6. SOLOMON AND THE GOOSE THIEF (A)

One day a man came before the king Solomon to lodge a complaint: "Prophet of God," he said, "I have neighbors that steal my geese, and I am unable to uncover the guilty party." Solomon summoned the faithful to prayer at the mosque and addressed them with a call to action. In the midst of his speech, he told them: "One among you has stolen the geese of his neighbor, then he entered the mosque with a feather on his head." The guilty man immediately rubbed his head and Solomon yelled out: "Arrest that man; it is him!"[11]

7. SOLOMON AND THE MAN WHO DISCOVERED A TREASURE (B)

One day, at the time when Solomon was barely thirteen years old, two men came before the court. Their litigation struck dumb all those present because of its rarity and put King David in a difficult situation. The plaintiff had in fact bought a piece of land from the accused and, while digging a cellar, had uncovered a treasure. He asked that the accused take back this treasure as he had bought the land without it, while the accused claimed to no longer have any right to it since he had known nothing of it and had sold the land along with all it contained. After giving the matter long consideration, David declared that each man should receive half of the treasure. Solomon, however, asked the plaintiff if he had a son, and when that individual said yes, he asked the accused if he had a daughter. He did have one daughter, and Solomon said: "If you really wish to end your litigation in a way that causes no harm to anyone, marry your children together and give it to them as dowry."[12]

8. THE MAN WITH TWO HEADS (C)

One day, Asmodeus, king of the demons, came to find Solomon and told him: "O king, you are regarded as the most learned of men. If you wish, I will show you something that you have never seen." The sovereign replied: "Very well, show me."

Immediately, Asmodeus started pulling up a rope that brought a two-headed man out of the depths. The monarch, astonished and somewhat amused at this sight, gave the command to lodge the man in his apartments. After which, he summoned his counselor Benaiah and told him: "Did you know that there were men living beneath us?"

"By the life of your soul, Lord King, I knew it, because I've heard Ahitopel of Gilonite, your father's counselor, state that there were men below us."

"What would you say if I showed you one?" asked Solomon.

"How did you manage to tear one of them from the depths of the earth? The distance between their world and ours is that of a five-hundred-year journey."

Solomon then summoned the man with two heads and when Benaiah saw him, he prostrated himself on the ground saying: "God be praised that he has given me to live until this day!" He then asked the man: "Who are you?"

"I am one of Cain's descendants," the man replied.

"Where do you live?"

"In an uninhabited world."

"Can the sun and moon be seen there?"

"Yes! We also work the fields and harvest them, and we own sheep and livestock."

"What side does the sun rise in your home?"

"In the west, and it sets in the east."

"Do you pray?"

"Yes, really, and we prefer your prayer."

"O Lord, while your works are varied, all display your Wisdom."

"If you like, we can return you to your own land."

"Do what you feel is best," he replied.

Then Solomon called up Asmodeus and told him, "Take this man back to his country." But Asmodeus, answered, "I cannot."

The man therefore settled down in Jerusalem and married a Jewish woman with whom he had seven sons. Six resembled their mother, but the seventh looked like his father because he had two heads. The man worked and reaped his lands and became the wealthiest of landowners.

The day came when he died, leaving all he owned to his seven sons. They told each other, "We are seven brothers so we will share the inheritance in seven equal portions." But the son with two heads said: "There are eight of us, and we should have a double portion of the inheritance."

They therefore went to Solomon and told him: "O Lord King, there are seven of us, but he who has two heads says there are eight because he wants our father's legacy to be split into eight parts so he can have two." After listening to their story, Solomon was deeply divided about what to do. He called the members of the Sanhedrin* to his side and asked them, "What are your thoughts on this matter?" But they told themselves, "If we say that the two-headed man should receive two portions, the king will think the opposite," so they refused to speak. "I will hand down my decree tomorrow morning," said Solomon. "So in the meantime, go to the Temple and ask God to shed some light on this problem."

The following morning, Solomon summoned the Sanhedrin together and said, "Have the man with two heads come to me," and he came. "Look," said the king, "if one of the heads knows what happens to the other head, then he is only one person, otherwise he is two. Bring me some hot water, old wine, and linen vestments." After he blindfolded the eyes on each head with the linen, he began pouring the old wine and hot water on one of the heads. "O lord," both heads yelled, "we are dying, we are dying, we are only one person! I swear it to you!" The Israelites who saw what Solomon had done were filled with amazement and trembled before him.[13]

---

*The Sanhedrin is the supreme council and tribunal of the Jewish people.

FIVE

Solomon's Possessions

While Solomon's ring is the best known of all the objects he owned, he also possessed other objects that are given brief mention in the Arabian literature. These notes contribute to the extraordinary fame of the son of David, Sulayman ibn Dawud, while revealing all that separated God's chosen one from common mortals. They made him an exceptional king because the ownership of objects like these were signs of his elect status and divine protection.

1. SOLOMON'S RING

After Solomon had performed his final duties to his father, he was resting in a valley between Hebron and Jerusalem when he suddenly lost consciousness. When he regained his senses, he saw eight angels before him. Each one had wings beyond count, all varied in form and color,

Fig. 5.1. Solomon's ring

49

and they bowed to the sovereign three times. When he asked them who they were, they replied: "We are the angels in charge of the eight winds. God, our creator and yours, has sent us to serve you and to make it so your power is exercised over us and the winds that are in our charge. In accordance with your will and desire, they will blow violently or become calm, and they will always blow to the side facing your back. When you give the order, they will carry you far above the earth and place you at the tops of the highest mountains." The leader of the angels then gave Solomon a precious stone on which these words were inscribed: "God is the power and the glory." The angel then told him, "When you have a command to give us, raise this stone toward heaven and we shall come at once to take your orders."

As soon as these angels departed, four more appeared who were greatly different in shape and appearance from each other. One had the face of an enormous whale, the next an eagle, the third that of a lion, and the fourth, a snake. They bowed deeply before Solomon and told him: "We are the sovereigns of all the creatures that live on land and in water, and we come before you on the orders of our master to give our support. Act toward us however you please; we shall place at your disposal and your friends, all the good and pleasant things God has graced us with, and against your enemies, we shall employ all the faculties we possess for causing harm."

The angel that commanded all winged creatures then presented Solomon with a precious stone on which was carved "All that Lives praises the Lord," and he said, "Thanks to the virtue of this stone that you need only raise above your head, you can summon us at any time and give us your orders."

Solomon did as the angel instructed, and he ordered him to bring a pair of all that lived in water, land, or air. The angels flew off at lightning speed, and in the space of an instant all possible creatures, from the largest elephant to the smallest worm, were brought into the king's presence. Solomon talked at great length with these various animals. They told him how they lived, and he listened to their grievances and took care of many of the abusive situations that existed between them. He conversed most of all with the birds, preferring them above all because of their sweet language that he understood as well as that of men, and because of the beautiful sentences they uttered.

In human language, the cry of the peacock means: "You will be judged in the way you have judged others." The song of the nightingale means: "Moderation in desires is the highest good." The turtle dove says: "For many creatures, it would be better if they had never been created." The hoopoe says: "He who has no pity for others will not find anyone who has compassion for him." The Syrdar bird:* "Convert sinners." The swallow: "Do good and you shall be rewarded." The pelican: "Blessed be the Lord in heaven and on earth." The pigeon: "Everything passes, God remains eternally." The eagle: "However long your life may be, it ends with death." The rooster: "Give thought to your creator, thoughtless men."

Solomon chose the rooster and the hoopoe to be his constant companions, one because of his ear-shattering and intrepid cry and the other because his gaze travels through the earth as if it were a piece of crystal. This meant that wherever the king traveled the hoopoe could always indicate where there was a spring to provide the necessary water, either for drinking or for performing the ablutions prescribed by the Law. Solomon then ordered the dove to raise its young in the temple that he had had built. Several years later, the posterity of this pair of doves was so numerous that all who visited this temple would make their way there beneath the shadow of the wings of these birds, even if they came from the most remote nooks of the city.

The next time Solomon found himself alone, he saw an angel appear before him whose top half looked like earth and his lower half like water. He prostrated himself before the king and said: "God created me so that I could let earth and sea know your commands. The Lord has ordered me to carry out your commands, and you can accompany me over land and sea. At your voice, the highest mountains shall vanish, and other mountains will surge up in the plains. Rivers and lakes will run dry, while dry fertile lands will be covered by water, if that is your will." Before leaving, the angel gave Solomon a precious stone with this inscription: "Sky and earth are the servants of God."

---

*[Possibly a pheasant. —*Trans.*]

Finally, another angel gave the son of David a fourth precious stone with the inscription: "There is no God but the one God, and Mohammed is His prophet." "With this stone," the angel told him, "you will gain dominion over the entire world of spirits, which is much more extensive than that of men and animals, and fills almost the entire space that lies between heaven and earth. Some of these spirits have faith and invoke the true God; the others are infidels. Some of them worship fire, others worship the sun, and others different stars. Many of them regard water as a deity. The first spirits gather around all pious men to protect them from all misfortune and sin. The others seek all the ways to cause humans harm, to torment them, and to lead them astray. This is quite easy for them to do because they can make themselves invisible or assume any form they please." Solomon wished to see the djinns in their natural, inborn state. The angel soared up through the air like a pillar of fire and then reappeared with a band of demons whose hideous appearance caused Solomon to shudder despite the power he held over them. He had not believed that such hideous beings could truly exist. One of them had a man's head placed on the neck of a horse and his feet were like donkey hooves; eagle wings were placed on a dromedary's hump and gazelle horns on the head of a peacock. Solomon implored the angel to tell him more as Djan, from whom all djinns descended, could only have one form. "This monstrous variety of shapes is the result of the debauched behavior of evil genies and their shameful relations with men, animals, and birds. Their desires know no bounds, and adultery and incest are everyday occurrences for them. As they reproduce over the generations, their original form degenerates," the angel explained.

Once he was back home, Solomon had the four precious stones given to him by the angels united on a ring so that he could exercise his sovereignty over the world of animals and spirits and over the land and the wind at his pleasure. His first concern was to make the demons submit to his authority. He summoned them to all come before him with the exception of Sakhr,* one of the most powerful genies who lived

---

*His name reflects the Arabic *sikhr,* "magic." The Latins named him Asmodeus.

hidden on an unknown island in the ocean, and Iblis,* the master of all evil spirits who God had granted complete freedom until Judgment Day.

Once the demons were gathered together, Solomon stamped them each on the neck with the imprint of his ring so he could, so to speak, brand them like slaves. He compelled the spirits or djinns to work for him and to build all kinds of public buildings on the model of the Temple of Mecca, which he had seen one day while traveling through Arabia, but larger and more costly. The wives of the djinns were obliged to cook, wash, spin, weave, carry water, and perform all tasks reserved for women. Solomon distributed the cloth they made to the poor. The dishes they prepared were placed on tables that covered a full square mile, and every day thirty thousand oxen, an equal number of sheep, and a vast number of fish and birds were consumed. By means of his ring, the king could procure the animals in whatever quantity he desired.

The demons and djinns were seated at tables of fire, the poor at wooden tables, the leaders of the people and the army had seats at silver tables, and the doctors and men renowned for their piety sat at tables made of gold and Solomon himself served them.[1]

2. THE LOSS OF THE RING

Solomon owned a ring that made him master of the universe, on which the high name of God was carved. The name of the mother of his sons was Djerade. Solomon trusted her more than any of his other wives. Every time he took off his ring when he went to do his business, he would entrust it to his wife to keep it until he returned. Now one day as God had decided, Solomon had given his ring to Djerade before retiring, and one of the great divs† took the form of Solomon. He had Djerade give him the king's ring and sat on Solomon's throne, and all submitted to his orders because of the ring. When Solomon

---

*The devil, *diabolos*. Iblis belonged to the angels called *aj-jinn*, created from blazing fire. Under the name of Al-Harith, he was one of the guardians of paradise.
†A demon from Persian beliefs that is often confused for a ghoul or genie.

returned and asked Djerade for his ring, she told him: "I gave it to you." Solomon denied it and they quarreled. Then Djerade said, "You are not even Solomon, the one sitting on the throne is Solomon. You are a div who has assumed Solomon's shape." He remained stupefied and left the house. Everywhere he went when he told people he was Solomon, they hit him and told him: "You are a div!" The div was sitting on Solomon's throne in Solomon's clothes and looked like him completely.

Feeling hungry, Solomon left the city and headed toward the sea. There he met some fishermen* and he told them he was Solomon. They bowed his head beneath a yoke and made him labor for them. No one offered him protection and he was hungry. That evening, they gave him two fish as payment and left it up to him to eat or sell them. He went into the city and sold one of the fish. He grilled the other fish and ate it with bread that he had bought with the money he got for the other fish. This happened the same way every day. He worked from morning to night for two fish. After forty days, God forgave him and restored his power.

During the time the div had sat on the throne he had made rulings that were not in accord with the Pentateuch like those of Solomon. Men knew that they were contrary to the law, but they dared say nothing out of fear. For their part, the divs went to their comrade and said: "Give us a souvenir, for they want to drive you away from here."

"What would you like?" he asked them.

"The magical science that Solomon has hidden."

He searched for it and gave it to them. They made a hole beneath the four feet of the throne and hid the books of magic and no one— excepting for the divs—knew about it. When Solomon regained his authority, these books remained beneath his throne. . . . some of these books remained in the possession of the children of Israel, and all that exists today comes from what they had.

Some time later, when men were suffering greatly from Solomon's absence, this div worked secretly with other divs to keep people far away. Then Asaph and the children of Israel got together. It was then that

---

*In the *Sippurim,* he turns up as a kitchen helper in the court of King Ammon.

Asaph told them: "I will ask the wives for more information." Asaph went into the king's apartments and asked his wives where Solomon was. They answered: "It has been a long time since he has come to see us." They then realized that it was not Solomon who was ruling, but a div. They then met to deliberate about how to kill the div. The other divs sought him out and told him: "Beware because men wish to bring about your ruin!" Then Asaph had the Pentateuch brought forth and summoned all the readers of this book. It is said that there were four thousand of them. They recited the Pentateuch in the presence of the div. He was unable to tolerate the reading of this book and fled. Afterward, people set off in search of Solomon.

The div, because he knew of no place where he could hide King Solomon's ring, tossed it into the sea. A fish swallowed it and through an act of Providence, this fish was caught that very same day in a net. That night, the fishermen gave Solomon two fish. Like every day he sold one and cut the other open to grill it for his meal. He then found the ring.[2] He slipped it on his finger and returned to his home. Men, demons, and birds all flocked to his side, and he performed works by the grace of God. Then he spoke to the divs: "Bring me that div!"

"He is hiding at the bottom of the sea," they replied. "We cannot catch him."

For several years, no one could capture him. Then a band of peris* went to the seaside and began loudly crying and weeping for Solomon. This same div, whose name was Dhadjar, shouted from the bottom of the sea: "What's your problem?"

"Solomon is dead," they replied.

The div then came out of the water and joined them. They grabbed him and brought him before Solomon. He ordered that he be placed between a stone and an iron slab, firmly tied there, and thrown back to the bottom of the sea where he will remain until the day of resurrection.[3]

It will be noted that the story of Sakhr is found in the *Kitab al-Mandal al-Sulaymani* written for exorcists and physicians for the

---

*The peris, in Farsi *pari*, are the descendants of the fallen angels in Persian mythology, but in *The Thousand and One Nights*, they are fairies.

purpose of diagnosing the type and origin of the ills their patients are suffering from. Some interesting variations appear in the *Kitab al-Mandal
al-Sulaymani*: Djerade is replaced by a female servant named al-Mawiyya,
and it is Solomon's wife who finds the ring in the fish. She places it in her
mouth and slips it into Solomon's mouth when she kisses him.

3. THE WEAPONS

Solomon is said to have owned a wonderful shield made from seven
different kinds of animal hide and surrounded by seven rings. Crafted
under celestial influence, the shield protected its bearer from charms
and enchantments. The son of David also had a flaming sword and an
impenetrable breastplate.[4]

4. THE CARPET

When most people speak of flying carpets, they are thinking more of
The Thousand and One Nights than of the legend of Solomon. In fact,
they are in reference to this king's dominion over the winds that carried him wherever he wished to go. The Qu'ran twice mentions this
mastery. The 38th sura, "Sad," reminds us: "We then tamed the wind
for him, which, on his command, blew modestly everywhere he wished"
(38, 36). There is also the 21st sura, "the prophets" (Al-Anbiya): "We
harnessed the impetuous wind that, by his command, headed toward
the land that We had blessed" (21, 81).

There is another explanation for the flying carpet that can be found
in *The Sun of Wisdom* (*Shams al-Ma'arif*), a thirteenth-century Arab
grimoire attributed to the Egyptian Sheik al-Buni. Jean Charles Coulon
stated that this "is the most famous work of magic in Islam."

There were four sealed Hebrew names on Solomon's carpet (*bisat
Sulayman*), and they were the obedient djinns and demons who
never revolted, even for the time it would take to blink. The carpet's
supporters who carried its full length were *effrits,* Solomon's greatest
viziers among the djinns, for he had three hundred viziers among

men and four hundred among the djinns. The four carpet bearers were the greatest of his human viziers, Asaf ben Barahiya, and the greatest viziers of the djinn, Tmryat, Hdlyag, and Shugal.

It is said that Solomon owned a carpet that was five hundred parasangs long.* Every time it was spread out, three hundred thrones of silver and gold were placed upon it, and Solomon ordered the birds to join their wings together in order to give him and his retinue shelter. It is also said that he had one thousand very beautiful houses made of crystal and that he had settled his wives in these houses. He had one thousand women: three hundred legitimate wives and seven hundred concubines. He then gave the wind the command to carry this carpet and all it held through the air for the distance of one mile—sometimes more, sometimes less. Everywhere he went he blotted out the sun for a length of one hundred parasangs, so that all the eyes of men could see was him. He remained for some time in Damascus and for some time in Jerusalem. In the morning he was in one city and in the evening, another. . . and this wind carried the carpet with all these people, on Solomon's command, without anyone feeling the slightest shudder.

Solomon decided to launch an attack on an idolatrous king whose kingdom was located on an island. It was a two-month journey by land between these two kings, and it was also necessary to cross the sea. Solomon prepared his carpet, sat upon it with his entire army, and crossed the sea until he reached this island. Then he attacked the king and slew him. He converted all the people and the army of this king to the true faith and took possession of all the king's property.[5]

5. SOLOMON'S NET

A Coptic prayer contains eight conjurations of demons, who are presented as blacksmiths and magicians, and indicates the kinds of illnesses they send. This prayer is known as "The Net of Solomon" (Marbabta Salomon). The text is in four sections. Only the first is translated here.

---

*Ancient Persian unit of distance that corresponds to roughly four miles.

The name of Walatta Gijorgis is a later addition—the name of the charm's beneficiary.

2. [...] Prayer concerning the net of Solomon, that God gave him to cast over the demons like a fisherman over fish, while saying:

3. Sadata'el of the net!

4. Then: I find refuge in Solomon's net.

5. Fasata'el. Amen!

6. Read: Dena'e, Az'ajat, Strong, Eternal.

7. Here is the word that comes from the place where Solomon abides:

8. Asu asu asu, taklasu taklasu taklasu, sulame zemlat.

9. I find refuge in the names Father, Son, and Holy Ghost.

10. Bind their hands and feet, darken their vision, annihilate their spells, and render [the demons'] poison ineffective Dask and Gudale,* Faus† and Seraj, and save us, O Solomon, from the hands of the smiths [*i.e.*, the demons].

11. Once when the demons had captured Solomon and presented him to their king, that king said:

12. "You have plunged us into great terror."

13. "What is your intention?" Solomon asked.

14. "If the praise of the Lord does not protect you, I will do whatever I like with you."

15. "You will not be able to do what you wish." Then the hidden king commanded that he not go anywhere near the soul or body of your servant, Walatta Gijorgis.[6]

6. THE THRONE

The Bible (1 Kings 10:18–20) was the first text to mention Solomon's throne. The Arabs then embellished this story, which came to the West by way of Byzantium. Today we know that the prototype of the son of

---

*Names of demons and diseases.

†This also means "medication, remedy" as well as *incantamentum*.

David's throne can be found in the story of Vikramaditya,[7] the Indian Solomon whose exploits have been recorded in Sanskrit literature and whose trace has even been found in Mongolia. This king was the owner of a wondrous throne given to him by Indra, the king of the gods. There were thirty-two figures sculpted on this throne. After his death, this throne was buried deep in the earth, for no one dared to sit on it. Several centuries later, the king Bhoja discovered it and wanted to sit upon it, but each time he tried, one of these figures would distract him by recounting one of Vikramaditya's exploits. Like Solomon, this king held dominion over demons known as rakshasa. Like him, he could travel through the air, but by means of automatons. The Somadeva,[8] "The Ocean of the Rivers of Tales," devotes the whole of its seventeenth book to him. According to Gilbert Gaulmin (1585–1665),[9] there was a *Book of Solomon's Throne,* printed in Paris in 1615, that is not available to us, but Marco Brösch discovered a *Tractatus de throno Solomonis* in a thirteenth-century manuscript housed in the library of Cues-Bernkastel Hospital,[10] which includes a description that corresponds with what the other accounts tell us.

The Book of Ceremonies (Ἔκθεσις τῆς βασιλείου τάξεως), written in Byzantium during the reign of Constantine VII Porphyrogenitus, tells us that the throne of the Magnaura was an imitation of Solomon's. In *Antipodosis,* Liutprand of Cremona (ca. 920/922–972), ambassador for Berangar, King of Italy, and Otho II, German Emperor, in Constantinople, described it as follows:

Near the palace in Constantinople there was a home of admirable beauty and grandeur; the Greeks call it Magnaura. . . . In front of the imperial throne stood a bronze but gilded tree whose branches were full of all kinds of birds. They too were bronze plated in gold, who all sang in their own way. The imperial throne had been crafted with such art that from one moment to the next it seemed low then high. Enormous lions, I don't know if they were made of metal or wood, but they were covered in gold, seemed to stand guard over it (*quasi custodiebant*), striking the ground with their tails, and growling with their jaws wide and their tongues moving.

For his part the Iranian Tabari (839–923) notes:

The throne of Solomon had four feet. It was made from red rubies
that had been worked in such a way to make four lions. Four
vultures were above Solomon's head whose wings were extended
so that they would cover Solomon in their shadow when he gave
audience. When he was not on his throne, these wings closed.
The four lions also formed a talisman. None but Solomon could
sit on this throne. When Nebuchadnezzar came to Jerusalem and
wanted to sit on it, he did not know how Solomon customarily
seated himself. Now, when he set foot on the throne, the lions
at its base each clawed his legs and crushed them. He fell to the
base of the throne senseless. He was given remedies and treat-
ment and was put back on his feet. After him, no one else ever
tried to sit on the throne.[11]

7. THE CHALICE

Wahb ibn Munabbibh (654–730), a native of Sana'a (Yemen) said this:

When Solomon drank, the djinns had a habit of making faces at
him because he could not see them; his carafe prevented him. As
this vexed him greatly, Sakhr made him glass vessels and he was able
to drink without losing sight of the shaytans.[12]

This goblet has a counterpart in the cup of Jamshid, the legendary
king of Persia who, like Solomon, could command genies (divs):

Jamshid was victorious over the divs and compelled them to work
for him. He commanded a large div to make him a cup (*djame*) that
would allow him, according to his wishes, see all the worlds and
every corner of the universe.[13]

There is another tradition about the cup in Romania in "The
Companion of the Quarryman."[14]

8. SOLOMON'S HORSES

One evening Solomon was presented with some rapid steeds who were standing on three feet with the fourth barely touching the ground and he said: "I preferred the goods of this world over mention of the Lord until the veil of night fell over everything. Bring them back to me," and he cut off their hocks and heads. He punished himself this way for having spent the day admiring them and forgetting the prayer of the *'asr.**

According to some, these horses had been bequeathed to him by his father David. According to others, they had been captured in an expedition against Damascus and Nisibis. They were so fast that he rode one of them to have lunch in Jerusalem and to return to Istakhar (Persepolis) in time for dinner.

It seems that Solomon bore scant respect for the precept from Deuteronomy 17:16 forbidding the king from acquiring more horses, which was one of the reasons for his posthumous punishment. Around 350, the Talmud explicitly states: "The king should not have many wives in order to not stray from the right path, but Solomon claimed the opposite."

We learn more about this in *The Testament of Solomon:*

> And I marched against the Jebusaeans, and there I saw a Jebusaean, daughter of a man, and fell violently in love with her, and desired to take her to wife along with my other wives. And I said to their priests: "Give me the Sonmanites (i.e., Shunammite) to wife." But the priests of Moloch said to me: "If thou lovest this maiden, go in and worship our gods, the great god Raphan and the god called Moloch. . . ." They told the maiden not to sleep with me until I complied and sacrificed to the gods. I then was moved, but crafty Eros brought and laid by her five grasshoppers for me, saying: "Take these grasshoppers, and crush them together in the name of the god Moloch and then will I sleep with you."
>
> And this I actually did. And at once the Spirit of God departed

---

*The late afternoon prayer of the five daily prayers in Islam.

from me and I became weak as well as foolish in my words. And after that I was obliged by her to build a temple of idols to Baal, Rapha, Moloch, and the other idols. I then, wretch that I am, followed her advice, and the glory of God quite departed from me. My spirit was darkened, and I became the sport of idols and demons. Wherefore I wrote out this *Testament,* that ye who get possession of it may pity, and attend to the last things, and not to the first.[15]

Among the Gnostic writings of the Nag Hammadi Codex, *The Testimony of Truth* contains a violent criticism of Solomon and his father:

Some of them fall away to the worship of idols. Others have demons dwelling within them, as did King David. He is the one who laid the foundation of Jerusalem, and his son Solomon, whom he begat in adultery, is the one who built Jerusalem by means of the demons, because he received powers.*

As it happens, Solomon was born from the union of David and Bethsheba, his wife (2 Samuel 12:24). While Jews and Christians condemned the great king this way, there is nothing similar in the works of Arab writers who totally overlook this criticism.

9. SOLOMON'S TREASURE

There was a house in Al-Andalus (Spain) that on coming to power, each king would seal its door with a padlock. . . . The land was conquered by Tariq ibn Ziyad. . . . In this dwelling was the table of Solomon (*ma'idat Sulayman*) that was made of gold and inlaid with precious stones. It also held the wonderful mirror that allowed one to see into the seven climates and which was made of a blend of substances. There was Solomon's golden chalice, a copy of the Psalms written in beautiful Greek letters on pages of gold adorned with gems, twenty-two books, all

---

*[Søren Giversen and Birger A. Pearson translation. —*Trans.*]

written in gold, including a Torah; another book made of silver containing the uses of plants and stones and the means for making talismans; another containing the art of color dyeing with the means for producing the colors of the hyacinth; and large baskets made of gold-stamped stone filled with the philosopher's stone of the alchemists.[16]

The 273rd Night of *The Thousand and One Nights* also mentions the quest for this table, but the city in which it was discovered is Lepta, and the description is consistent with that of fairy tales: the table is made of emerald and covered by chrysolith plates and golden goblets.

10. SOLOMON AND THE PHILOSOPHER'S STONE

We have said that Solomon had the perfection of this stone and knew by divine inspiration the great and wonderful properties of it to constrain the devils. And therefore, as soon as he had made it, he decided to make all the Spirits appear before him. But first, he made a wonderful, great cauldron of brass, which was no smaller than the whole circuit of the Forest of Vincennes, but that it wanted half a foot, or there about . . . that it must be somewhat rounder, and it was needful to be so great, for to serve that purpose that he had in mind. And after the same manner he made a cover, so close and just, as was possible. And in like manner, he caused a hole to be cast in the ground large and deep enough to bury his cauldron. When he had prepared all these things, by virtue of the stone he made all the Spirits that were dispersed in this world, little and great, beginning with the emperors of the four corners of the Earth, come before him. Then he made the kings, dukes, earls, barons, lords, knights, esquires, captains, heads of bands, petty captains, foot soldiers, and those on horseback come. When they all came, Solomon commanded them to get into the vessel that was buried in the ground. The Spirits could not gainsay, but were fain to go in, but you may well think that it was with great grief. As soon as they were all in, Solomon caused the cover to be set on and glued fast with the glue of sapience, and therein leaving the devils, caused it also to be covered with earth, until the hole was filled up. His mind and purpose was that the world should be no more infected, that men might afterward live in peace and tranquility, and that all virtue and godliness might reign upon the Earth. . . . But what happened after a long time? As kingdoms chance to change, the towns and cities decay, and new are built. So there was a king who had a great desire to build a city and fortune would that it came into his head to raise it in the exact place wherein these devils were enclosed. This king set people to work to make this city, which he would have mighty, strong, and invincible. Therefore, it required terrible and deep foundations to make the walls. The ground breakers dug so low that one among the rest discovered the cauldron wherein these spirits were. After he had stricken upon it, and his companions did perceive it, they thought they should have been made rich forever, and that there was hidden some inestimable riches. . . . Now these brasiers and batterers had beaten upon it so long, that they beat out a great piece of the cover and made a way to go in, but it was no sooner open then the devils, you may be sure, strived to get out by heaps, making such a noise and cry, that the king and all his people were so amazed with fear that they fell down as if dead. These Spirits got to their feet and away they went, every one to his old corner, but that perhaps some of them were amazed to see the countries and kingdoms altered and changed since their imprisonment, by means whereof, they were fain for a time to stray as vagabonds.[17]

A counterpart to this story is found in the Gnostic text, *The Testimony of Truth,* passed down through the Codex of Nag Hammadi. It says:

> When he had finished building, he imprisoned the demons in the temple. He placed them into seven water pots. They remained a long time in the water pots, abandoned there. When the Romans went up to Jerusalem, they discovered the water pots, and immediately the demons ran out of the water pots, as those who escape from prison. And the water pots remained pure thereafter.[18]

The manuscript of the *Clavicula Solomonis de secretis,* which has been kept in Warsaw, seems to be based on the same tradition.

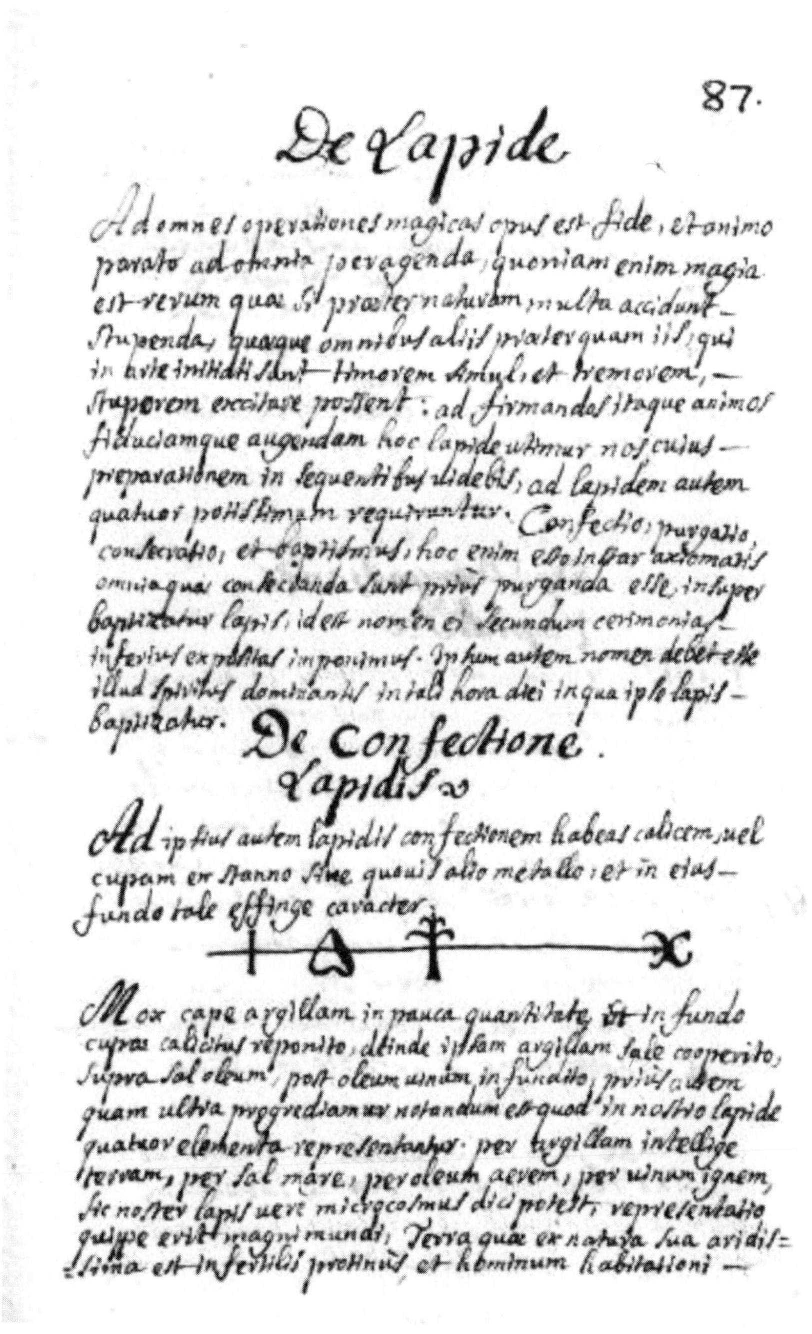

87.

De Lapide

Ad omnes operationes magicas opus est fide, et animo parato ad omnia peragenda, quoniam enim magia est rerum quae si praeter naturam, multa accidunt stupenda, quaeque omnibus aliis praeterquam iis, qui in arte initiati sunt timorem, tumult, et tremorem, stuporem excitare possent: ad firmandos itaque animos fiduciamque augendam hoc lapide utimur nos cuius praeparationem in sequentibus videbis, ad lapidem autem quatuor potissimum requiruntur. Confectio, purgatio, consecratio, et baptismus, hoc enim esse instar axiomatis omnia quae conficienda sunt prius purganda esse, insuper baptizatur lapis, idest nomen ei secundum ceremonias infervius expositas imponimus. In hunc autem nomen debet esse illud spiritus dominantis in tali hora diei in qua ipse lapis baptizatur.

De confectione Lapidis ∞

Ad ipsius autem lapidis confectionem habeas calicem, vel cupam ex stanno sive quovis alio metallo: et in eius fundo tale effinge caracter.

$$ \dagger \quad A \quad \dagger \qquad\qquad \maltese $$

Mox cape argillam in pauca quantitate, et in fundo cupae calicis reponito, deinde ipsam argillam sale cooperito, supra sal oleum, post oleum vinum infundito, prius autem quam ultra progrediamur notandum est quod in nostro lapide quatuor elementa repraesentantur, per argillam intellige terram, per sal mare, per oleum aevem, per vinum ignem, sic noster lapis vere microcosmus dici potest, repraesentatio quippe erit magni mundi, Terra quae ex natura sua aridissima est infertili prottinus, et hominum habitationi —

Fig. 5.2. The Stone

11. THE LIBERATION OF THE DJINNS

Without the second half of the thirteenth century, *The Dialogue de Placides et Timeo* follows a source similar to the one used by Bonaventure des Périers but makes no mention of the Philosopher's Stone.

> The wise king Solomon imprisoned the infernal spirits called devils, about which we will say a few words. I would like to say that, thanks to his intelligence and cunning, he enclosed all the devils of hell inside a glass vessel. He overcame them and knew that they could stand up in the vessel although it was not at all large. They remained inside it as long as it was intact, but long after Solomon's death came the Babylonians, who wished to build a city. While digging the foundations for its walls, they unearthed this vessel, and thinking that it contained a treasure, they broke it. Then all the devils got out and were no longer captives, nor will they ever be again.[19]

The *Bibliotheca anecdotorum* (fourteenth century) gives us another version of this glass bell jar: "Solomon then conjured all the demons and imprisoned them in a small glass bottle that he sank into the depths of the sea. . . . After that, a lame demon who had not entered the flask because he arrived too late helped all the other demons get free."[20] This tale is a form of evil etiology—in fact, once freed, the demons could resume their pernicious activities!

SIX

Solomon's Literary and Scientific Works

1. THE POEMS

If we know Solomon best through his Book of Wisdom, the Christian apocryphal texts also inform us that he wrote odes. Forty-two have come down to us in Syriac and likely date from the third century.[1] They do not correspond at all with what we are told by the Byzantine historian Michael Glycas in his *Annals* (twelfth century). According to him, Solomon wrote five thousand odes on everything created by the earth and on all the animals. As it happens, Flavius Josephus tells us the same thing:

> He also composed *Books of Odes and Songs,* a thousand and five. *Of Parables and Similitudes,* three thousand. For he spake a parable upon every sort of tree, from the hyssop to the cedar, and in like manner also about beasts, about all sorts of living creatures, whether upon the earth, or in the seas, or in the air. For he was not unacquainted with any of their natures nor omitted enquiries about them but described them all like a philosopher and demonstrated his exquisite knowledge of their several properties. God also enabled him to learn that skill which expels demons, which is a science useful and sanative to men.

The author of the Odes took up all the traditional elements connected with Solomon. He was a miracle worker, an exorcist, beloved by God, and an "anointed messiah."

2. THE PROVERBS

The oldest part of the Proverbs was attributed to Solomon who, according to 1 Kings 1–5:12, pronounced three thousand proverbs testifying to his enormous wisdom. Typical of the wisdom literature of Israel, the Proverbs include two (25–29) that were collected by Ezekias around the year 700. Adolf Erman gathered the counterparts of the Proverbs 22:17–24, 42 and showed their Egyptian origin by comparing them to a papyrus containing the teaching of the scribe Amenemope, son of Karnaht (ca. 1300–1075 BCE).[2]

The following proverb can be read in this large compilation: "A virtuous woman is a crown to her husband, but a shameless woman is a rottenness in his bones." In the second collection we find: "A door turns on its hinges, a sluggard on his bed." Both collections are characterized by the expression of a humane, secular wisdom.

It should be noted that the Proverbs were translated and recast in the dialogues of Solomon and Marcolfus.[3] There are versions in a number of languages, including Latin, English,[4] and German. The dialogue

Fig. 6.1. Amenomope, *Book of Proverbs*, Papyrus 10474 of the British Museum

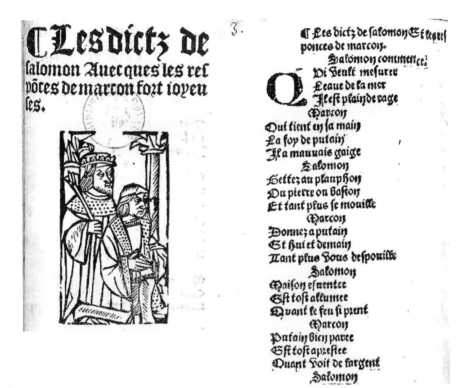

Fig. 6.2. The Words of Solomon

pits Marcolfus, whose role is to be systematically contradictory, against the wise sage Solomon. The madman advances a counter argument reflecting his folly against eleven of Solomon's wise observations.

We see them again in the twelfth century in the Count of Brittany's *De Marcoul et de Salomon*[5] and in *Veez cy une desputacoun entre Salomon ly saaye et Marcoulf le foole*.[6] In the fourteenth century we see them in *Enseignement de li sages Salemons et Tholomé nous enseignent pour venir au sauvement de l'âme*.[7]

Geoffrey Chaucer (1340–1400) cites Solomon's Proverbs ten times in one of his *Canterbury Tales*.[8] Rabelais parodies the Proverbs by writing "He who has no adventure, has neither horse nor mule, so sayeth Solomon."[9]

The German *Solomon and Morolf* is quite different from the texts I just mentioned. Most likely written toward the end of the

twelfth century but passed down by manuscripts from the last third of
the fifteenth century, it is an adventure novel whose plot is as follows:
at Solomon's request, Morolf sets off toward the east to bring back
Solomon's runaway wife. The story is very similar to the Ukrainian
tale *The Tzar Solomon and His Wife* and the Karelian story "The Tsar
Vassili Okulovich and the Tsarina Solomonida" (see part 3, section 11,
pages 207–13). Frederic Vogt's meticulous research lists all the variants
of this text. In his opinion, this legend came from the Jewish world
into Byzantium, and then into Russia and Germany, whose accounts he
summarized and analyzed.[10]

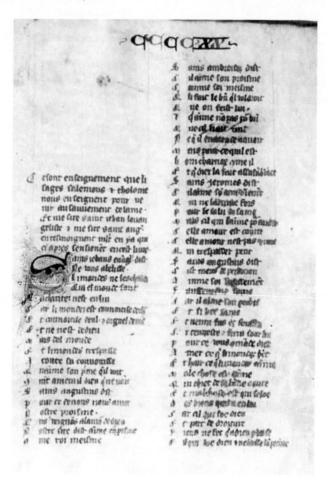

Fig. 6.3. Teaching of Salomo and Tholomé
(Paris, National Library, French manuscript 24432).

3. THE DIALOGUE OF
SOLOMON AND SATURN

Solomon and Saturn is the title given to four texts written in Old English, two in verse and two in prose, that are introduced as an exchange of riddles between King Solomon, representing wisdom, and Saturn, prince of the Chaldeans, described as a pagan. It begins with the question: "How many forms are assumed by the devil and Our Lord when they confront each other?" (*Ac hú moniges bleós bið ðæt deófol and se Pater Noster ðonne híe betwih him gewinna?*) This gives rise to the following list.

Forms of the Devil	Forms of God
Child	Holy Spirit
Dragon	Stinger called *Brachia Dei* (arm of God)
Darkness	Light
Wild Animal	Whale named Leviathan
Horrific dreams	Celestial vision
Evil woman	Celestial breastplate
Sword	Gold breastplate
Thorn bush	Silver initial
Hammer	Silver eagle
Serpent	Christ
Venomous bird	Gold eagle
Wolf	Gold chain
Wrath	Peace
Evil thought	Pure spirit
Form of death	Lord

The text uses Our Father in a dual sense. It is both God and the *Pater noster,* the prayer being a combat weapon against the devil, the cunning one (*laða gæs*), the enemy (*feond*), and his machinations (*Wælnita heap, bealwe bocstafas*): "Therefore with this luminous prayer cause the blood of the devil to boil so that its drops fall on him."[11] This is what opens the heavens, extinguishes the demon's fire, and so forth. The right hand of the *Pater noster* resembles a golden sword that shines brighter than eleven of the constellations in the sky.[12]

But where is the Solomonic magic in all this? It seems to be missing entirely, and yet, the *Dialogue* uses runes to fight the devil! Each of the runes listed is accompanied by its actions, for example:

A (ᚠ) pursues it with great strength and strikes it. T (ᛏ) tortures it and stabs its tongue, strangles it, and tears its cheeks. E (ᛗ) afflicts it . . . then comes S (ᛋ), the prince of angels. . . ."

The dialogue in verses ends with an admonition: "Think before you draw the blade of your sword."[13]

In the prose fragment in the Cottonianus Vitelius manuscript, A.XV in the British Museum collection, Saturn asks about several things:

Tell me, he asked, where was God sitting when he created the heavens and earth?

He was holding onto the wings of the wind.

Then the text speaks of Adam:

From what was his name formed?

From four stars.

What were their names?

I shall tell you: Arthox, Dux, Arotholem, Minsymbrie.*

Of what substance was Adam, the first man, made?

Of eight pounds by weight (*of vii punda gewihte*).

Tell me, what were their names?

---

*More precisely: Anathole, Disis, Arctos, Mesembrios. In the Middle Ages, there were a huge variety of spellings. They are the names of the four cardinal points.

And Solomon cited the earth, which gave him his flesh; the fire, which gave him his blood, the wind, which gave him his breath, the foam, which gave him the inconsistency of his moods, the grace, which provided his fat and growth, the blossom, which is responsible for the different kinds of eyes, the dew, from when he draws his sweat, and the salt, which is why his tears are salty.[14]

Solomon last answered Saturn's questions about holy historical figures such as Noah, Mary, Eliseus, as well as on the four rivers of paradise, and so forth.

4. THE PSALMS

The eighteen psalms of Solomon[15] are the result of pseudepigrapha and are preserved in a dozen Greek manuscripts and four Syriac manuscripts. They describe the siege of Jerusalem, then its occupation (I–II), and present Solomon as a messiah. Relying on historical data, J. Viteau proposes these as the dates on which these psalms were written:

Psalm I, circa 64–63	Psalm X, circa 63–55
Psalm II, circa 48–47	Psalm XI, circa 63–60
Psalm III, circa 63–60 or 69–64	Psalm XII, circa 69–64
Psalm IV, circa 69–64	Psalm XIII, circa 63–60
Psalm V, circa 63–55	Psalm XIV, circa 63–60
Psalm VI, circa 63–55 or 69–64	Psalm XV, circa 63–60
Psalm VII, circa 63–62	Psalm XVI, circa 63–55
Psalm VIII, circa 63–62	Psalm XVII, circa 63–60
Psalm IX, circa 63–55	

The eighteenth psalm is different from all the others as it discusses divine charity, the reign of the messiah, and the stability and regularity of the course of the heavenly bodies:

11. Our God is great and glorious, he dwells in the highest heaven;

12. It is he who set the stars on their course
    for the division of each day into seasons
    and they never depart from the path He appointed for them.

13. They pursue their path each day out of fear of God
    from the day that God created them, and thus forevermore.
    Since the beginning of the world, they have never left their course
    except when God so commanded them
    by the order of His servants.[16]

Apocryphal psalms written in Hebrew have been discovered in caves number 4 and 11 in Qumran, and the question of their origin as Jewish or Greek is still a source of contention among researchers.[17] In the fragment of the Arabic text, David confirms that all the psalms are his and that he alone is capable of reciting from memory the fifteen Songs of Degrees. He next gives Solomon this recommendation:

Keep God's commandments, Solomon my son, study the law of the Lord, and walk before him with a perfect heart. God has chosen you and made you king over the people of Israel. Bestow justice as I did and be constant, and the Lord will be with you as he was with me for forty years. I recommend, Solomon my son, that you observe my testament in memory of me and that you display the mystery that I have seen concerning the Lord and his Mother the Virgin who came from our tribe. For me, I beg him for pity on his creature in this world and to grant me his mercy.

Once David said all this to his son Solomon; he stopped speaking and died happily in his old age. Solomon gave him a grave in a magnificent sepulcher, as was appropriate for one of his rank. He interred him close to his fathers while giving thanks to God to whom belongs the action of grace and praise ceaselessly and eternally.[18]

5. THE HERBAL

Michael Glycas mentions Solomonic remedies that use herbs with charms, and, in 1747, Daniel George Morhof spoke of an Arabic herbal by Solomon (*Salomonis herbarium*)[19] that taught the user to perform medical miracles, but outside of these mentions, we have not found the barest trace of this book. It should be noted, though, that Solomon's seal (*sigillum Salomonis*) is the name of the plant whose botanical name is *polygonatum* (πολυγόνατον) and *convallaria polygonatum*. *The General History of Plants*[20] calls it "Solomon's signet." As for the "Solomon's Seal," this is the name of various monocotyledon plants of the genus *polygonaton* that is sometimes called "*muguet des pauvres*" (poor man's lily of the valley).

78 Du Signet de Salomon.   Chap. LXVII.

LA FORME.

Le large Signet de Salomon, a les tiges longues, rondes: Les fueilles longues, verdes, plus grandes, plus lõgues, & plus polyes que les fueilles de Laurier, entre lefquelles pendent à queues cour tes, belles fleurs verdaftres, longues & creufes, trois ou quatre enfemble, tellement que chafque queué porte communement plus de fleurs que de fueilles : les fleurs peries fe tournent en bayes rondes, verdes au commancement, & puis noires, femblables au fruiêt de l'Hierre, ou aux Cufines. La racine eft longue, de la groffeur d'vn doigt, noüeufe, blanche, aiant plufieurs fibres, & faueur au commancement qu'on le goufte douce, puis apres vn peu acre & amere.

Le Signet eftroiêt, n'eft point fort different à l'autre, finon que fes fueilles font plus eftroiêtes, & ne viennent point feparément, mais quatre ou cinq fortans d'vne ioinêture au tour de la tige, bien pres en forme d'eftoille. Les fleurs font plus verdatres, & le fruiêt plus noir. La racine plus petite & plus grefle, au refte femblable à la fufdiête.

LE LIEV.

Le large Signet de Salomon, croift en ce païs és bois fecs & haut efleués. Le fecond vient aufsi aux montaignes & bois, mais principalement en Alemaigne. icy on ne le trouue finon planté aux iardins des Amateurs des herbes.

LE TEMPS.

Ilz fleuriffent tous deux en May & en Iuin.

LES NOMS. ●

Le Signet de Salomon fe nomme en Grec πολυγόνατον : en Latin *Polygonatum* : és Boutiques *Sigillum Salomonis*: en haut Aleman ꟗeiſꟗ ꟗurꟗ, c'eft à dire Racine blanche; en bas Aleman Salomons ſegⱨel.

LE TEMPERAMENT. ●   ●

Le Signet de Salomon eft de nature chaude & feche, abfterfiue, & quelque peu aftringente.

LES VERTVS ET OPERATIONS.

La racine de Signet de Salomõ pilée confolide & guerit les playes fur lefqlles elle eft applquée

La mefme toute nouuelle, pilée & induiête ou le ius d'icelle, efface toutes lentilles, taches, meur triffures(puenâtespar eftrebaftu, tôbé, ou hurté) foit en la face, foit en toute autre partie du corps.

Cefte herbe ne la racine d'icelle ne font point vtiles à prédre par dedens le corps, comme efcrit Galien.

Pfyllion.   Herbe aux pulces.

Fig. 6.4. Jacques Daleschamps, Jean Desmoulins,
Histoire génerale des plantes (vol. 2, Paris: Borde, Arnaud & Rigaud, 1653)

Anne Regourd found a *Book of Solomon's Binding Spells and Other Useful Remedies* (*Kitab al-Mandal as Sulaymani li-algam'wa-gayrihi min al-adwiya al-nafi'a*) in the Arab tradition, and she provides a list of the medicinal plants found in these manuscripts.[21]

According to Johann Zwinger,[22] Solomon allegedly wrote some "sermons on trees, from the cedar in Lebanon to the hyssop that grows out of walls" (1 Kings 4:33), which, in fact, means from the largest to the smallest, because, for the Hebrews, the cedar is the symbol of majesty and the hyssop represents humility.

6. THE MEDICAL BOOKS

Connected directly with plants, physicians have gleaned remedies from the books inspired by Solomonic texts, and Michael Glycas notes that "doctors from many nations extracted a wealth of commentaries from his books." Some traditions even assert that Hippocrates and Galen were among their number. According to Suidas, his book on the healing of disease was likely destroyed by King Ezechias when he saw how it was being misused. It was once carved on the door of the Temple and contained remedies for all illnesses.[23] Karl Preisendanz viewed Solomon as a master of healing magic, astrology, and demonology.[24]

Pseudo-Justinian noted in the fourth century: "Many remedies for the body's illnesses were discovered by pious men and by King Solomon. However, not a single infidel knows how to heal the soul."[25]

In the fifth century, bishop and historiographer Theodoret of Cyrus[26] wrote that in the Solomonic writings it is possible to learn how to treat certain diseases with hyena bile, lion fat, beef blood, and snake meat, for these products were regarded as being apotropaic.

In the seventh century, the physician Asaph the Jew (Assaf Ha Yehudi) published a *Book of Medicines* (*Sefer refouoth*) that borrowed its title from the treatise by Ezechias which, according to tradition, was either hidden or destroyed. The Talmud cites this same book but attributes the authorship to Solomon. It was allegedly hidden by Ezechias. Maimonides (1138–1204) considers this book to be a magical anthology of healing.[27]

A fourteenth-century Dutch book of folk remedies states that Solomon allegedly claimed that "menstrual blood is a very dangerous substance."[28] It is common knowledge that this blood was widely used in black magic.

At the beginning of the sixteenth century, a birthmark at the base of the nose or on the forehead was called Solomon's knot (*nodus Salomonis*), and it was supposed to be a sign of bad luck.

7. THE *LIBER SALOMONIS*

The Sloane manuscript 3826 (folio 2 r57) contains a book said to be dictated by Solomon to his scribe Clarifaton. The book contains seven treatises:

Clavis, dealing with astronomy and the stars;

Ala, on the properties of several stones, gems, and animals;

the *Tractatus thymiamatu,* on suffumigations;

the *Treatise on Time,* indicating the year, the day, and the night of every magic operation described in this book;

the *Treatise on Cleanliness and Abstinence;*

Samain, in which all the heavens are named along with their angels, and all magic operations and workings that can be made with them;

and the *Book of Virtues,* with the properties of the magical arts, its figures, and their organization.[29]

SEVEN

Solomon's Explorations

1. SOLOMON'S DESCENT TO THE BOTTOM OF THE SEA

Being wise, and even very wise, Solomon conceived of the idea to travel down to the bottom of the sea to see what was there and what was lacking. He had a very large bottle manufactured and sat down inside it. Once his servitors had tied a rope to the neck of the bottle, they brought it out into the open sea and then sent it sinking toward the ocean floor. He had given them instructions that they would pull him out as soon as he tugged on the rope when he was underwater.

Having heard of what was going on, Solomon's sister grew very scared that he would drown. She raced to the sea and threw herself in to pull her brother out. "Lord," she cried, "don't let me die until I have found my brother! Change me into a fish so I can find him and pull him back to shore, then, if you wish, leave me in the sea for eternity." And, lo a miracle! God changed the lower half of her body into a fish and arranged matters so that she would live eternally in the sea seeking her brother Solomon and never finding him. And truly, she who had become half fish and half woman dwelled in the sea. Many sailors caught sight of her and would chase her saying: "If you are looking for Solomon, young lady, he is with us. Come onto our boat and you will see." Once she heard the name Solomon, she would swim behind the boat for several days until she became exhausted and abandoned the ship.

Meanwhile, Solomon had reached the bottom of the sea where he looked with wonder at the order that ruled among the fish. When they waged war, they made terrible preparations with an eye to battle. Solomon saw men, aquatic horses, and other marvels in the sea. Once he had come to the sea floor, he saw an immense fish swimming by. It spent three days and three nights near Solomon's bottle, and never in all that time did he catch sight of its tail. Next to this huge fish there were rows of billions of fish arranged in square detachments, and in front of every square there was a larger fish that was in command like some pasha in an army. The huge fish pushed the bottle when he swam too close, therefore shaking the rope as well. The servitors holding the other end immediately pulled the bottle back up with the very wise Solomon inside. He told the old men that made up his council of all that he had seen.

Since that time, the wise Solomon arranged his armies like those of the fish that he had seen in the sea. With such a formidably organized army, Solomon conquered all the kings and forced them to pay him tribute. Eventually, all other kings imitated the arrangement of Solomon's army.[1]

This story brings to mind an episode from *The Romance of Alexander,* a text that was translated into all Western languages, in which he descends to the bottom of the sea. The tale of Tsar Vassili Okulovich and the Tsarina Solomonida is reminiscent of another version of this descent to the ocean floor (see part 3, section 11, pages 207–13).

Solomon ordered his wife to seal him inside a chest and to let the chest sink to the bottom of the sea while making sure to not let go of her end of the chain. But she did not obey, and he remained at the bottom of the sea. Devils chanced to come to the shore and began quarreling over several objects: a hat that makes its wearer invisible, a staff that hits by itself, and a flying carpet. They agreed to submit to Solomon's judgment and fished out the chest he was in. Once he was back on the shore, he crossed himself and they fled, leaving their booty behind.[2]

2. SOLOMON AND THE YOUNG MAN
IN THE GLASS DOME

It is said that one day Solomon had a desire to learn how deep the sea was and what could be found within it. He chose one hundred demons (*assaytanes*) out of those who were most skilled. From this hundred, he kept fifty. Out of this fifty he took twenty-five, then twelve of this twenty-five, and from the twelve, six, and from the six, three.

He gave orders to one of the three to go visit the seas, observe what he found there, and to watch what the sea creatures did. After traveling through all the seas, the demon saw nothing but fish, the bigger ones eating the smaller ones. He returned to report on his mission to King Solomon, son of David—*alahi salaam* (peace be upon him)—and described what he had seen in the ocean. The king sent another demon with orders to sound the bottom of the sea. The demon set off but was never able to reach the bottom. On his way he met an angel (*almalaque*) in the sea who asked him: "Where are you going, cursed demon?" The demon replied: "Solomon ordered me to sound the bottom of the sea, but I could not reach it." The angel said: "How could you reach it when no one but God has any knowledge of it? One hundred years have already gone by since I myself, in this same spot, saw a sailor who was repairing a timber on his boat that had been broken in a storm. He dropped his tool and it fell into the water. This tool has still not reached the bottom!" He left as soon as he finished telling the demon this.

Continuing his sea voyage, the demon eventually stumbled upon a dome (*alcuba*) made of green glass. It was attacked by the waves and the fish, which were unable to damage it in any way. He returned to tell Solomon about what he had seen and informed him of his discovery of the green glass dome. When he learned of this, Solomon summoned one hundred demons and ordered them to go find this green dome in the sea and bring it back to him.

The order was executed, and the demons deposited the dome at King Solomon's feet. There was a young man (*mancebo*) clad in white inside the dome. King Solomon spoke to him: "Young man, what is the reason you are inside this green glass dome?" The young man replied:

"O king, you should know that my parents were quite elderly. I took care of them as they had for me when I was a child. I washed them and kept them clean as if they were babies. My father died first. When my mother was at death's door, she prayed to God to spirit me out of the world, so that after her death I would not be corrupted by the desires and vices of this world and lose the merit (*aquel gualardon*) that I had earned. God granted my mother's prayer: two angels came to take me in His Name, and they placed me in this green glass dome in the middle of the sea.

The king asked: "How long have you been there?"

The young man replied: "For twenty-six years."

The king asked him: "How do you feed yourself? How do you quench your thirst?"

"Every morning a white bird brings me a white substance in his beak that serves me as food and drink."

The king then asked: "Young man, how can you tell day from night?"

He answered: "See you, O king, this white groove. When its whiteness grows more intense, I know that it is day."

The king asked: "How do you know when it is night?"

The young man responded: "When this black groove expands, I know that it is night."

The king asked: "O young man, would you like to stay here with me?"

The boy replied: "No, I ask that you put me back where I was, so that what God has planned for me will be realized."

The young man then went back into his dome then shut the door from inside. The demons took it and dropped it back in the sea, right where they had found it.[3]

3. SOLOMON IN THE AIR

One day when Solomon was shining in all of his royal glory, his throne rose up into the air, carried aloft by the wind. Above the throne, a cloud covered him in its shadow,*[4] and beneath stretched a carpet carried by

---

*Another tradition tells how the birds flying over the carpet woven by the djinns protected him from the sun.

a multitude of men and genies. When they passed over Mecca, a fakir caught sight of him and his entire escort. He shouted out: "O praise-worthy God, what glory you have given to the son of David!"

When he heard these words, the prophet Solomon ordered the wind to stop, then, calling to the fakir, he said: "Swear to you by the God who has given this glory to the son of David, if you speak one time *La ilahah illa-lahou** you shall obtain a more brilliant glory in the other world than that of the son of David on earth."[5]

The story of Tsar Vassili Okulovich (see part 3, section 11, pages 207–13) is quite close to this story by Bukhari of Johore, but a basket replaces the carpet, and two noi, gigantic birds similar to the roc of the Arabian tales and the zuzœlœ of the Tartar tales, carry it through the air.[6] Researchers have also noted the kinship of this flight with what the great Persian poet Djemschid (ca. 940–1020) said:

> Djam-Chid decided to have a special seat made for him. It would then be used traditionally for the coronation of the kings of Iran. The artisans set to work to create this throne (*takht*), which is still known under the name of Tahkté-Dam-Chid. They crafted a gold throne encrusted with jewels. Djam-Chid mounted his throne and commanded the divs to hold it in the middle of the air so that every-one could admire it.[7]

---

*"There is no god but God."

Solomon and the Djinns

The thirty-fourth sura of the Qu'ran, Saha, quotes Allah as speaking the following words:

> And to Solomon [We subjected] the wind, its morning [stride from sunrise till midnoon] was a month's [journey], and its afternoon [stride from the midday decline of the sun to sunset] was a month's [journey] (i.e., in one day he could travel two months' journey). And we caused a fount of (molten) brass to flow for him, and there were djinns that worked in front of him, by the Leave of his Lord. . . . They made for him whatever he desired: stately buildings, images, basins like water-troughs and huge, built-in cauldrons.

There is another book of this nature, *The Book of Contracts Concluded with the Whole of Djinns and Genies by Solomon, Son of David,* which was mentioned by Ibn Qayyim ash-Shibliyya,[1] but this book is not available for study, unfortunately.

1. THE DJINNS

When God summoned the genies to Sulayman, the angel Gabriel [Djebrail] made the following proclamation: "Djinns* and Satans

---

*The djinns (Hebrew: *azazil*) were the first inhabitants of the earth. They caused harm and God sent an army of angels who pushed them back to confinement on islands. They are the descendants of Iblis, who became the devil.

(*shayatin*) answer the call of Sulayman ibn Dawud (Solomon, son of David)." They came from all the mountains, caves, valleys, and deserts, saying: "Here we are. Here we are." The angels drove them forward like a shepherd drives his flock until they were all gathered before the king in obedience and submission. They consisted of twenty-four thousand categories and Sulayman saw their colors: There were black ones, red ones, speckled ones, white ones, yellow ones, and green ones, coming in the size and shape of every animal. Some had a lion's head on an elephant's body, others had a trunk and tail, and yet others had horns and hooves. The king was greatly amazed at the sight of all these shapes, and he prostrated himself while paying homage to the Most High: "My God," he said, "strip away the terror that you have inspired in me." He then questioned the djinns about their natures, food, and drink, and all answered him. He divided them between various professions: some cut rocks, stones, and trees; others dove into the sea, built palaces; and some extracted minerals and precious stones.[2]

Fig. 8.1. Djinns, Zakariya ibn Muhammed al-Qazwini, The Wonders of Created Things and the Curiosities of Existing Things (*Aja'ib al-makhluqat wa ghara'ib al mawjudat*).

2. THE FATE OF THE REBEL GENIES

A man set sail for India with several others. They sailed until a wind arose that pushed them onto some land in the middle of the night. When the light grew in the East, they saw, emerging from the caves of this country, bands of entirely naked black men who were like wild beasts, for they could not understand a word that was spoken to them. They had one among their kind who was a king and understood Arabic. . . . The sailors went into the town and met a fisherman who was casting his net into the sea to catch fish. He then pulled it back out. It held a vessel of lead-sealed brass sealed with the seal of Sulayman ibn Dawud.* He picked up the vase, broke it, and a blue smoke rose from it into the air. A strange voice could be heard saying: "I repent, prophet of God!"

A being horrible to gaze upon emerged from this smoke. It was a terrible being whose head touched the mountain. It then vanished before their eyes. The people in the boat felt as if their hearts would explode in their chests, while the people of this land took no notice of it whatsoever. One man went to see the king and asked him about it. "Know this," the king replied, "this was one of the djinns that Sulayman ibn Dawud, in his wrath, imprisoned in a vase and then sealed with lead before having it thrown into the sea. When a fisherman casts his net, he often pulls up one of these vessels. When it gets broken, a genie comes out whom, imagining that Solomon is still alive, asks his forgiveness and says: "I repent, O prophet of God."[3]

This story can be also seen in *The Thousand and One Nights* with "The Fisherman and the Genie." The genie in it is called a *marid*, meaning a rebel demon (see the Qu'ran 37:7).

3. SOLOMON AND THE DIVS

When Solomon was angry at a div, he ordered him bound and placed inside a large stone, then sawn in half along with that stone. Then God

---

*Engraved with God's name, this ring makes it impossible to break whatever carries its imprint.

gave Solomon a fountain of copper and bronze as is reported in the Qu'ran.[4]* No one before him owned its like. Inside this fountain he had the divs crushed together, after which, he ordered them to be cast into the sea. It is said in the Qu'ran: "And others [divs] were bound with chains. Such are our gifts, spread them or refuse them without realizing, and so forth."[5]

4. SOLOMON AND ASCHMEDAI (ISRAEL)

When King Solomon wished to build the Temple in Jerusalem, he was discomfited by procuring stones of the necessary size because it was mandated to avoid the use of all iron tools, as metal was generally intended for manufacturing weapons of war. He therefore summoned the sages of his kingdom to consult with them on this matter. They answered him: "There is a worm the size of a grain of barley called the *shamir* that can carve the hardest of stones. Moses already used it to carve the name of the twelve tribes on the precious stones of Adam's breastplate." In a transport of joy, Solomon cried out: "I thank you from the bottom of my heart, wise men! But tell me, where might I gain possession of this insect?"

"O our king and master," the sages replied, "we cannot give you any counsel on this matter, so compel the demons to appear before your throne. They will surely be able to tell you."

The king immediately made all the demons appear before his throne and asked them where the *shamir* hid. They replied: "O king, we have no idea either, only our king Asmodeus, chief of all demons will be able to tell you."

"Then I shall hold you prisoner here until you tell me where the home of your elder Asmodeus is."

After several days of captivity, the demons said they were ready to let him know the location of their ruler. "Very far from here," they told Solomon, "in the middle of the forest at the foot of a mountain is where the prince of demons lives. That is where he has dug a well filled with

---

*The word *qatar,* which can be found in the Qu'ran, means liquid copper.

the clearest spring water. To guarantee the purity of the water, he has placed a heavy stone that bears his seal over the well opening. Everyday he climbs into the sky to learn of heaven's decisions. Toward evening, he returns to Earth, thirsty because of this long journey. He delights in this pure, cool drink but not without making sure that the seal of the well is intact. Then he puts everything back in order and vanishes. That, O king, is all we can tell you. With your great wisdom, you will see what you need to do."

Solomon immediately summoned his loyal counselor, the valiant warrior Benaya, and gave him a gold chain on which the name of God was engraved, and several goatskins filled with a precious wine. Thus equipped, Benaya set off with several companions to fulfill a mission that was as difficult as it was dangerous.

After walking for weeks and weeks, crossing raging rivers, and climbing steep mountains, they finally reached the forest indicated by the demons and found the well of Asmodeus there. They quickly got down to work. They took great pains to not touch the lid that bore the seal of Asmodeus. They pierced a hole in the side of the well through which they poured the old wine into the water. They then put everything back into order so that no one could see that anything was amiss. Benaya and his companions hid in the forest to await the return of the prince of demons.

Toward evening, the demon returned from heaven. Benaya and his people were terrified by his tall size and horrific appearance, but it did not cause them to lose their courage. As was customary, Asmodeus began examining his well, and when he was satisfied that everything was in order, he removed the cover so he could drink. But barely had the liquid touched his lips when he realized the fraud: "Ah! It's wine!" he shouted. "I don't drink wine. Wine steals consciousness and disturbs reason. A wise man doesn't drink wine." But his thirst tormented him so strongly that he wished to at least dip his lips into the liquid. "One sole drop," he told himself, "should not cause any harm." He brought the bowl to his mouth but instead of one drop, he swallowed two, then three, then four. He barely had time to realize what he had done when the sweet beverage had entirely filled his gullet.

The effects of the wine were not long in making themselves known. The demon fell into a deep slumber. When they saw this, Benaya and his companions came out of hiding and carefully approached him whereupon they attached the chain bearing the name of God around his neck. When Asmodeus got up and saw the chain around his neck, he grew angry and tried to tear it off, but Benaya told him: "You will never be able to break this chain, which is stamped with the name of all powerful God. For now, you are in my power."

Hearing these words, the leader of the demons transformed and followed Benaya and his men with good grace. During this journey, some odd incidents occurred. One day, the demon sat with his back against a tree, but at the first contact with this evil spirit, the tree was uprooted. Another day, when seeking to rest, Asmodeus leaned against a small house in which a poor widow was living. Hardly had his body touched the wall when the entire house began to shake. In terror, the poor old woman raced outside begging him to have mercy on her and her poor dwelling. Continuing their journey, they chanced upon a marriage procession. Then Asmodeus began to moan and groan. "Why are you crying?" Benaya asked.

"Because I know the young bride is going to die tomorrow."[6]

Passing by a cobbler's shop, they heard a man ordering a pair of boots that would last for seven years! Asmodeus cried out: "A pair of boots* for seven years! But this man has but seven days to live!"[7]

En route, they also met a drunken man who, having moved off their path, came close to falling into a ditch which would have killed him. Asmodeus made a vigorous effort and managed to pull the man out of his perilous plight. Benaya, having expressed his surprise at seeing such charity on the part of the head of all demons, was answered by Asmodeus: "I know full well that this drunken man is a great sinner. I did him this favor so that he will have received his compensation for the small good that he had done on this earth and that his future life will hold nothing in store for him but punishment."

Another day, they encountered a man in the fields who was hunting

---

*The Russian text says sandals.

for treasure using witchcraft. When he saw him, Asmodeus burst out laughing: "There is a man who is looking everywhere for treasure and doesn't know that there is one hidden beneath the house he lives in.[8]

They finally reached Jerusalem. Brought immediately to the palace of King Solomon, the king of demons drew in front of the throne a square four cubits long and in full wrath, addressed these words to the monarch: "Look, once you are dead, you will have to be satisfied with a piece of land no bigger than this, and now, not content with having caused so many lands to submit to your authority, you wish to again subjugate the demons!"

Solomon answered: "Don't get worked up, demon! It is not out of ambition or greed that I have called you before my throne but only because I desire your advice for a work I wish to undertake in the honor of God. For I know that you honor God like us. So please hear me out. Before his death, my father David charged me with building the Temple of God that he was unable to build. But because I am forbidden by the Law from using iron tools to carve the stones I need, I find myself in a very uncomfortable situation. However, I have learned that there is a little worm, the *Shamir*,[9] which by its touch alone can cut even the hardest stones, and that you alone are able to procure this wonderful insect for me. Therefore, I had you brought before my throne."

"My king and master," Asmodeus replied more calmly, "let me inform you that I have no power over the *Shamir*. It was the Spirit of the Sea that entrusted that power to the wood grouse, and that bird swore he would guard it well."

After Solomon heard this response, he sent Benaya in search of this wood grouse so he could gain possession of the *Shamir*. Benaya made his preparations to accomplish this difficult mission. In addition to the necessary foodstuffs and equipment, he added a glass bell jar to his baggage. After countless searches through wild, wilderness lands where few humans had ever set foot, he finally discovered the nest of the bird on the top of a tall mountain, on the peak of a bluff. He immediately took out the glass bell jar and placed it over the nest. Then he hid behind the trees with his companions.

When the wood grouse came to feed its young, Benaya was unable to get near them. After wearing herself out trying to take care of her clutch, she flew off and returned a few minutes later carrying the *Shamir* worm in her beak. She placed it on the bell jar, which burst into pieces at first contact with the insect. Then the grouse tried to pick the worm back up with its beak, but Benaya and his men jumped out yelling so loudly that she dropped the *Shamir*. Benaya quickly grabbed it and fled with his companions.

Solomon was then able to begin construction of the Temple. The *Shamir* cut all the stones that were needed, and seven years later, the building was completed.[10]

Before continuing, we should note that Gervase of Tilbury, who wrote his *Otia imperialia* from 1209 to 1214, provided us with another form of the *Shamir* legend:

Solomon chose the men of Biblos to sculpt and polish the marble and stocks used to build the temple. As it happens, according to Jewish tradition, to cut these stones more quickly, Solomon had the blood of a small worm that was called a *Tanir*.* The marble, moistened with its blood, was easy to cut. Here is how it was discovered: Solomon owned an ostrich that had a chick. Because he had imprisoned the young bird in a glass bowl, the ostrich, seeing its chick but unable to reach it, went into the desert and brought back a small worm whose blood she used to smear the glass, which then broke into pieces.[11]

During this time, Asmodeus remained Solomon's prisoner who had kept him close at hand so he could be consulted whenever a difficult situation arose. But one day Solomon said: "I have acquired great science in divine matters and profane affairs, but I would like to add to my store of wisdom everything that makes you superior to simple mortals."

"Remove this chain that I am wearing around my neck and put yours in its place," Asmodeus replied, "and I will then satisfy

---

*Depending on the authors, the name of this worm varies: *Thamur, Tanir, Shamir.* The Arabs call it *Samur,* and a crow replaces the ostrich.

your curiosity, and you will learn many wondrous things."

Solomon, elated at the thought of learning these secrets and at being initiated into the mysteries, hastened to grant the chief of the demons' request. But hardly had the demon been freed of his chain on which the name of all powerful God had been carved when he regained his full strength. He grabbed the king and launched him into space so forcefully that the king fell back to earth thousands of leagues away[12] in India.

When Solomon returned to his senses, he saw to his surprise that he was in an unknown land among foreign folk. However, with great courage, he began the long journey home. The first few weeks were not too hard on him because he still had a little money, and his shoes and clothing were still in good condition. When he experienced some moments of weakness, his trust in God sustained him. But soon, when he had exhausted all his resources, the rich and powerful King Solomon was obliged to knock on doors like any other poor beggar. When he said, "I am Solomon, King of Jerusalem," nobody put any stock in his words and they made fun of him.

Finally, after long years of traveling, he reached Jerusalem. He immediately presented himself to the Sanhedrin, the supreme court of the holy city, and said, "It is I, Solomon, king of Jerusalem, don't you recognize me?" But here, too, they took him to be a madman. This was because, after his disappearance, Asmodeus had assumed the appearance of the King of Israel and governed in his stead without anyone seeing through the deceit.

However, as Solomon continued to assert his rights and said things that were evidence of great wisdom, the Sanhedrin decided to examine his case. Their decision was bolstered by certain suspicions that had arisen concerning the fake Solomon. For example, his servants had long been intrigued at the sight of their master going to bed without removing his shoes. To understand this peculiarity, you should know that demons that assume the appearance of human beings can transform their entire body except for their feet. Asmodeus had rooster feet and he took great pains to keep anyone from seeing them.

So, the new Solomon was led into the palace to be placed in the presence of the alleged monarch. When Asmodeus saw the true king Solomon entering the room, he let out a scream that caused the land of Israel to shake from the entire city of Jerusalem, all the way to Jericho. Then he grew to such gigantic proportions that he broke through the ceiling of the palace until his head touched the clouds, and he suddenly vanished.

But King Solomon, fearful of the prince of demons' revenge, had himself guarded every night when he went to bed by sixty warriors chosen from among the heroes of Israel, as it is said in the Song of Songs (3:7–8): "Behold, it is the couch of Solomon! It is surrounded by sixty brave men of the mighty men of Israel, each of them wears a sword at his side to dispel the terrors of the night."[13]

The quarrels between Solomon and Asmodeus enjoyed considerable success with the Jewish community of Prague. In the nineteenth century, Wolf Pascheles (1814–1857) collected an echo of it in the volume of his *Sippurim** which comprises moral tales.[14]

5. SOLOMON AND ASCHMEDAI (INDIA)

It is said that no man should boast of his wisdom,[15] but Solomon boasted of it on his throne when he said, "There is no one wiser than I." It is also written (5 Moses XVII, 7) that "The king should not have many wives so that he may not stray from the path of righteousness," but Solomon said, "I will have many wives and I will remain on the path of righteousness." What did Yod† do in similar circumstances? He stood before God's throne and said: "Lord of the World, have you ever written a needless letter?"

"No!"

"You see, Solomon has thrown me out; he possesses one thousand wives and has transgressed your law."

**Sippurim:* "400 leagues." In one variant, Aschmedai takes Solomon into his enormous mouth and spits him at this distance.

†The son of Yehoyada, a priest in the Hebrew Bible.

"I am going to look into this matter and help you get back your rights."

He called Aschmedai,[*16] the king of the demons: "Go to the home of Solomon, steal his ring, assume his appearance, and seat yourself upon his throne," and Aschmedai obeyed.

The children of Israel mistook him for Solomon when he wandered through the towns and villages saying: "I, the preacher, am king." The people told each other, "What a madman! The monarch is sitting on his throne and this preacher is claiming to be the king!" This went on for three years. God then said, "I have given Yod justice." During these three years, Aschmedai visited Solomon's wives. Eventually he went to see one at a time she was unclean. Seeing him, she said, "How your habits have changed!" He stopped speaking. "You are not Solomon," she said.

He then went to see Bethsheba, the king's mother, and said: "I desire this and that[†] from you."

"Then you cannot be my son," she replied.

She went to the home of Benayahu[17] and told him of this. He was horrified, and rending his garments, responded, "God preserve us! If that is what he is like, then he is not your son who sits the throne but Aschmedai, and the young wanderer is Solomon." He had him summoned and asked him: "Who are you, my son?"

"I am Solomon, son of David."

"How did this happen to you?"

"One day when I was at home as usual, a tornado carried me away and, since that time, I have been acting as if bereft of my senses, this is why I have been wandering here and there."

To make sure that Benayahu believed him, Solomon told of a past event that only the people present knew about. Benayahu convened the members of the Sanhedrin. Aschmedai was arrested and stripped of Solomon's ring. The king resumed his former appearance and regained possession of his throne.[‡18]

---

[*]The name of the king of the demons appears as Asmoth, Ashmédaï, Asmoday, Asmodeus, Aesma, Asmadai, Asmodius, Asmodaios, Hasmoday, Chashmodai, Azmonden, Sidonay, or even Asmobée in various texts.

[†]"This and that" is a euphemism for sexual acts.

[‡]In the Bible, Asmodeus is called "the worst of the demons" (Tobias III, 8).

The *Talmud of Babylon*[19] (mid-sixth century) tells the tale of how Solomon tricked Aschmedai into lending his aid for building the temple. He kept him in his power thanks to the chain that he had slipped around his neck.

One day when Solomon was alone with this demon, he said: "It is written that God brought Jacob out of Egypt with the speed of a buffalo.[20] Our wise men tell us that 'speed' means angels and 'buffalos' means demons. What would you like to have from me?"

"Remove my chain and give me your ring, and I will show you my power."

Solomon unchained him and gave him his ring, which Aschmedai swallowed. He then touched the sky with one of his wings and the earth with the other, and cast Solomon four hundred parasangs* away. Solomon wandered from door to door saying, "I the preacher was King of Jerusalem." When he went before the Sanhedrin, the sages said: "A mad man never changes his speech, what could this mean?" They questioned him: "Did the king make you ask this?"

"No!"

They next questioned the king's wives: "Does the king come visit you?"

"Yes," they replied.

He asked if they had looked at his feet. "He always comes with them covered by his garment," they said. He then learned that this Solomon only wanted the unclean women and even Bethsheba. The sages set Solomon back upon his throne, gave him back his ring, and a chain on which God's name had been carved. If Aschmedai sees it, he flees.[21]

6. SOLOMON AND THE DRAGON

A curious poem of two hundred fifty-eight verses, which has been dated back to the eleventh century, provides its own description of the

---

*A parasang is a historical Iranian measure of distance.

winning of the *Shamir*, most likely based on a text in Latin. Here, a dragon replaces Aschmedai and his capture, thanks to an intoxicating drink, is very reminiscent to that of the djinn Sakhr.

Solomon was the son of David and ruled after him. God granted him His grace and told him to choose whatever he wished, wealth or wisdom, for he esteemed him above all other men on earth. Solomon replied: "Lord, you know I must take care of my subjects and render judgment as well as You. If you grant me wisdom, I shall live honorably and achieve what is most dear to me." The voice then said, "As you have renounced wealth and chosen wisdom, I shall grant you great honors and expand your powers to such an extent that your like shall not be found in any other kingdom." The gallant David, first sovereign on this earth, built a dwelling for God. Solomon finished it and adorned it out of his love for the King of Heaven.

As told by his writings, a man named Jerome had discovered something quite disconcerting in a book of Archely[22] that the Greeks still possess. It told him of wonders.

A dragon grew in Jerusalem and was emptying all the springs of the city. The cisterns were empty, and men were plunged into the deepest distress. Solomon was powerful and acted with wisdom. He ordered people to fill a cistern with mead and wine, the best that had ever been drunk. After the dragon drank all of it, he fell asleep and was bound.

The all-powerful holy one spoke through the dragon's mouth and told Solomon: "Lord, free me and I will display my great reverence to you in your church. If you wish to believe me, you will build it in one year. Cut my bonds."

"Explain yourself," said Solomon, "or I will have you killed."

"There is an animal in the forest of Lebanon. Capture it and make a rope from it. It will be so sharp that it will cut a piece of marble in two like a razor."

Solomon was delighted and acted wisely: he cut the beast's bonds and banished it beyond the land's borders, then, with his men, went to the forest of Lebanon. To his great joy, he flushed out the animal and then tracked it for three days before capturing it. He commanded it to be carried with them, and this is why the temple of Jerusalem was built without the use of iron.[23]

The paths taken in the handing down of legends can sometimes by quite surprising. Eight centuries later, René Basset collected this form of the legend from Algerian Berbers:

It is told how once upon a time a dragon flew down to a spring above Cherchel. It had children. One day these hatchlings came out of the cave to play. The children of the town came there and hit them, killing four. Their father learned of this and immediately grew wrathful and spit poison into the water. All the people of the town that drank this water were poisoned and died. The survivors lodged a complaint with Solomon. He took pity on them and accompanied them back to their home. There, he slit the throat of a rooster, took its head, stuck it over his own, and went to visit the dragon. He gave him his promise that he would not harm him: "You shall have nothing to fear as long as this head sits upon me." The dragon believed him, placed his head on the pommel of the saddle that retreated at once, pulling the dragon with him. The beast came out of his hold and when they reached Metidja, the prince slew him. He hurled himself on the tail of Solomon's horse and cut it clean off. The king quickly fled to Hamman Righa where he commanded the djinns to heat the water and wash away the dragon's blood that had spilled on him.[24]

7. SOLOMON'S BOOK OF MAGIC SPELLS FOR COMMUNICATING WITH THE DJINNS

This Yemenite book names the twelve tribes of djinns and describes both their habitats and functions and the names their leaders. It advises practitioners how to diagnose the type and origin of the ills that are afflicting their patients and how to exorcise them. The manuscript transcribed by Anne Regourd contains the *mandal,* in other words, the depiction of the leaders of the tribes:

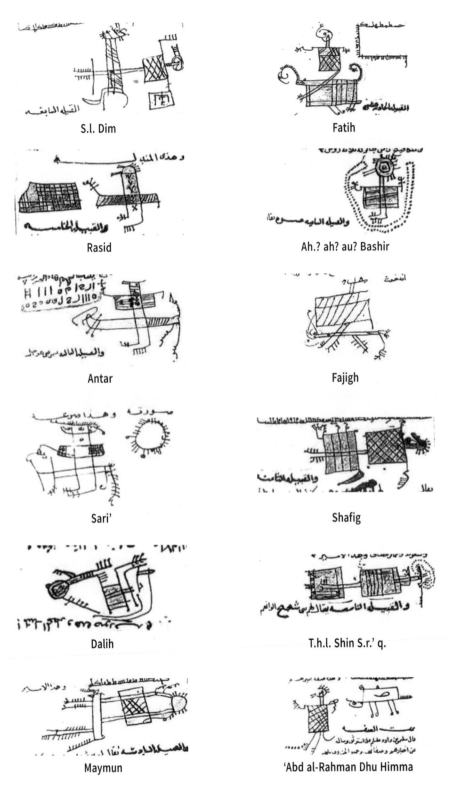

Fig. 8.2. The leaders of the twelve tribes of djinns.

After he captured Sakhr, Solomon interrogated him about the twelve tribes of djinns, and the demon gave him extensive descriptions. What is interesting here are primarily their descriptions, which I will give in the order of the tribes.

1. They have white faces, black hair, and are hairy; they dwell in deserts and ruins.
2. They are black, their eyes are slits, and they dwell in stables, lower stories, and in household vessels, such as cauldrons, for example.
3. They are white, have bull's horns, and live in fields, caves, and ruins.
4. They fly between heaven and earth, look like birds, and are Muslims.
5. They are black and as big as palm trees. They live in remote places.
6. They are not described; they dwell in the lower parts of houses or in excavations and are deaf and dumb.
7. They are the impious and most filthy of djinns; they live on ships and in the seas, and they yelp like dogs and donkeys.
8. They dwell in the clouds and appear in unwholesome and unhealthy places.
9. They have the coloring of human beings, live in ruins, and eat the dead.
10. They are the color of dust and live in water mains and streams.
11. They have large heads and are colored like snakes. They live in the wadis* and the caverns. They are liars.
12. These are the descendants of [the archangel] Iblis. They have big heads and are androgynous.

The description of their food makes them monsters. Some of them eat blood and worms from piles of garbage while others eat coals,

---

*A wadi is a riverbed or valley that is dry most of the year except for during the rainy season, when it becomes an oasis.

cinders, slag, and dead bodies. All seek to cause harm to humans and take possession of them, whether by charm, perfidy, or violence, but fortunately magic spells (*kitab*) exist that make it possible to exorcise them. There are also protective spells (*hirz*).

The description of the consequences of being possessed by a djinn reveals that they are quite often personification of illnesses. They cause feelings like pins and needles, and they are responsible for urinary incontinence, vomiting, weeping, dizziness followed by red skin rashes, the skin turning black, the loss of reason, false labor, jaundice, and aging.

The Sins of Solomon

Among Talmud scholars, the harshest against Solomon appear to have been the oldest ones, those that are known as the "repentants" (Tannaim).

The Midrash of Bamidbar Rabbah, written in the seventh century, recounts an old belief gleaned from the Mishnah, the oldest part of the Talmud. It aspired to seeing the whole of Israel gaining access to Eternal Life with the exception of a few great sinners:

> They also wished to add to these three names [of great sinners] that of Solomon; but then the image of David appeared before them and prostrated itself (in supplication). They paid no attention to it. Next, a fire streamed forth from the Holy of Holies and devoured everything around it. They paid no attention to it. After that, a celestial voice rang out and told them: "Have you seen a man skilled at his task? He who built my house before his own, and not only that, but he who spent [only] seven years to build my house and thirteen to build his: should he be held accountable to folk of obscure rank?"* They paid no attention to it. But when the celestial voice finally said to them: "Is it up to you to choose and not Me? Speak of what you know!" they ceased to include him among their number [of the condemned kings].¹

---

*Meaning, should this king be subject to judgment by common men?

In the seventeenth century, Johann Zwinger wrote a study on Solomon's sins and was not very kind to him. He condemned him for his lust, idolatry, and magic, which, according to Zwinger, made him an atheist![2]

1. PRIDE

The Talmud, written around 350, cites a passage from Jeremiah that says: "Let not the wise boast of their wisdom" (Jeremiah 9:22). But it was Solomon who boasted: "No one is wiser than I" and God stripped him of his throne and sat Aschmedai (אשמדאי) upon it. Aschmedai is Sakhr in the Arab traditions.

> Solomon had asked Asmodeus: "How are you superior to me?" Asmodeus told him: "Take this chain off of me and give me your ring, and I will demonstrate my superiority." Solomon freed him and gave him his ring. Immediately Asmodeus swallowed it and then propping himself with one wing on heaven and the other on earth, he drove him four parasangs away. In his new situation, Solomon told himself again and again: "What advantage does man gain from all the effort he makes beneath the sun? Here is the fate of all my labor," and went from door to door saying: "I, Kohelet, I was king of Israel in Jerusalem." Eventually he came before the Sanhedrin and the rabbis asked why he stubbornly continued to sing the same refrain. To get to the bottom of this matter, they told Benaya that his master had summoned him, but he replied that he had not been called. They asked his wives if their husband the king continued to come visit them. When they answered yes, they advised them to look at his legs. They answered that he was always covered and that he wished to exercise his rights as a husband no matter what condition they were in and that even his mother was not spared from his demands. The rabbis then gave him a ring and a chain on which the name of God was carved. When Asmodeus saw Solomon he flew away. Despite that, Solomon was always scared of him and this is why it is said that he always had sixty warriors around his bed—because of his fears.[3]

Solomon's sin was known as far away as Egypt. One of the Coptic manuscripts of Nag Hammadi (Upper Egypt) discovered in 1945 and dating from the fourth century, the Second Treatise of the Great Seth, notes: "How ridiculous that Solomon believed he had been anointed and was compelled to be proud by the Hebdomad."*[4] In Romania, Solomon's pride was even the subject of a folktale.[5]

2. IDOLATRY

1 Kings 4–6 tells us that Solomon fell into idolatry because of his wives who turned him to foreign gods, like Astarte and Milkom, the god of the Ammonites. The Arabs also have this tradition. In his *Summary of Wonders,* Ibrahim ibn Wasif Shah says that Solomon slew King Sidoun—who was also a magician served by genies—married his daughter, and became idolatrous.[6] Tabari (839–923) tells us the following tale:

> The king had a daughter and there was no one more beautiful than she on the earth. Solomon carried her away, but she wept constantly from grief at the loss of her father and every time Solomon went to see her, he found her with tears in her eyes and sorrow in her heart. She refused to yield to his desires and refused to speak to anyone. He then summoned the djinns and deliberated with them. They told him: "We have a method." They then made a marble statue that perfectly resembled the father of the young woman. Others said that it was he himself who commanded them to make this fig-ure. When the young woman saw this statue that looked like her father, she was quite happy and had a royal throne crafted like the one her father had when he was king. She would never leave it and worshipped it day and night, although she spoke and was friend-lier toward Solomon. She was therefore worshipping her father's statue, but no one knew, neither Solomon nor anyone else, except for Asaph, son of Berakhya. Asaph was never summoned to an

---

*Meaning, the God of the Old Testament who was above the seven heavens.

audience in Solomon's palace, but he would show up there from time to time without warning, and this was how he knew that the young woman was worshipping the statue. Asaph knew the high name of God and it was he that arranged everything in Solomon's house. Because Solomon was a powerful king, no one dared speak before him, neither men, women, nor young lads and girls, while no one feared Asaph, so people hid nothing from him.

So, Asaph sought out Solomon and said to him: "O prophet of God, grant me permission to go to the temple and make my devotions for my time is approaching and I wish to leave a good memory." Solomon granted him this. Some time passed while Asaph remained in the temple without visiting the king. Solomon finally summoned him and asked: "Why have you not come to see me?"

"Because your house holds an idol," he replied.

Solomon ordered the statue to be broken and the young woman to be punished. He immediately donned a clean robe and said: "O Lord, you know that it is unworthy of the son of David that in the houses of my kingdom people worship someone other than you after all the good that you have heaped upon them. I knew nothing of it; come lend me your aid," and he wailed, asked forgiveness, and wept.[7]

It will be noted that Tabari doesn't know the king's name, but the *Book of Solomonic Mandal* (Kitab al-Mandal al Sulaymani), a Yemenite book of exorcism whose Latin translation spread throughout the medieval West,[8] tells the same story. Here Solomon weds the daughter of the idolatrous king of the city of Sus.

The author of the Gospel of Truth from the Nag Hammadi codex goes even further and accuses David and Solomon of idolatry and claims Solomon was the fruit of an adulterous union.[9]

This accusation of idolatry traveled through the centuries. During the fifteenth century, the inquisitors Jacobus Sprenger and Henri Institoris mention it twice in *The Hammer of the Witches,* but exempt Solomon of any responsibility:

For in this way Solomon showed reverence to the gods of his wives. And no one can be excused on the ground that he does this through fear; for Saint Augustine says: "It is better to die of hunger than to be fed by Idolaters."

Again, Solomon showed reverence to the gods of his wives out of complaisance and was not on that account guilty of apostasy from the Faith; for in his heart, he was faithful and kept the true Faith.[10]

In the seventeenth century, Johann Zwinger devoted chapter six of his long study of Solomon's sins to his idolatry (*De idolatria regis Salomonia*) and raised questions about the magic and atheism of the son of David.[11]

3. LUST

A recurring reproach in the texts is the accusation of lust. Solomon did not only have several wives—Tabari speaks of a thousand—but also, according to Michael Glycas, three hundred concubines.[12] He had no hesitation about sending Pharsalo and Sauel*[13] and his armies, as well as his demons, in pursuit of a virgin. Futhermore, it was one of these wives who was responsible for his fall into idolatry.

1 Kings 11 says: "But King Solomon loved many strange women, together with the daughter of the Pharaoh, women of the Moabites, Ammonites, Edomites, Zidonians, and Hittites. . . . And he had seven hundred wives, princesses, and three hundred concubines, and his wives turned away his heart." In 1696, Johann Zwinger wrote lengthy expositions on Solomon's relationships with women.[14] The king transgressed the orders of Deuteronomy: "Neither shall he multiply wives to himself, that his heart turn not away" (17:17), a prediction that could not be any more accurate as it was because of a woman that Solomon became an idolater.

---

*It will be noted that Sauel may be the angel or the demon Sauel that is found in magic incantations.

TEN

Solomon and the Queen of Sheba

The story of Solomon and the queen of Sheba, Bilquis (Balqis, Bilqil) has enjoyed a surprising celebrity and has come down to the present in several forms. The Qu'ran (27:16–44) offers a lengthy exposition on the queen of Sheba:

Solomon was the heir of David. He said, "O men, we have been taught to understand the language of the birds, and all parts of all things have been given us. This is truly a real blessing. Gathered together to serve Solomon were his obedient soldiers of djinns and humans, as well as the birds; all lined up in ranks."

He smiled in amusement at her statement, and said, "My Lord, let me give thanks for the blessings You have bestowed upon me and my mother and father, and to do a righteous work that pleases You. Allow me by your mercy to enter into the company of Your righteous servants." He inspected the birds, and noted: "Why do I not see the hoopoe? Why is he missing? I will punish him severely or sacrifice him, unless he gives me a good excuse."

He did not wait for long before the hoopoe returned with news: "I found that a woman is their queen; she has been heaped with every blessing and possesses a magnificent throne.

"I found her and her people bowing before the sun not Allah.

The devil has embellished their actions and diverted them from the right path; they are not well guided.

"They should have been prostrating before Allah, the One who causes all that is hidden in the heavens and earth to emerge, He who knows everything you conceal and everything you reveal. Allah: there is no other god beside Him; the Lord of the Immense Throne."

Then Solomon said, "We will see if you told the truth or if you are a liar. Take this letter from me, give it to them, then stand apart from them and watch how they respond."

The Queen said: "O nobles! A letter has been sent me. It comes from Solomon and says: 'In the name of Allah the Merciful, the Very Merciful, do not be arrogant toward me but come to me in complete submission.'"

She said: "O nobles! Advise me on this matter; I shall make no decision unless you are present (to counsel me)."

They replied: "We are keepers of dread strength and formidable power, but command belongs to you, so think over what you would command."

She said: "In truth kings, when they enter a city, they bring about its ruin and humble those who are its most honorable citizens. Such is how they act. But truly, I will send a gift to them and see what reply the messengers bring back."

Then, when [the delegation] came to Solomon, he said, "Have you brought me wealth? What Allah has given to me is far better than what He has given to you, but you are happy with your gifts. Return to them. In truth we shall come to them with armies that they will have no power to resist, and we shall drive them out from there in disgrace, and they will be scorned."

He said: "O chiefs! Which of you can bring her throne to me before they come to me in submission?"

A powerful djinn replied: "I will bring it to you before you rise from your place. And this is truth because for such a task I am indeed strong and trustworthy."

One who had the knowledge of the Book said: "I will bring it to you in the twinkling of an eye." Then when he saw it settled beside him, he said: "This is by the grace of my Lord that He may test me on whether I am grateful or ungrateful; and whoever is grateful, he is grateful only for his own soul, and whoever is ungrateful, then surely my Lord is self-sufficient and He is generous." And he said [again]: "Render her throne unrecognizable to her, and we shall see whether she is guided or if she is of that number who are not guided."

When she came, she was asked, "Is your throne like this?" She replied, "It seems that this is it." [And Solomon said]: "We received the knowledge before this and we already decided to submit. And that which she used to worship outside of Allah has prevented her [from being a true believer] for she was of a disobedient people." And she was invited to enter the palace. Then, when she saw it, she thought that it was deep water and bared her legs. Then Solomon said, "This is a palace paved with crystal." She said, "My Lord, indeed I have wronged myself and I submit with Solomon to the will of Allah."[1]

Fig. 10.1. Solomon welcomes the Queen of Sheba.
Rudolf von Ems, Weltchronik (fourteenth century)

1. SOLOMON AND THE QUEEN OF THE SOUTH (ETHIOPIA)

The mother of King Menelik was a Tigré* who was known as Queen of the South [Etiyë-Azeb]. During this era, the Tigrés worshipped a dragon and made the following sacrifice to it: each of them in turn had to give the dragon their eldest daughter and an entalim† of mead and another of milk. When it was the Queen of the South's turn, she was tied to a tree. Seven saints‡ came and sat in the shade of the tree. She began to cry and one of her tears fell upon them. They then looked up and asked her:

"Who are you? Are you Mary or a human being?"

"I am a human being," she replied.

"Why are you tied up here?"

"So that the dragon may devour me."

"Is he in the other side of the hill or this side?"

"On this side."

When they saw the dragon, Abba Chahama grabbed his beard, Abba Garima said, "He frightens me," and Abba Mentelit said, "Take him!" and hurled himself on the dragon and struck it. Next, they hit it with their crosses and killed it. Once they had slain it, its blood spurted out onto the Queen of the South all over her foot, turning it into a donkey's hoof. Next, they freed her and told her: "Go back to your village."

When she got there, not knowing the dragon was dead, the village people chased her away. So, she climbed up a tree, where she spent the night. The next day, she went back to the village and told the villagers: "Follow me! I am going to show you that he is truly dead." They accompanied her and when the found it lying down dead, they said to each other, "She should be our sovereign as God did not allow her to become the dragon's prey." Once she had been named queen, she appointed a young woman like herself to be her minister.

She had heard said that in Jerusalem lived a king named Solomon.

---

*Inhabitants of the Ethiopian province of the same name.

†Around 300 liters.

‡Variant: seven angels.

Anyone who went to see him would be healed of their ills. "If you went to see him, as soon as your foot passed over the threshold it would be like it was before," they told her. Once she heard this, she bound up her hair to look like a man, and her servant did the same. Both equipped themselves with swords and set off. When they drew near the palace, a herald told Solomon: "The King of Abyssinia is here." "Bid him enter," the king ordered.

The Queen of the South and her servant presented themselves before the king, and she grasped his hand and thanked him. He commanded that bread, meat, and mead be brought out, and they sat down to eat. During the meal, the women ate and drank little out of modesty, which made Solomon suspect that they were women. When night fell, he gave the order that two beds be prepared for them in the same chamber, one facing the other. He took a skin full of mead, hung it over the room with a bowl underneath, pierced a hole in the wineskin because he was in the habit of keeping his eyes half open while he slept and shutting them when he was awake. During the night while they were resting, he slept with his eyes half-closed. The two women told each other, "He is not sleeping; he is awake and watching us. When will he go to sleep?" He woke up and closed his eyes. "Now, he is sleeping," they said, and began licking the honey out of the bowl. He was then certain that they were women and went to them and lay with each of them. Each told him, "You deflowered me." He held out a silver staff and a ring to each of them, saying, "If it is a woman, may she take the silver staff and join me; if it is a man, may he take the ring and join me." The Queen of the South grabbed a mirror, then they each returned to their own land, pregnant.[2]

We should note that Solomon had children with the Queen of the South. The Falashas, the Ethiopian Jews, whose name means "exile" or "immigrant," considered themselves to be their descendants.

2. THE STORY OF SOLOMON AND BILQUIS

Solomon loved to mount expeditions against the infidels. One day he learned that there were idolaters in Yemen. He immediately had his carpet readied, lined his army upon it, and commanded the wind to carry the carpet from Syria to Yemen. His path led him by the Hadj. When they came to Mecca, he commanded the wind to land the carpet, and he made the progression around the temple. "From this place a prophet will emerge from the Arabs," he said. "His residence will be in Medina as will be his tomb and there will be no man on earth before God more noble than he." Then he left Mecca and the Hadj. His path crossed through a burning desert; the heat was very strong, and his men suffered from thirst. Solomon wished to learn if there was water in the area that he could cause to gush forth. The only thing on earth that knew the places that held it was the hoopoe (*hudhub*).[3] Solomon sought the hoopoe from among the birds and when he could not find it, said, "Why don't I see you here?" It so happened that the hoopoe had left and was now in the territory of Sheba held by Bilquis. A queen ruled over this entire land of Sheba. It was said that not since the death of Joseph had there been such a beautiful creature, because her mother was a peri and her father a prince. The hoopoe saw Bilquis on her throne that was eighty cubits long by eighty cubits wide; its base was made of red gold set with rubies and pearls. Solomon's hoopoe saw another hoopoe there and approached it. "Who are you, where do you come from, and what audacity brings you here?" the other hoopoe asked. Solomon's hoopoe told her of the power of his master and his army. The other hoopoe told him, "This queen worships the sun."

The hoopoe headed back to Solomon, but the other birds came to meet him, saying:

"Solomon wants to punish or even kill you."

"What else did he say?"

"Unless you have an irrefutable excuse, then he will think about letting you live."

Then the hoopoe went before Solomon who asked him, "Where have you been?"

"I have learned something that you know not," the bird replied. "I return from Sheba with news. I found there a woman who rules over men. She owns all manner of things, and she has a large throne. I have seen that she and her people worship the sun to the exclusion of God."[4]

Solomon was amazed and said, "I will certainly learn if you are telling me the truth or lying. Go back with this letter." He wrote a missive and gave it to the hoopoe, who took it in his beak before setting out. He reached the land of Sheba by the morning.

Bilquis was sitting on her throne surrounded by her servants. The hoopoe tossed Solomon's letter in their midst, then perched in a tree. Bilquis was surprised and said: "This must be a great king who has birds under his command." She next called her army to assemble, showed them the letter, and opened it. Solomon had written her in these terms: "In the name of a charitable and merciful God! Do not set yourself against me out of pride but come to me and become believers." This letter was quite short and laconic because Solomon was proud and despised infidels. He was only ever haughty in his attitude toward them.

Then Bilquis bid her leaders and nobles to enter and said to them: "O lords, give me your advice on this matter. I will make no decision without you."

"We are strong and powerful, but yours is the power to command us."

"What do you think?"

"Do you know what kind of man Solomon is?"

"We know that he is a great king in Syria who follows the religion of the children of Israel and practices the law. He is a prophet of God, and the divs, the peris, the wind, the birds, the wild animals, and the ferocious beasts all submit to him."

"When the kings invade a city, they destroy it. . . . I will send presents and we shall see what my envoys bring back. If he accepts the present, I will know that he seeks for the goods of this world; if he doesn't accept it, then I will know that he is a prophet and that he is just."

Bilquis next sent a messenger with two bricks, one of gold and the other of silver, a golden box holding an unpierced ruby—at this time no one possessed diamonds which were capable of piercing rubies. Bilquis then told her envoy, "Ask Solomon what is in this box. If he tells you, then ask him what is needed to pierce the ruby?" She also sent one hundred boys and one hundred girls. "Ask him as well what is the water that does not come from the earth or sky but quenches thirst." The envoy then left with these presents.

While the envoy was still on his way there, Gabriel came to see Solomon and told him what was coming and the answers to Bilquis's questions. The king commanded that the entire extent of his carpet be covered with silver and gold in the form of bricks, similar to those carried by the envoy of Bilquis. He arranged the people in tiers on the carpet, took a seat on his throne, and ordered the messenger to be admitted. When the messenger saw the large number of gold and silver bricks, he was ashamed to give Solomon the two bricks from Bilquis but set them aside and presented the other objects. Solomon told him, "You brought two silver and gold bricks," and the envoy admitted it was so. Then Solomon saw the presents and asked, "Do you wish to help me with your treasures?" The envoy then gave Solomon the message from Bilquis. The king responded: "This water that does not come from earth or sky is perspiration. If you make a horse gallop and it sweats, and you collect this sweat in a cup, the person who drinks of it will quench his thirst. You cannot quench your thirst with any other kind of sweat but that of the horse, because all other sweat is salty but that of the horse is sweet. When you drink it, your thirst is quenched, but when you drink something salty, your thirst increases. As for this box, it holds a large and unpierced red ruby the like of which has never been owned by any sovereign."

"What can it be pierced by?" the envoy asked.

Solomon ordered the divs to go fetch a diamond and pierce the ruby with it. Then he ordered bread to be brought forth before the meal. He had a vessel brought in with water for hand washing. Custom was that when water was spilled on the hands of women, they held out their palms while men presented the backs of their hands. It was by this means that Solomon was able to tell the boys from the girls that Bilquis had sent him. Then Solomon sent back the messenger without accepting any of the gifts he had brought. After his departure, the king remained at the same place.

Next, Bilquis gathered her army together to go before Solomon and accept the true faith. Every time they made a trip, whether long or short, she had her throne sealed up inside the last of seven apartments on each of which she had had a lock placed. The last was guarded by one thousand men, and she kept the keys by her side.

The distance to Solomon's location was two days' travel. Once Bilquis had completed one day's travel, Solomon knew of it and said: "O lords, who among you shall bring me her throne before they arrive and adhere to the faith?" A djinn called Ifrit told him, "I will bring it before you even have time to make a move, for I am strong and loyal enough to be equal to this task." Asaph, who knew the science of the Book, said, "I will bring it to you before you can even blink an eye." Asaph was one of the great men of the children of Israel, a descendent of Levy, the son of Jacob, and one of the tribe of prophets, and he knew the high name of God. Asaph, son of Berakhya, prostrated himself before God and invoked him by his high name. At that very moment, Solomon saw the throne in front of him. This made him quite happy, and he said, "Change this throne so we can see if she has good guidance, so that we know if she will recognize it when she sees it."

The divs were jealous of Bilquis and wished to turn her aside from Solomon's heart. She was quite beautiful and possessed no flaw except for a few goat hairs on her legs.[*5] Solomon wished to see her legs to make certain of this himself. He ordered the divs to build a palace with a crystal pavement before it that was one hundred cubits long by one hundred cubits wide, and to pour water beneath the crystal so that when she saw it, she would think it was all water. Solomon took his position and to reach him, Bilquis had to cross over this pavement. She therefore did what every woman would do when they go into the water; she hitched up her pants and uncovered her legs. Solomon saw them and was both surprised and satisfied. Even today, it is still customary to see the leg of the woman one wishes to marry. . . Solomon did not want anyone else to see her legs, so he told her, "Cover your legs, there is no water here, it is crystal." Next, Solomon took her as his wife and sent her to his harem. The entire army of Bilquis converted, and the queen gave it to Solomon along with her entire kingdom.

Then Solomon had the hair pulled from Bilquis's legs, but it pulled off the skin at the same time. The divs then manufactured a compound

---

*Researchers believe that one of Queen Zenobia's characteristic features was transposed on her. In Arab tradition, Queen Zenobia was known as The Hairy One (al-Zabba').

of chalk and arsenic for removing the hairs. So, Solomon was the first one to ever use this compound for hair removal. He possessed five objects that were unknown to the kings before him: ointment for hair removal, the hot bath, the art of piercing pearls, the art of diving, and the art of melting copper. Solomon later had a son by Bilquis.[6]

The crystal pavement reappears in the *Romance of Alexander* (beginning of the eighth century). Bilquis's hairy legs or even her donkey's hoof makes her a witch for some authors,[7] but for others, like the prince Omayyade Chalid ibn Yazid (died 704), she was one of the eight women renowned for teaching alchemy: "And among these scholars, here are the most famous: Maria, Tadusiya, Autasiya, Cleopatra, Aulashaniya, Wahhada, Bilquis, and Barbar."[8]

This story is also found in the *Targum Sheni* (the Second Targum), a collection of sermons in Aramaic on the Book of Esther that is first cited in the eleventh century but whose composition most likely goes back to the seventh or eighth centuries.[9]

In his *Testament,* Solomon writes: "Also came Sheba, queen of the South, a witch of immense learning, and she prostrated herself before me."[10] In Ethiopian traditions, the Queen of Sheba is a semi-demonic creature, the daughter of a king of Himyr and a djinniya* according to Zamakhshari, or the king of China and a peri, according to the Tabari's Persian summary, and the sign of this demonic nature is her animal foot. *The History of the Kings of Gondar* (Ethiopia, fifteenth century) depicts Solomon speaking to the queen:

"Your foot, I've been told, became like that of a donkey and yet there is no horn on your foot."

"You were told the truth," the queen answered, "but when I entered your palace, I struck the wood of the threshold and the horn fell off."[11]

In one manuscript of Honorius Augustodunensis's *Image of the World,* the Queen of Sheba had goose feet (*pedes anserinos*).[12] The

---

*A female djinn.

wood of the threshold was from the Cross of the Lord. This legend also appears in the work of Jacobus Voraginus as we shall see.

Fig. 10.2. The Queen of Sheba Meets Solomon: *Boec van den houde* (Holland, fifteenth century)

Fig. 10.3. Solomon and the Queen of Sheba, Ethiopian painting

3. THE DISCOVERY OF
THE TRUE CROSS

During the Middle Ages, the legend of the Queen of Sheba merged with that of the discovery of the true cross according to Jacobus Voraginus (died 1298) which is reminiscent of another tradition presented of the Scholastic History (*Historia scholastica*) of Pierre le Mangeur (Petrus Comestor, died 1179). Gervase of Tilbury (around 1152–1234) was inspired by the same legend.[13] In France, the Queen of Sheba is depicted with goose feet, like the Queen Pedauque, near the Priory of Saint-Pourcain, in the church Sainte-Bénigne of Dijon, Sainte-Marie de Nesles (Champagne), and Saint-Pierre of Nevers.

> Solomon, treasuring the beauty of this tree, ordered it cut and placed in the house of the Lebanese forest. However, as reported by Jean Beleth, it could not be placed anywhere and no place could be found suitable for installing it as this tree was sometimes too long or sometimes too short, and if it had been cut based on the dimensions of the place where one wished to place it, it would have looked so short that it would have lost all value. In irritation the workers

Fig. 10.4. Piero della Francesco (died 1492), Adoration of the Sacred Tree and the Arrival of the Queen of Sheba at Solomon's Palace.

discarded it and set it over a waterway so that people wishing to cross it could use it as a bridge.

Now, when the Queen of Sheba came to hear the wisdom of Solomon and wanted to cross this waterway, she saw in her mind that the Savior of the World was hanging from this wood, and so refusing to cross it she began to worship it immediately.

One can read in the *Scholastic History*, however, that the Queen of Sheba saw this wood in the house of the forest and, once she had returned home, she informed Solomon that a man would one day be hung from this wood whose death would bring about the destruction of the kingdom of the Jews. Solomon therefore ordered the tree's removal from its present location and had it buried deep within the depths of the earth. Subsequently, this was the location of the probatic bath in which the Nathanites or subdeacons washed their victims.[14]

ELEVEN

Solomon and Death

1. MEETING THE ANGEL OF DEATH

After seeing the queen of ants, Solomon ordered the djinns to take
another path so as not to disturb the ants during their prayers.
When he came to the border of Palestine, he heard someone praying:
"My God, you who chose Abraham for a friend, deliver me soon
from this sorrowful life!" Solomon went down to the person and
saw that he was a very old man all hunched up with all his limbs
trembling.

"I am an Israelite of the tribe of Judah."

"How old are you?"

"God alone knows. I counted the years up to three hundred, and
another fifty or sixty years could have gone by since then."

"How is it that you have lived to an age that no one has reached
since the time of Abraham?"

"Once upon a time, I saw a comet during the night of Alkadr,* and
I made the insane wish to meet the greatest of all the prophets before
I died."

"You have reached your goal. Prepare yourself to die, for I am the

---

*Laylat al-Qader, "The night of Fate," also known as "The night of Power" or "the night
of Majesty" is one of the last ten nights of the month of Ramadan on an odd-numbered
day.

king and prophet Solomon to whom God has lent his power as to none other before me."

At these words, the angel of death appeared in the form of a human and took the soul of the old man.

"You must have been already prepared to get him so quickly," said Solomon.

"How wrong you are," the angel replied. "Know that I rest on the wings of an angel whose head is ten thousand years beyond the seventh heaven and whose feet are planted at a depth that is five hundred years beneath the earth. If God permitted, he could swallow up the earth without making the slightest effort. He has his gaze permanently fixed on the tree Sidrat al-Muntah,* which has as many leaves as there are men on earth, and each one bears an individual's name. With each birth, a new leaf appears with the name of the newborn, and when a man reaches the end of his life, a dry leaf falls while at the very same moment I am already present to collect his soul."

"How do you do this and where do you go?"

"Gabriel accompanies me when a believer dies, the soul is then wrapped in green silk cloth and my companion, a green bird, breathes it in.[1] It then remains in paradise until the day of judgment. I take the souls of sinners by myself and carry them in a crude woolen fabric smeared with pitch to the gate of hell where they will live in the midst of horrific emissions." Solomon thanked him for the lesson and begged him to hide his own death from all men and all genies. Then he washed the corpse, buried it, and prayed for its soul and the lessening of his sufferings when the angels Ankir and Munkir examined it.[†2]

It is told that Solomon, son of David, wished to see the angel of death in order to form a bond of friendship with him. Hardly had he expressed

---

*Sidrat al-Muntahā, the "Lotus of the boundary," is a tree that marks the end of the seventh heaven. It flowers to the right of God's invisible throne.

†These two angels ask the deceased to identify his god and faith, and they strike him if he does not give them a suitable answer. There is a similar situation in the "judgment of the grave" (*chibut hakeber*) among the rabbis.

this wish, when the angel introduced himself after emerging from under his throne.*3 "Who are you?" Solomon asked.

"The angel of death," the figure answered.

Solomon fainted. The angel begged God to give him the power to see him. God revealed that he should place his hand on his chest. No sooner had he done this than Solomon came back to his senses and said: "O Angel of Death. I see that you're a gigantic creature. Do all of God's angels look like you?"

"My foot," the angel replied, "rests on the shoulders of an angel whose head crosses through the seven heavens and goes beyond them by a distance of a five-hundred-year march. He has his mouth open, his voice raised, and his hands outstretched. If God allowed him to put his lips together, his mouth would encompass all that exists between heaven and earth."

"But what you are describing is enormous!" said Solomon.

"O prophet of God," the angel continued, "what would you say if I described other angels of immense stature or rather, what would you say if you saw me in the form I assume when I come to seize the souls of infidels?"

"Have you come to me as a visitor or an abductor?" Solomon asked.

"As a visitor," the angel replied.

Solomon became the friend of the angel of death, who would come sit with him every Thursday until sunset. One day, Solomon told him, "I see that you are not even-handed in your dealings with people: you take this person and leave that one." The angel replied, "The question is no more informed than the person asking it. In fact, there are books in which the names of those to be taken are inscribed. The inscription of these books takes place each year on the Night of the Sentence, which falls in the middle of the month of Shaban. Those who profess the oneness of God are those whose souls I grab with my right hand. The soul

---

*"God has an angel whose feet present right through the entire earth and fills the surrounding air with his head reaching just beneath the throne. He is the one that holds the soul of Mohammed in his hand. If a bird were to be cast into the space that extends between the nape of his neck and his ear lobe, it would take him seven hundred years to cover that distance," says Ibn-Ishaq and el-Waqidi.

is gleaned in silken fabric steeped in musk, then it is brought aloft to Illiyyun.[4] Meanwhile, I grab the souls of infidels with my left hand. They are sent down to Sijjin* wrapped in resin.[5]

2. THE DEATH OF SOLOMON

Several months after the death of Queen Bilquis, the angel of death appeared to Solomon with six faces. One was on the right, one was on the left, one in front, and one behind, and one on top of the head and one below. Solomon, who had never seen him in this guise, was startled and asked him: "What is the meaning of these six faces?"

"With my right face," the angel answered, "I come to fetch the dwellers of the East; with the left, those of the West; with that on top, I seek the souls of the inhabitants of heaven; and with the lower, the djinns in the depths of the earth; with that in back, the souls of the peoples Gog and Magog;† and with that in front, the believers, of which you are one."

"Do angels have to die?"

"All that lives shall die once Izrafil‡ sounds his trump for the second time. Then I will slay Gabriel and Michael before perishing myself on God's command. All that will remain will be God alone who shouts: 'To whom does the world belong?' without anyone being there to answer. It is only after forty years have passed that Izrafil will resurrect in order to blow his trump for the third time and awaken all the dead."

"And who will emerge from his grave first?"

"The prophet Mohammed who later will give birth to the descendants of Ishmael. Izrafil and Gabriel and the other angels will go to his tomb in Medina in person and call him: 'Soul that is purest and most noble of all, go back into your unblemished body and restore it to life!' He will step out of the grave and shake the dust from his head. Next,

---

*A prison in the lowest depths of Hell.

†Jadjubj and Madjudj, the impure peoples.

‡Izrafil is the one that halts movement and separates souls from their bodies. No one is taken before they have reached the age that was set for them. He is called "the Master of the Trump" because he will announce the end of the world.

Gabriel will greet him and show him Borak,* the winged horse that is ready for him, as well as a standard and crown that God has sent him from heaven.

"Then he tells him: 'Come to the house of your Lord which is also mine, you who are chosen above all creatures, the gardens of Eden are already adorned for you and the houris, full of desire, await you there.'† He then seats him on Borak, puts the heavenly standard in his hand and the crown on his head, then brings him to paradise. It is only after this that the rest of humankind is called back to life. . . .'"

"When will the resurrection take place?" Solomon asked.

"God alone knows, but certainly not before Mohammed, the last of all prophets, has appeared. Before this, the prophet Isa [Christ], a child of your line, will preach the true faith, be elevated to godhood and reborn; the peoples Yajuj and Majuj will break down the wall behind which Dhu-l-Qarnayn (Alexander the Great) imprisoned them,[6] the sun will rise in the west, and there will be many other wondrous phenomena."

"Let me live until the construction of the Temple is complete, for if I die, the djinns will cease work."

"You have used up your time and it is not within my power to extend your life for a second."

"Very well, then follow me into the crystal hall."

The angel accompanied Solomon into a room with walls made of crystal. Solomon prayed, then leaning upon a staff begged the angel to take his soul while he was in that position. Once the angel had taken his soul, his death remained hidden from the djinns for another year until the Temple was completed. Once his staff, eaten by worms, collapsed, and Solomon fell to the ground, they realized that he had died and, to avenge themselves, they hid all kinds of grimoires behind his throne. They did their job so well that more than one gullible individual believes that Solomon was a magician. But he was a prophet of

---

*The mount of the prophets, *al-burāq* brought by Gabriel to carry Mohammed from Mecca to Jerusalem.
†The virgins of paradise.

God about whom the Qu'ran says: "Solomon was not an ill-doer, but the demons were, and they taught magic to men."

Then, when Solomon was lying on the ground, the angels carried off his body and his ring, and hid them in a cave where they keep watch over him until Judgment Day.[7]

3. SOLOMON'S TOMB

According to Ibrahim ibn Wasif Shah, who wrote his *Summary of Wonders,* around the year 1000, Solomon's tomb is in a castle on an island in the ocean.[8] The *Book of the Wonders of India* (*Kitab 'adjaïb al-Hind*) by Bozorg bin Shahriyar of Ramhormoz, places it on the Andaman Islands in the Indian Ocean, whose indigenous inhabitants have historically been falsely maligned as cannibals. Bozorg's story was confirmed by that of a merchant named Sulayman in 851:

> There is a golden temple containing a tomb on the larger Andaman Island. It is an object of veneration for the inhabitants. It was their great respect for this tomb that induced them to raise the gold temple above it. The inhabitants of both islands come there in pilgrimage, and they say it is the tomb of Solomon, son of David, may God bless both their names! They add that this monarch had asked God to place his grave in a place where the men of his time were unable to go, and that God granted him this favor and chose to put it on their island.[9]

Tabari has a much more detailed account:

> The prophet answered: "The tomb of my brother Solomon is in the middle of a sea that forms part of the great sea, in a palace carved out of the rock. This palace holds a throne on which Solomon has been placed in the same position he held during his rule. The royal ring is still on his finger, and everything is such that one would say Solomon is still alive. There are twelve guardians on this island that keep watch over Solomon day and night. No human being can reach

the site of the tomb of this noble man because the journey requires spending two months at sea. It is also said that since Solomon's death, no living thing has made it to his tomb except for two people, one of whom was Affan and the other Bulukiya.

It is said that Affan made his way there in search of Solomon's ring and that he brought Bulukiya with him as a travel companion. They set off and finally reached the spit we have described after infinite efforts and hardship. Finally, when Affan sought to remove Solomon's ring, he was struck by lightning sent by all powerful God and utterly consumed. Bulukiya retraced his steps and spread word of what had happened.

Solomon appears to be alive because after he died, he held himself upright for an entire year, propped up by his staff, and no one knew if he was dead, sleeping, or alive. Finally, a white ant gnawed through the staff, causing it to crumble and Solomon to fall. Confusion ran wild then among the divs, peris, and humans. Then these different beings removed Solomon's throne and carried it to the center of this island in the middle of the sea that we just described.[10]

One of the accounts of the legend provides more details about the discovery of the tomb. In it, Bulukiya meets an individual named Affan who was highly versed in the occult sciences and wished to take possession of Solomon's ring. Solomon's body lay in a tomb beyond the seven seas that could only be crossed by smearing one's feet with the sap of a certain herb that made it possible to walk on water. It so happened that this herb could only be plucked in the presence of the serpent queen. They picked it, crossed all the seas, and entered the tomb, but when Affan tried to take Solomon's ring, an enormous serpent reduced him to ashes.[11]

The Egyptian historian and jurist Nuwayri (1268–1332), author of an encyclopedia with the title *Everything One Could Wish to Know about the Belles Lettres* (*Nihayat al-arab fi finun al-adab*), closely followed the account in *The Life of the Prophets* by Tha'labi (died 1035) while making a few changes: the serpent is small, yellow, and named Tamlikha; the tomb is located in the middle of the second sea; and

Solomon is depicted as a young man with long hair and a serpent over his head.

4. THE POSTHUMOUS PUNISHMENT OF SOLOMON

Several fathers of the church, Tertullian (*Adversus Marcionem* II, 23), Saint Cyprian, Saint Augustine (*Contra Faustum* XXII, 81), and Gregory the Great in his *Moralia in Job* (II, 2), rank Solomon among the damned.[12] In a Latin life of Saint Edward the Confessor, contained in a thirteenth-century collection of the lives of the saints in the library of Corpus Christi College in Cambridge, England, we can read this little history:

Two Englishmen went on pilgrimage to Jerusalem. There they made their prayers and offerings, then for better or worse, and at the cost of some exhausting effort, they made their way to Mount Sinai. Flowing at the foot of the mountains not far from this place is a river that comes out of Paradise. The pilgrims decided to follow it back to its source. But going this way and that, they kept going astray. Finally, after wasting many days wandering to no purpose, they came upon a wall that they were unable to cross at any point. Its length was beyond estimation and its height was infinite. However, when going along the Euphrates, they spotted an arch that stood over the river; the waves beneath it boiled violently. "What are we going to do?" they asked each other, "Where can we cross? Perhaps the Angel of Counsel who guided us through the desert can also us direct us through the water." They then dipped their hands in the water and found it lukewarm. They took off their clothes, and quickly dove into the water, leaving the arch behind him. They then went ashore on the other side and saw right before them a leafy and shadowy forest. They went in and came upon a palace that was so old it was falling into ruin. They could see many chambers and large halls. Crossing through each of them, they could find no one living there.

Finally, when they came to the last chamber, they suddenly stumbled upon a person of noble bearing whose pleasant features were noteworthy. When he saw them standing there trembling, he offered them comfort with these words, "What is your nation? What is the reason for such a long trip? It has been quite a long time since I have seen anyone here, and I have been in solitude for all these many years. But keep hurrying along; once you have gotten to the other side of this forest you will see a royal city in front of you, full of all the delights of life and salvation. If you manage to find lodging there for one night, you will enjoy without any tarnish the abundance of all goods." They asked him his name. He told them, that born of David, he was commonly known as King Solomon. Having seriously inspired the wrath of God, he was doing penitence, struck by this punishment [which they saw] until Judgment Day. Having heard these words, the pilgrims were moved by contrition in their hearts; they asked his permission to leave and left.[13]

5. THE PENITENCE OF SOLOMON

The legend continued to grow and change with new and strange addition that eventually gave it the appearance of a fantasy that any Gothic novel author would have been proud to call their own. You be the judge after reading this text:

There was a man who strove to find a method for talking to the devil. He went to a number of places seeking information. . . . He was advised to make his way into the wilds of Scotland, and he did just that. There he was told of an old woman with a reputation for meddling in such matters. He spoke to her, and she told him that she would take care of the matter: "Do you see this old, broken-down castle, where there is naught left but the walls and floors, full of thorns and brambles. Against the wall a corbel* is leaning as if

---

*A cut stone (ashlar) sticking out of a wall that is used to support a beam. The word corbel is related to the word *corvus*, meaning crow or raven in Latin, because the support structure looks like the beak of a raven.

propping up a beam, and there you must wait, without any fear. You shall find a man that looks like a Moor of Mauritania in Africa; ask him what you will, he will answer."

The journeyman made his way to the castle and waited there for some time. Then a kind of bier or coffin on two large stones was brought in. This coffin held an entirely naked man who was then placed over the corbel. The man then saw more then ten thousand crows coming his way. They tore this person to pieces and ate all his flesh until there was nothing left but bones. Once that was done, the bones were placed back in the coffin and carried away. Next, the journeyman saw the so-called Moor of Mauritania come in. This was the figure the old woman had told him about and he asked him:

"Who is that person?"

"That's King Solomon," the Moor replied.

The journeyman then questioned the Moor to learn if Solomon was damned, and he was told no, but that he would suffer this penitence and torture every day as if he were still alive until the end of the world.[14]

TWELVE

Solomon among the Sabaeans

In the ninth century, "Sabaean" designated a community who worshipped the stars and planets, and were living in Harran,[1] the city formerly known as Carrhae in northern Mesopotamia. This community was believed to be the primary crucible of the occult sciences—especially magic and astrology. It is marked by an extraordinary syncretism of Babylonian cults and beliefs of Greek origin. The city was dedicated to the worship of the Moon goddess, Sin, and Jupiter was worshipped there under the name of Bel. A Sabaean describes his religion this way:

> Our way of calling upon the divine majesty is manifest, our religion intelligible. Since the earliest times, our elders, because they sought a means of being introduced, made representations corresponding to the houses above, based on the relationships and attributions that they respected both in form and substance, and in accord with the time and styles, in figures. Anyone who sought the favors of the corresponding higher houses through the representations of these figures was obliged by them to wear such a ring, and such a garment, and use such an incense, and to present such a request, and to speak such a spell. This is how they sought the favor of the spirituals (forms without revealed matter), and through them that of the Lord of Lords and the Cause of Causes.[2]

There were scholars, philosophers, and writers in this community that gave their own version of the Solomonic legend. Here I am reproducing one based on Nicolas Sioufi's version, and I have added subheadings to make it clear.[3]

1. THE CARPET

Solomon was both king and prophet. He had two reigns. The first lasted for nine hundred years during which he had jurisdiction over the angels of heaven. During the second reign, which only lasted one hundred years, he was sovereign of the entire earth. Humans, djinns, animals, birds, and fish, all of whose languages he understood, were subject to his commands. He wore a ring on his finger given to him by Pthaïl that he only needed to rub to get whatever he wished. In addition, he owned a large carpet that transported him, with no effort and with very little time, wherever he wished to go—even to the sun, where he went on excursions from time to time. After sitting on the carpet, along with the people he wished to accompany him, he only had to rub his ring and strike the carpet with a wand for it to suddenly take off as fast as lightning.

Great actions illustrate the time of Solomon's rule over the earth. Until that time, evil angels had wielded great power over humankind, and they tormented them in countless ways. The victims of this torment turned to the monarch to ask him to deliver them from these invisible enemies. Solomon then captured most of these evil spirits. He put them into bottles that he then hermetically sealed with his seal and had cast into the sea. Since that time, people have recovered peace and tranquility.

2. SOLOMON'S PUNISHMENT

One day, when Solomon, surrounded by his court, climbed aboard his carpet, he was filled with a feeling of pride when thinking of the great power at his disposal. As soon as this sense of vanity filled his mind, the carpet collapsed under the weight it was carrying and the prophet king along with all his people fell. Most of his people died from this fall. As soon as he was back on the ground, the king noticed the absence of his ring that had been suddenly removed by divine command as punishment for his sin.

Solomon's features also underwent a major transformation at this time, which made him unrecognizable to his subjects. His people became wed to the idea that their king had been abducted by the angels, and all the efforts used by the disgraced monarch to convince the world of his true identity only served to increase the mockery his claims inspired. Disavowed and driven away by everyone including the members of his own family, the poor wretch sought refuge in the desert where he lived with the wild beasts. After suffering for quite some time the rigors imposed by hunger and the cold, Solomon took the chance, in order to earn his living, to take a job with a fisherman. This individual gave his daughter's hand in marriage to the king and they both continued to pursue their modest career to support their joint household.

A year had passed since Solomon had fallen from grace when one day, on cutting open the belly of a fish he had just caught, he found his famous lost ring inside. He immediately dropped into the river to make his ritual ablutions, went back to land, and addressed Alaha (Allah) in a fervent prayer on his sincere desire to repent. As soon as he finished praying, he rubbed the ring that he had already slipped onto his finger and his former appearance as the prophet king believed to have been abducted by the angels was instantly restored. He returned to his palace where he was welcomed with great joy and all the honors due to a master who had just been found anew. A short time after Solomon had reclaimed his throne; he received a letter from Pthaïl* in which he was urged to go conquer the city of Chaddad-ben-Aad.

This city Arem (Irem, Iram)†4 sought to imitate the earthly paradise and was said to be located in the deserts of Yemen. Tabari tells how an expedition set off in search of this paradise and found Chaddad dead, clad in seventy gold brocade robes.

---

*He ruled over the Hadhramaout and the Adites.
†Irem or Iram, "the city of pillars" (Iram ḏāt al-ʿimād).

3. THE CITY OF CHADDAD-BEN-AAD

Solomon set out to immediately carry out the order he had been given and led his troops before the city. All the walls were piled high with dirt. They could see, though, the tops of the walls that were excessively tall and made this city impregnable. Solomon summoned some birds to whom he gave orders to fly over the fortifications to explore the city and return to him with news of what it looked like inside. The strongest fliers soared high in the air without being able to reach the top of the walls. They fell back, worn out with fatigue, and all of them in the end had to admit their inability to fulfill his orders.

At that moment, the conqueror found himself in quite a predicament and did not know what to do. A tiny bird, no bigger than a sparrow, which the Sabaeans call Tizkholo in their tongue, came to bow down before Solomon and offer him his services to enter the city. "All I ask," he said, "is that you put your strongest and sturdiest bird at my disposal so he can carry me on his back for as far up as he can fly. I will then take care of the rest." The bird that would serve as a mount was immediately chosen and the puny Tizkholo installed on its back. The little bird's weight caused the other bird no discomfort whatsoever. They rose higher and higher through the air, and after they had covered a vast distance, the Tizkholo could see that his bearer was tired. He gave the bird permission to leave by telling him to go back down to the ground, and he continued his flying higher all alone. Every time he grew weary, he took refuge in a small hole to rest and then resumed his journey. In this way, he finally arrived at the top of the walls and entered the city that seemed deserted through a gap in the wall. He found an old man burdened with years in an apartment and hastened to greet him. This individual returned his greeting and asked him if he desired anything.

"I have come," replied the bird, "on behalf of Solomon to ask you how to gain entry into this city."

"I am not able to tell you," replied the old man, "but you will find a man older than me in this place, who will be able to satisfy your curiosity."

The Tizkholo went to find the second old man who sent him to see a third old man who was even older than he. As soon as he heard the name of Solomon, he demanded with urgency where this monarch was.

"He is at the foot of the walls to your city," the bird answered.

"Go tell him," the old man said, "that the gate to this city is located in the middle of the wall that faces the Pole Star and that he need only order his djinns to clear away the clumps of dirt that conceal it from his eyes. Once this gate has been completely uncovered, he shall give the wind the order to blow violently and the two doors in the gate will open before him."

The little bird returned to Solomon and reported on his mission.

The order to start clearing the gate was given to the djinns at once. They began to work, but they were unable to complete the job successfully given the huge encumbrance. Solomon gave the wind the responsibility to finish the job and to open the doors. The task imposed on the aerial element did not take long and the gate opened. The prophet king then entered the city with his army and found the three old men who had been visited by the Tizkholo waiting for him. They introduced themselves to the conqueror and offered him their homage. Solomon asked them what they were doing in this deserted city. "We are alone here," they told him, "and it was our mission to guard this city until your arrival."

The monarch then entered the palace of Chaddad and found all its inhabitants had been transformed into statues. All the chambers were decorated with precious stones, most notably a large reception room in which he found the statue of Chaddad seated on a throne.* The throne had been carved from a single block of precious stone. Solomon asked the old guardians who were accompanying him to recount the story of Chaddad.

"Chaddad," the oldest one replied, "had been made the universal sovereign of the earth by the sun. He was heaped with riches by the daystar and undertook the construction of the city and palace that you are now seeing. Once he had settled in, he became excessively proud of his great power and sought to make himself a god. He planned to slay the sun and

---

*Contrary to the Sabaeans, the Muslims claim that Chaddad never lived in this city.

take its place. He grabbed his bow and shot an arrow high into the sky. It fell back dipped in blood. This arrow was shown to the inhabitants of this city as proof positive of Chaddad's claims and from that day forward he was looked upon as the dominant power on heaven and earth. This behavior of Chaddad and his subjects, who truly recognized him as a god, excited the wrath of Alaha who struck the land with drought and a great famine afflicted the country. Driven by hunger, a large crowd came to petition Chaddad, as if to a god, with a request for something to eat. "If the earth refuses you the petty grain you are asking for," he responded with his customary pride, "I am rich enough to feed you even with precious stones. Enter my palace and you will find stores full of these stones among my treasures. Take as many as you like; you can have them ground for food while you are waiting for the earth to give you wheat." When they heard this response to their pleas, which rang both of pride and impotence, the subjects of the mad king opened their eyes and began to see how false his claimed divinity was. They left this land and scattered to other countries, until the time came that Chaddad remained alone with those whose statues you have seen. As for the three of us, we refused to embrace Chaddad's impious belief. We withdrew to a cave to continue to worship Alaha who sent us our daily food through a miracle. When he saw the king and his supporters persist in their blind error, the furious Alaha changed them into stones, and they have remained in the state in which you saw them since that time. We were alerted by a secret voice that you would come one day to take possession of the city we had been charged with guarding until your arrival so that we may turn it over to you." Once they had finished telling their tale, the three old men, whose mission was now over, hailed the conqueror and returned to their apartments, where they died.

4. SOLOMON'S DEATH

Solomon sat in contemplation for some time and began reflecting on the sad effects of pride. He recalled his own past disgrace and the loss of his ring, which was simply the result of this vice. He then humbled himself again before Alaha and again repented for the sin he had committed.

At the moment he was buried in these reflections, he suddenly felt that his ring had been mysteriously removed, and he died on the spot. His companions, horrified by this unexpected death, arranged the king's body in the palace where it can still be found today, and hurriedly left the city to return to their own country with the army.

5. THE DEATH OF CHADDAD

Chaddad wished to enter into the city Iram of [thousand] pillars.[5] "I have come to what Houd* announced to me after death and I possess it." But when he tried to enter, God on high ordered an angel to counter the Adites with a shout of wrath. In the blink of an eye, the angel of death seized their lives, and they fell face down upon the ground. Then God caused this city to vanish from the sight of men. However, in the land where it had been built, during the night gold, silver, and precious stones shining like lanterns could be seen. But when someone went to the spot, they could find nothing.[6]

---

*A prophet.

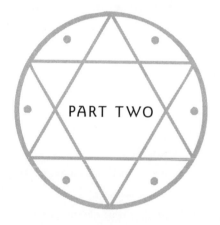

PART TWO

THE MAGICIAN

It is magic that has played the greatest role in the enduring memory of King Solomon. His reputation as a magician dates back to his prowess as an exorcist. The historian Yossef ben Matityahou HaCohen, better known as Flavius Josephus (37/38–100), tells us this:

> He composed such incantations also by which distempers are allevi-
> ated. And he left behind him the manner of using exorcisms, which
> drives away demons so that they never return, and this method of
> cure is of great force until this day. For I have seen a certain man
> of my own country, whose name was *Eleazar* (Ἐλεάζαρ), releasing
> people that were demoniacal[1] in the presence of Vespasian, his sons,
> his Captains, and all of his soldiers. The manner of the cure was
> this:* he put a ring that had a root of one of those sorts mentioned
> by Solomon to the nostrils of the demoniack, after which he drew
> out the demon through his nostrils, and when the man fell down
> immediately, he abjured him to return into him no more, making
> mention of Solomon and reciting the incantations which he com-
> posed. And when Eleazar would persuade and demonstrate to the
> spectators that he had such a power, he set a cup or bason full of
> water a little way off, and commanded the demon, as he went out
> of the man, to overturn it, and thereby to let the spectators know
> that he had left the man. And when this was done, the skill and
> wisdom of Solomon was shown manifestly. For which reason it is,
> that all men may know the vastness of Solomon's abilities and how
> he was beloved of God, and that the extraordinary virtues of every
> kind with which this King was endowed may not be unknown to
> any people under the sun. For this reason, I say it is that we have
> proceeded to speak so largely of these matters.[2]

---

*Solomon was reputed to know every remedy. Julie Filippi collected a strange heal-
ing method in Corsica: "First the sign of Solomon is made over the ailing part of the
patient's body, then it is covered with a good layer of oil that is then covered with flour
or starch powder. On the second or third prayer, the oil and flour is removed."

This episode was known far and wide, and a number of Byzantine authors set the tone. Michael Glycas, for example, replicates Flavius Josephus's account exactly.[3]

The *Kitab al-Falasifa,* attributed to Ḥunayn ibn Isḥaq (800–873), depicts Solomon traveling by zephyr to an island of wise genies who are the keepers of occult knowledge.[4]

In *The Key of Hearts* (*Miftah el-Qulub*), a tenth-century Persian manuscript, we find this observation:

> In truth, Solomon was the greatest of all magicians. He ruled over the birds and the beasts, and over all men from the highest to the lowest."

In the thirteenth century, Gervase of Tilbury noted that "Solomon taught how to enclose demons in rings and, thanks to seals, magical spells, and exorcisms, to summon and imprison them."[5]

During the Middle Ages, Solomon passed as being the founder of the *Ars notoria* (The Notary Art),[6] a form of nondemonic ritual magic that summoned spirits to obtain favors, which God was supposed to have revealed to him. This science makes it possible to acquire the seven liberal arts and to use prayers, lists of obscure words presented as Aramaic, Greek, and Hebrew, and geometric figures called "notes."[7]

In Romania, the lexicon reveals that Solomon's connection to magic remains. *Solomonie* means spell, and a wizard is a *Solomonar.* Furthermore, Romanian people know of the imprisonment of devils in jars sealed with his seal.

A large number of grimoires have circulated under the name of the son of David. Let's start with the oldest one.

THIRTEEN

The Testament of Solomon

Over a dozen Greek manuscripts, none later than the fifteenth century, have transmitted *The Testament of Solomon*[1] (ΔΙΑΘΗΚΗ ΣΟΛΟΜΩΝΤΟΣ) into the present. Julian Véronèse notes: "From one manuscript to the next, the lessons diverge to such a huge extent that the reconstruction of a standard text appears illusionary, whereas even the oldest manuscripts (ca. 1225) are relatively close to 'point zero,' located around 1180."[2] McCown[3] has shown that the text is characterized by an extraordinary syncretism of Assyrian, Babylonian, Iranian, Jewish, Hellenistic, and Christian elements.

Two clues suggest that it has had other titles. The Byzantine historian Michael Glycas mentions a *Book of Genies* attributed to Solomon, in which this latter forces the demons to show themselves in all their forms and to reveal their true nature. These demons are enslaved by a pact and banished to certain places,[4] which specifically brings what the *Testament* says to mind. Its authors show the son of David summoning demons and compelling them to reveal their names and pernicious actions, as well as the means needed to make them powerless. This takes place in two stages. The first focuses on describing a series of evil spirits. Generally, they are monstrous, in keeping with an ancient adage that says a hideous body is the seat of a black soul, but we should note that he assigned them a specific task of building the Temple of Jerusalem.*

---

*"I condemned some of these demons to the heavy construction work of the Temple of God. I shut others up in prison. I commanded the others to whip up the fire to manufacture gold and silver."

The second stage describes a series of thirty-six decanic demons.

The Coptic Gnostics offer us a second clue. In *The Untitled Text* from the codex of Nag Hammadi, appears the following passage:

> Then Death, being androgynous, mingled with his (own) nature and begot seven androgynous offspring. These are the names of the male ones: Jealousy, Wrath, Tears, Sighing, Suffering, Lamentation, Bitter Weeping. And these are the names of the female ones: Wrath, Pain, Lust, Sighing, Curse, Bitterness, Quarrelsomeness. They had intercourse with one another, and each one begot seven, so that they amount to forty-nine androgynous demons. Their names and their effects you will find in the *Book of Solomon.*[5]

In the Arab countries, the influence of the *Testament* made itself felt especially in the work of the Baghdad bookseller and calligrapher, Ibn al-Nadim (died 995 or 998). What he writes in fact is this:

> Names of the effrits (*al-'ifrit*) that appeared before Solomon, son of David. They are seventy in number. They state that Solomon, son of David, blessings upon him, sat down and summoned the chieftain of the djinns and demons (*shayatin*), whose name was Fuqtus. He had them pass in review and Fuqtus told him the name of each of them and their actions against the descendants of Adam. He had them swear an oath and sign a pact. When he adjured them with this pact, they would answer and act. The pacts were the names of God.[6]

Ibn al-Nadim clearly followed the same source as Michael Glycas—a demonology treatise such as the *Testament*. He also mentions in passing Ibn Hilal and his Book of the Commentary on *What the Demons told Solomon, son of David and the Pacts that He Made against Them.*[7]

> Solomon learned that once night fell, a boy working on the construction site of the Temple of Jerusalem was victim of attacks from a demon named Ornias. This demon stole half of his food, half of his salary, sucked the thumb on his right hand, and prevented him

from growing. Solomon went to the Temple and after praying there for many long hours, received a ring holding a precious stone on which a seal, the pentalpha, had been carved, from the Archangel Michael. Michael told him, "With this you will shut away all the world's demons—male and female—and with their service, you shall build Jerusalem," Solomon lent his ring to the child who marked his chest with the seal and led the demon before Solomon who interrogated him. "Who are you?" he asked, and the demon replied: "Ornias."

"Tell me, demon," ordered Solomon, "you are subject of which sign of the Zodiac?"

"To the water bearer. I stifle those who are hungry with desire for the virgin nobles of the earth, but in the case where there is no sleeping arrangement, I change into three shapes. For someone desperately in love with a woman, I transform myself into a female comet, I take control over men while they sleep and play with them; after a little while I regain my wings to fly away to celestial regions. I also appeared like a lion obedient to all demons."

Solomon pressed his seal on him and condemned him to cut stones for the Temple. He also ordered him to bring him the prince of all the demons.

Then the beautiful demon Onoskelis* who strangles men with a bridle and engages in hostilities with what she was gifted by nature: "Nevertheless, I often associate with men in the guise of a woman," she added, "and above all those whose skin is black because they share my star with me." Solomon ordered her to spin hemp for the ropes used for building the house of God.

Then Asmodeus introduced himself. He is connected to the star that is called the Charot or the Dragon Child. "My function is to conspire against all newlyweds to prevent them from coupling together," he said. "I divide them entirely by multiple disasters and I spoil the beauty of virgin women and smother their hearts. . . I

---

*This means "Donkey foot," another name for Empusa. The Byzantines saw this figure as a child-eater who had a bronze foot.

carry men away in crises of anguish and desire even though they have their own wives who they abandon and go out day and night with others who belong to other men with the goal of having them commit sin and fall into murderous designs." And, at Solomon's request, he added, "The liver and gall of a glanos fish send me fleeing when they are smoked over the ashes of the tamarisk." Solomon commanded him to construct the flooring of the Temple.

Solomon summoned Belial to appear, a fallen angel who henceforth governs Tartarus and destroys kings, inspires the religious to lust and heresies, inspires envy, murder, and sodomy among humans. Among the Hebrews he is neutralized by the holy name of God Emmanuel, and among the Greeks by a row of numbers whose sum is 644. Solomon ordered him to cut the marbles of Thebes.

Fig. 13.1. Jacobus of Teramo, Belial, Munich (Bayerisches Staatsbibliothek, Cgm 48, folio 45v, 85v).

Fig. 13.2. Jacobus of Teramo, Belial before Solomon,
(Das Buch Belial, Augsbourg, 1473).

This convocation has been widely depicted in the iconography of manuscripts and incunabula.

Belial had a son who lived in the Red Sea or the Dead Sea, and Solomon ordered Belial to bring him, but the other wished him to be accompanied by Ephippas, who would pull his son up from the depths.

Then appeared Tephras who brings darkness upon men, lights the fields afire, and demolishes dwellings.* He lives in the horn of the moon when it is in the South, and the name of the archangel Azael gives mastery over him. Solomon imposed on him the task of measuring the stones and tossing them to the workers laboring in the upper part of the Temple.

Seven female spirits of the thirty-three elements of the Astral Chief of darkness then introduced themselves and gave their names: Deception, Strife, Combat, Jealousy, Power, Error, and The Worst of All. Their stars are pale and seven in number, which correspond to the Pleiades.

Name	Action	Neutralization By
Deception	Laying of traps, deceptions	Lamechalal
Strife	Brings weapons to the spot	Baruchiachel
Combat	Quarrels, slander	Marmarath
Jealousy	Lack of sobriety, division of couples, scattering of families; lifts up tyrants, topples kings, helps rebels	Balthial
Power	Causes people to fall into error, digs through graves, leads errant souls far from all piety	Asteraoth
Error	Imposes the yoke of Artemis	Uriel
The Worst		the Locust

Solomon commanded them to dig the foundations of the temple to a length of two-hundred-fifty cubits.

Then Envy introduced himself. He was a headless demon with human limbs, whose "specialty" was the devouring of heads, and who also caused serious and incurable sores and mutilations to feet. The procession continued with Staff (Rhabdos) who brought a green stone for the adornment of the Temple; with Lion Bearer, who Solomon gave the charge of bringing in wood from the forest; with a three-headed

---

*This spirit had the power to reduce the convulsions of dropsy. The sufferers of this illness had to pray using three names: Bultala, Thallal, Mechal.

dragon who manufactured the bricks; with a demoness named Obisuth, who Solomon had hung from the door of the Temple by her hair; with Pterodrakon who carves the marbles; and with Enepsigos, a prophetic spirit who tells Solomon:

"After a time, your kingdom shall be broken, and again in season this Temple shall be broken into pieces, and all of Jerusalem shall be defeated by the King of the Persians and Medes and Chaldeans. And then the vessels of this Temple, which you are making now, shall be made to serve other gods; and just like them, all the jars in which you have imprisoned us shall be broken by the hands of men. And then we shall go forth here and there in great strength and scatter ourselves across the world. And we shall lead the inhabited world astray for a long season, until the Son of God is stretched upon the sign [the cross]."

Then came Kunopaston—a horse in front and a fish behind—who Solomon had shut up in an earthenware jar that was placed in the Temple. Then came a spirit with sword in hand. When questioned, he replied:

"I sit close to the men who pass among the tombs and at an unexpected moment I assume the form of the dead. If I catch any one of them, I destroy him immediately with my sword. But if I cannot destroy him, I cause him to be possessed by a demon, so he devours his own flesh and his hair falls from his chin."

Then came the thirty-six demons of the decans: each gave his name, identified his specialty in the causing of ills and misfortune, as well as the name or ritual that would cause them to flee. Here they are as they introduced themselves in the Paris manuscript.

In the case of Atrax and Bouldoumech, an exorcism is given in the form of a charm. To ward off Nathaoth (variant: Naoth), Mardero, Alath Nephthada, Akton, and Enenuth, *The Testament* tells how to make a protective amulet.

In his study of these demons of the decans,[8] Wilhelm Gundel explains their names and origins, clearly showing that they provide splendid examples of syncretism. For example, Rhyax comes from Hebrew and means "Lord;" Ichthion and Horopel (variants: Horopolos, Aropolos), "the Press," come from the Egyptian decans.

Demon of the Decan	His Activity	How to Neutralize Him
1. Ruax	Empties men's heads	Michael
2. Barsafael	Causes migraine	Gabriel
3. Arotosael	Attacks the eyes	Uriel
4. [missing]		
5. Ioudal	Causes hearing loss	Uruel
6. Sphendonael	Causes tumors and tonsillitis	Sabrael
7. Sphandor	Paralyzes the nerves of the hands, breaks bones, sucks out the marrow	Arael
8. Belbel	Twists hearts and minds	Arael
9. Kurtael	Causes colic and suffering	Iaoth
10. Metathiax	Kidney pains	Adonanel
11. Katanikotael	Discord among couples	amulet
12. Saphathorael	Drunkeness, partisanship	amulet
13. Bothothel/Bobel	Nervous disorders	Adonanel
14. Kumenatel	Shivering, torpor	Zoroel
15. Roeled	Cold, stomach pains	Iax
16. Atrax	Fevers without cure	Exorcism
17. Ieropael	Convulsions	Charm
18. Buldumech	Hostility in couples	Charm
19. Naoth/Nathath	Sits on the knees	Amulet
20. Mardero	Incurable fevers	Amulet
21. Alath	Coughs, respiratory problems in children	Amulet
22. [missing]		
23. Nephthada	Dysuria	Amulet
24. Akton	Rib and muscle pains	
25. Anatreth	Stabs the entrails with burning sensations and fevers	Arara Charara

Demon of the Decan	His Activity	How to Neutralize Him
26. Enenuth	Removes conscience, causes teeth to fall out	Allazool
27. Pheth/Axiopheth	Causes hemorrhages	Exorcism
28. Harpax	Causes somnolence	Kokphnedismos
29. Anoster	Causes uterine pain, bladder pain	Marmarao
30. Alleborith	Causes the swallowing of fish bones, lingering disease	Cough
31. Hephesimireth		Seraphim, Cherubim, ointment of oil and salt
32. Ichthion	Muscle paralysis and damage	Adonaeth
33. Agchonion		Amulet, subtractive spell
	Sleeps among swaddling clothes	Alpha & Omega
34. Autothith	Inspires resentment and fighting	
35. Phthenoth	Gives the evil eye	Drawn eye
36. Bianakith	Makes flesh rot, desecrates abandoned houses	Aleph Tav Inscription over door

1. AMULETS

You must write a name on either a piece of paper, the pages of a book, a tin plate, or copper taken from a boat, and tie it around your body, your kidneys, your neck, or hang it from the door of your house.

Here are four examples:

No. 20. Mardero: "If someone write on the page of a book: 'Sphener, Rafael, go away, do not drag me away, do not flay me,' and ties it round his neck, I retreat at once."

No. 21. Alath: "If anyone writes on paper: 'Rorex, chase Alath away,' and ties it round his neck, I depart at once."

No. 23. Nephthada: "If someone writes the words 'Iathoth, Uruel,

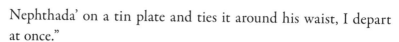

Nephthada' on a tin plate and ties it around his waist, I depart at once."

No. 36. Bianakith: "If a person writes 'Melto, Ardu, Anaath' over his front door, I shall flee from that place."

2. REMEDIES

To cure the illness caused by a decanic demon, ingredients and incantations are used:

No. 26. Enenuth: "If someone writes 'Allazool pursues Enenuth' and ties the paper on his person, I will go away at once."

No. 29. Anoster: "If someone crushes three laurel seeds in pure oil and covers themselves with it while saying 'stop by Marmarao,' I will retreat at once."

No. 31. Hephesimireth: "If you throw salt that has been rubbed in your hand with oil and spread over the patient while saying 'Seraphim, Cherubim help me,' I will leave at once."

For Agchonion (no. 33), a subtractive charm that takes a textual form that resembles a cluster of grapes must be used. This is a common procedure in ancient Greek magic:

Lycurgos

ycurgos

kurgos

yrgos

gos

os

3. EXORCISMS AND CHARMS

It is hard to tell the difference between exorcism and charm in the *Testament* because they rely upon the same technique. Here are the relevant examples:

No. 16. Atrax: "If you wish to imprison me, chop up coriander and smear it on your lips while reciting the following charm: 'The fever is like dust. I exorcise thee by the throne of the God on high, retreat from dirt and abandon the creature fashioned by God.' And I retreat at once."

No. 17 Ieropael: "If someone speaks these three names in the victim's right ear, 'Iudarize, Sabune, Denoe,' I will leave at once."

No. 18. Buldumech: "If someone writes the names of Solomon's patriarchs on a piece of paper and places it in the entrance hall of their house, I shall leave at once. And legend written shall be as follows: 'The God of Abraham and the God of Isaac, and the God of Jacob commands you to leave this house in peace,' and I depart right away."

No. 19. Nathath: "If someone writes 'Phnunoboeol drives Nathath away and doesn't touch his neck,' I retreat at once."

No. 27. Pheth: "If someone exorcises me in wine, sweet-smelling and undiluted by the eleven ages (aeons), and says: 'I demand and urge Pheth (variant: Axiopheth) to stop by the eleven ages,' then give it to the patient to drink, I retreat at once."

4. AN INTERROGATION

As a proper demonology treatise, the *Testament* stages the interrogation of Ornias, which we saw in the beginning of this chapter. While passing before a father and his son, Ornias laughed because he knew the child would die before his father. Solomon then asked him:

"Tell me how you know that?" and the demon replied: "We demons ascend in the firmament of heaven and fly among the stars and we hear the sentences that are levied on the souls of men and directly we come, and whether by force of persuasion, or by fire, or by sword, or by some accident, we conceal our act of destruction. If a man does not die by some untimely disaster or by violence, then we demons transform ourselves in such a way as to appear to men and be worshipped in our human nature."

5. THE OTHER ELEMENTS OF
THE *TESTAMENT*

The text includes a letter from Ardaes, king of Arabia, who requests Solomon's aid against an Aeolian spirit: "Early in the morning there a certain wind begins to blow until the third hour. And its breath is cruel and terrible, and it strikes down man and beast." Solomon sent one of his servitors with this order:

"Saddle your camel and take a leather wineskin, and take this seal as well. Go into Arabia to the place where the evil spirit blows and take the flask with the signet-ring in front of the mouth of the wineskin and hold them in the spirit's path. And when the wineskin is fully puffed up, you will know that the demon is in it. Then quickly knot the wineskin's mouth and seal it securely with the signet-ring and tie it carefully to the camel and bring it to me. And if on the way it offers gold, silver, or treasure to you in return for letting it go, see

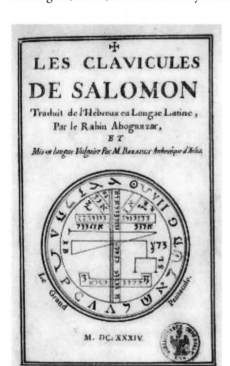

Fig. 13.3. The Other Elements
of the Testament

that you are not swayed, but arrange things without promising to release it. And then if it points out to you places where there is gold or silver, mark the places and seal them with this seal, and bring me the demon."[9]

Again we see Ephippas,[10] who was mentioned earlier in the *Testament*, who speaks in favor of major alterations to the text. Ephippas can move mountains, so King Solomon asks him to lift a stone and deposit it by the entrance to the Temple. The demon tells him that he needs the help of Abezithibod, one of his fellow demons living in the Red Sea. With his aid, Ephippas suspended a pillar in the sky. The day it falls back to earth will be the end of the world.

The Testament ends with Solomon falling into idolatry because of a woman who sent him five locusts with these words: "Take these locusts and shred them together in the name of the god Moloch and then will I wed you." Solomon lost all his wisdom and built a temple filled with the idols of Baal, Rapha, Moloch, and others.[11]

In the *Veritable Clavicles of Solomon,* a work claiming to be the Latin translation of a Hebrew text by the rabbi Abognazar, we find a fragment of the Testament in French:

O my son Roboam,* seeing that of all the sciences there is none more useful than the knowledge of celestial movements, I have thought it my duty, being at the point of death, to leave you an inheritance more precious than all the riches I have enjoyed. In order that you may understand how I have arrived at this degree (of wisdom), it is necessary to tell you that one day when I was meditating upon the power of the Supreme Being, the Angel of the Great God appeared before me as I was saying, "O how [great and] wonderful are the works of God!" I suddenly beheld, at the end of a thickly shaded vista of trees, a light in the form of a blazing star, which said unto me with a voice of thunder: "Solomon, Solomon, be not dismayed.

---

*Roboam is the son of Solomon and the information in a large number of grimoires is intended for him.

The Lord is willing to satisfy your desire by giving you knowledge of whatsoever thing is most pleasant to you. I order you to ask of Him whatsoever you desire." Whereupon, recovering from my surprise, I answered unto the Angel, that according to the Will of the Lord, I only desired the gift of wisdom, and by the Grace of God I obtained the enjoyment of all the celestial treasures and the knowledge of all natural things.

It is by this means, my son, that I possess all the virtues and riches that you now see me enjoy, and in order that you may be willing to be attentive to all which I am about to relate to you, and that you may retain with care all that I am about to tell you, I assure you that the Graces of the Great God will be familiar to you, and that the celestial and terrestrial creatures will be obedient to you and a science which only works by the strength and power of natural things, and by the pure Angels which govern them. The latter of which I will give you the names in order, their exercises and particular employments to which they are destined, together with the days over which they particularly preside, so that you may arrive at the accomplishment of all, which you will find in this my Testament. In all of which I promise you success, provided that all your works only tend to the honour of God, Who has given me the power to rule, not only over terrestrial but also over celestial things, that is to say, over the Angels, of whom I am able to dispose according to my will and from whom I am able to obtain very considerable services.

After this prologue, Solomon gets to the crux of the matter and gives us a wealth of information about the notions of the world during these remote times:

First it is necessary for you to understand that God, having made all things in order that they may submit to Him, wished to bring His works to perfection by making one being that participates in the Divine and in the Terrestrial. That is to say, humankind, whose body is gross and terrestrial while their soul is spiritual and celestial, to whom He has made the whole earth and its inhabitants subject, and to whom He has given the means by which they may render the Angels familiar, as I call those celestial creatures of whom some are destined to regulate the motion of the stars, others to inhabit the elements, others to aid and direct human beings, and others again to sing continually the praises of the Lord. You may then, by the use of their seals and characters, render them familiar to you, provided that you do not abuse this privilege by demanding from them things which are contrary to their nature; for accursed be he who will take the Name of God in vain and who employs for evil purposes the knowledge and good with which He has enriched us.

I command you, my son, to carefully engrave in your memory all that I say to you, in order that it may never leave you. [F adds: *ou du moins, je t'ordonne que* ("or, at least, I order that. . . .")] If you do not intend to use the secrets that I now will teach you for a good purpose, I instead command you to cast this Testament into the fire. Do not abuse the power you will have of constraining the Spirits, for I warn thee that the beneficent Angels, wearied and fatigued by your illicit demands, would execute the commands of God to your sorrow, as well as to that of anyone who with evil intent would abuse those secrets which He has given and revealed to me. Think not, however, O my son, that it would not be permitted for you to profit by the good fortune and happiness which the Divine Spirits can bring you. On the contrary, it gives them great pleasure to render service to humankind for whom many of these Spirits have great liking and affinity, God having destined them for the preservation and guidance of those terrestrial things which are submitted to the power of humans.

There are different kinds of Spirits according to the things over which they preside: some of them govern the Empyrean Heaven, others the Primum Mobile, others the First and Second Crystalline spheres, others the Starry Heaven. There are also the Spirits of the Heaven of Saturn, which I call Saturnites; there are Jovial, Martial, Solar, Venusian, Mercurial, and Lunar Spirits. There are also (Spirits) in the Elemental spheres as well as in the Heavens: there are some in the Fiery Region, others in the Air, others in the Water, and others upon the Earth,* which can all render service to that man who learns their nature, and knows how to attract them.[12]

6. INFLUENCE OF THE *TESTAMENT* ON ARABIC LITERATURE

Elements of the narrative structure of the Testament can be found in the medieval Arabic literature, and I shall provide some examples.

Abu Bekr Muhammed ben 'Abdullah al-Kisa'I, who died around 799, collected passages from the Testament together in a curious work with the title *Tale of the Description of the Shaytans Gathered Before Solomon, Son of David*:

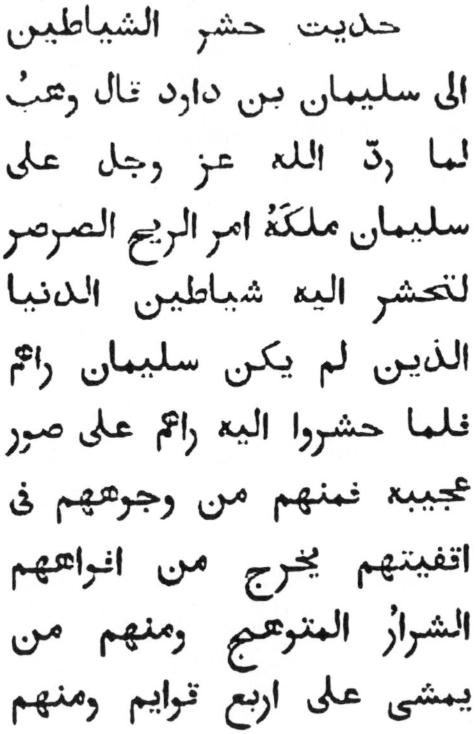

حديث حشر الشياطين
الى سليمان بن داود قال وهب
لما رق الله عز وجل على
سليمان ملكة امر الريح الصرصر
لتحشر اليه شياطين الدنيا
الذين لم يكن سليمان راهم
فلما حشروا اليه راهم على صور
عجيبه فمنهم من وجوههم فى
اقفيتهم يخرج من افواههم
الشرار المتوهج ومنهم من
يمشى على اربع قوايم ومنهم

Fig. 13.4. Beginning of al-Kisa'I's text

---

*The cosmology he describes here is in line with the widely popular Platonian geocentric understanding of the Earth's place in the universe.

Fig. 13.5. Djinns and Shaytans. Left, Library of Bordeaux, ms. 1130
Right, Munich Staatsbibliothek. Arab Codice 464

Wabb tells us:

Once God had given Solomon his throne, he commanded the
winds to gather together all the demons of the world the sovereign had not yet seen. Once before him, he could see their strange
forms. Some had their faces on their shoulders and burning sparks
flew from their mouths, others walked on all fours, while others
had blue eyes, green faces, and black bodies. Some had faces like
dogs and the bodies of elephants with their buttocks in the center; they brayed like donkeys. Among them, Solomon saw a demon
that was half dog and half cat with a large snout. Solomon asked
it: "Who are you?"

"O prophet of God, I am Mahr ben Hafaf ben Qilha;b ben Jaz'am
brought by Noah."

"What is your function?"

"Gaming and drinking," it replied. "I am he who presses the juice of the grape and offers it to drink as wine. Whoever drinks it becomes drunk. I dwell in one of the valleys of India. I incite men to drink, play the harp, the lute, the castanets, and all kinds of games, to lie, to falsify, to murder, and to commit all sins against All-powerful God."

At this point, Solomon looked at each of these tempters of men and ordered them to be shackled and chained.

Then he went by another demon that was even more terrible than the first. It looked like smoke with a blazing fire shooting from its throat. It was a repulsive vision and barked like a dog.

"Who are you?" Solomon asked.

"Halhal, the sword bearer of Iblis."

He was extremely ugly, blood dripped from every hair, and a sword and a cutlass hung from his belt.

"What do you do?" Solomon asked.

"No blood is spilled unless it is by me and the chain you see around my neck is made from the blood of Adam."

Solomon ordered that he be bound, but the other begged him: "Don't do that, O prophet of God, do not bind me. I am going to gather all the giants of the earth together and swear to you that I shall cause no harm as long as you live." Solomon accepted his oath then allowed him to leave for he was obedient henceforth.

Then the son of El-Harit, Murra, appeared in the form of an ape. He had claws like scythes and held a harp. Solomon asked him, "Who are you?" He told him, and then Solomon asked: "What are your duties?"

"I am the first to have created this harp and played it. It is the only instrument that provides pleasure."

"Peace be upon him!" said Solomon, and he gave the order to bind him. This is how he bound so many demons.[13]

Leaning on a variety of authors, Zakariya ibn Mohammed al-Qazwini, who was born in Qazwin (in present day Iran) around 1203 and died in Baghdad around 1283, wrote *Marvels of things created and miraculous aspects of things existing (Ajā'ib al-makhlūqāt wa-gharā'ib al-mawjūdāt)*. He recounts how Gabriel summoned the djinns together to be introduced to Solomon. They came out of their caves, mountains, hills, valleys, deserts, and swamps, driven by the angels like shepherds drive their flocks. Together they formed four hundred and twenty groups. They were then made submissive to Solomon. The son of David gazed at their strange aspects. They were black, white, yellow, red, or piebald, and they had the shapes of horses, mules, and lions. They had trunks, tails, claws, and horns. Solomon then questioned them about their faith, their families, their habitats, their food, and the reason behind their peculiar forms. They answered: "we are different because of the diversity of our rebels (marid), their mixture with us, and our marriages with their descendants." Solomon contemplated them and saw they had ill intentions, but angels armed with clubs intervened. Solomon had them tied up and imposed various tasks on them: working metals, extracting stones from the cliffs, chopping down trees, and building fortresses; their wives were compelled to weave and spin silk and wool, and make saddle blankets.[14]

Fig. 13.6.
The djinns
introduced
to Solomon.

Al-Qazwini also cited extracts from the Book of the Israelites (Kitab al-Isra'iliyat), by the Yemenite Wahb ibn Munabbih (654–730),[15] a collection of stories concerning Biblical figures. He describes Solomon's meeting with the djinns and shaytans. Some had two heads, some had a lion's head on an elephant's body, some had their faces facing backward and spitting fire, and some walked on all fours.

"Who are you?" asked Solomon to the first one.

"Mihran ibn Hafan ibn Filan."

"What do you concern yourself with?"

"Song and the preparation of wine; I prompt the desire to sing and drink among the children of Adam."

The king ordered him to be bound.

Another djinn appeared, black, ugly, and barking, blood dripping from his hair and his body had a repulsive aspect.

"Who are you?" asked Solomon.

"Halhal ibn Mahlul."

"What do you do?"

"I spill blood." The sovereign had him tied up.

A third came before the king. He looked like an ape with claws like scythes and he held a harp.

"Who are you?" asked Solomon.

"I am Murra ibn al-Harith,"

"What do you do?"

"I was the first to introduce the playing of the harp and no one can get pleasure from listening to music unless I allow it." Solomon had him bound.[16]

The overall structure is the same as in the *Testament,* but we are given the impression that Wahb ibn Munabbih was satisifed with supplying just a few examples. Furthermore, he left out everything that smacked of magic.

Fig. 14.1. *Hygromancy of Solomon.*
On the left, the lamen,[1] the ring, and the sign needed to etch on the glove,
On the right, the signs to wear on the shoes and on the cloth covering the lamen.
British Museum, Harley manuscript 5596, foilo 33r–v.

FOURTEEN

Solomon's *Hygromancy*

The oldest manuscripts of *The Hygromancy of Solomon* (also commonly known in English as the *Magical Treatise of Solomon*) date from the fifteenth century, but the core material goes back to the sixth century. I am following the Paris manuscript, which contains:[2]

1. The astrological part with the planetary rulers of the days.
2. The angels and demons that rule over the hours and days of the week.
3. Solomon's advice to his son Roboam:

Roboam, I engrave for you here a method of knowing most exactly what must be known at all costs at the time when you wish to work your will. First speak the prayer to the planet present at that hour, then conjure the angel and the servant, which is to say the demon.

4. Prayer to God for obtaining the submission of the planet Saturn though names:

God eternal, independent power that organizes all for our salvation, grant us grace so that I may submit this planet to my will. Planet Saturn, I conjure your path, your air, your descendance, your heaven, your shine, and your energy by these names: Gassial, Agounsael, Atasser, Veltoniel, Mentzatzia, so that you may give me your grace and energy and power at the hour when you're dominant."

5. A prayer to Zeus:

Lord God, all powerful Father, creator of things visible and invisible, ruler of rulers and king of dominators, grant us the strength of your grace so that Zeus submits to us, for all is possible with you, Lord. Zeus, I conjure your wisdom, your knowledge, your healing energy, your heavenly journey, over which you walk by the names that follow herein: Anoph, Orsita, Atnox, Onivegi, Atziniel, Ankaniti, Tyneos, Genier, Kaniptza, so that you may pour your grace over me in this work I am performing.

6. A prayer to Ares:

Terrible god, unspeakable god, invisible god who has not and cannot be seen by any human. God who caused the abysses to shudder and reduced the living to the dead, grant us your grace so that we can gain submission of the planet Ares. Ares of fire, I conjure the god who created intelligible substances and the entire army of fire; I conjure your energies, your journey, and your shine by the names that follow herein: Outat, Nouet, Choreze, Tinae, Dachli, Ambira, Noliem, Siet, Adichael, Tzanas, Plesym, so that you may pour your grace over me in this work I am performing.

Other manuscripts are more complete and include exorcisms of the demons of the cardinal points, the requirements for subjugating evil spirits, a parchment that needs to be written on in the blood of a bat, bird, or bull, the use of perfumes and clothing, then the text lists other techniques for compelling spirits to appear.[3] Solomon explains to Roboam how to ritually dominate demons and demonstrates this by invoking the ones of the four cardinal points, identified by the names of the four winds.[4]

FIFTEEN

The Keys of Solomon

Starting in the thirteenth century, numerous grimoires began circulating under the name of *Clavicula Solomonis, The Little Key of Solomon*. This is the date cited by Peter Abano (1257–1315) when he mentions this work. There are one hundred and thirteen manuscripts bearing this title, which cover the span from the fifteenth to eighteenth centuries and are written in a dozen different languages. The Greek version,[1] from which the Latin translations are derived, are vouched for by around fifteen manuscripts with various titles—*Magic Treatise of Solomon, The Little Key of the Art of Hygromancy*[2]—and the text consists of two parts, each with about twenty chapters.

A long Latin text of three books can be found in a manuscript in the Narodowa Library:[3]

1. The Secret of Secrets
2. The Pentacles of the Apparitions
3. The intelligences of the planets and their spirits. Stones.

Let's look at this in greater detail.

The first book provides various magical recipes for making it rain and thunder, and to prevent freezes and heatwaves, followed by techniques for opening anything that is closed in the following manner: take a lodestone, make the sign of Saint Andrew's Cross over it three times, draw a circle around the stone and a square within the circle, and so forth.

Let's take two examples. If someone wants to make rain, they need to take natural or artificial sea water and put it in a circle made on the ground in the manner described in the chapters on the circle. Put the Heliotrope stone in the middle of the circle and a magic staff on the right side. Write the characters of Bechard on the left side and Eliogaphatel in the middle, and holding the staff, say: "Eliogaphatel, the sky is composed of clouds, may they resolve into water." Once these words are spoken, the rain will fall abundantly.

To have as many gold pieces as you wish, prepare as many rounds of virgin parchment as coins you want to have. Glue them together, each made with the dimensions of the coin of the region that you want. Then make the circle on a table and the three characters of Chaunta, and raise all the pieces of parchment up high and say these words by the keyhole of your room holding a wand: Chaunta, Ferala, Sadain, If, Gluth, Temterans, Tagam, Seranna, Fount, Eritherem, Elibanoth, Nerohin. Say this in the evening, and sleep for an hour on your bed, not thinking of the coins. Then, instead of those of parchment, you will find genuine gold ones.

More standard are the means of gaining a woman's love or of killing an enemy using the heart of a rooster born in May, over which is spoken the words "Remaner adhuch / Calemturch archalth / Elestor" before stabbing it.

The second book deals with everything that is necessary for the magician. First, he must invoke the supreme and ineffable name on which all that lives on earth and in heaven depends, including the spirits, both good and evil (*tam boni quam mali*), and prepare the "tools," meaning the circle, the pentacle, the sword, the holy water, the garment, the fire for suffumigations, the blood and ink, and the virgin parchment. Next, the time and place of the operation must be chosen to summon the spirits. Several pentacles are drawn: the first makes it possible to acquire science; the second, prophecy; and the third makes it possible to be in two or many places at once (*Ut homo reperiatur in pluribus locis*); the others make it possible to become invisible, to know the present, past, and future, and to win great honors.

The third book deals with the names of the intelligences and their planets:

Planet	Intelligence	Spirit
Sun	Michael	Fabriel, Vstael, Turnel
Moon	Gabriel	Madiel, Anael, Vetael
Mars	Samael	Amabiel, Iasel, Galdel
Mercury	Raphael	Vianuel
Jupiter	Sachiel	Mielis, Turmiel, Ruduel, Iarihael
Venus	Anael	Castiel, Assatiel, Gutriel
Saturn	Cassiel	Guadoliel, Sagum, Tamael, Mustalfiel, Uriel, Periel, Assaidi

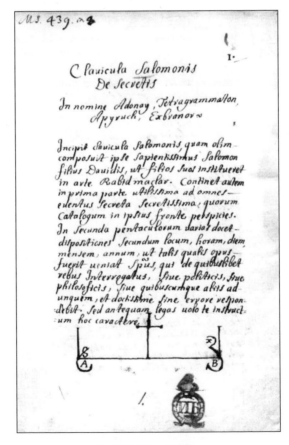

Fig. 15.1. Moon Spirits

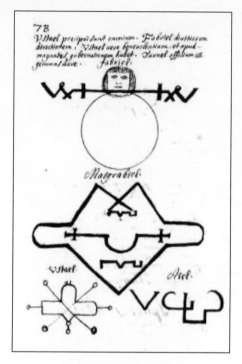

Fig. 15.2. Satellite Spirits

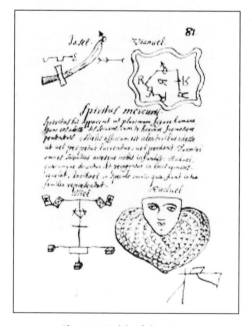

Fig. 15.3. Spirit of the Moon

Fig. 15.4. Spirit of Mercury

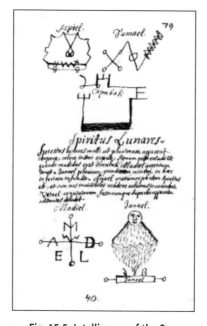

Fig. 15.5. Intelligence of the Sun

Each spirit has a specific function. For example, Uriel must be addressed for sowing discord, and Guadoliel and Sagum for exciting women to have coitus. Iasel, meanwhile, provokes quarrels between brothers and wars between people. Every spirit also possesses servants called "satellites." For example, Fabriel Masgrabiel, has the obedience of Ustael, Aiel, Sapiel, Tumael, and Capabali.

The third book ends with instructions on the use of stones in magical operations. Four terms summarize the approach to follow: *Confectio, purgatio, consecratio,* and *baptismus.*

Armadel's version of the *Keys of Solomon,* preserved in the Landowne Manuscript 1202 4to of the British Library, provides a different list from the one we just looked at of the spirits or intelligences that govern the thirteen heavens. Each spirit is the specialist of one or more domain.

Oririel	Possesses theology, metaphysics, writing, religion, prophecy.
Magriel	Astronomy, astrology, art of divining by expressions, conjunctions, and oppositions; teaches the composition of marks and characters.
Uriel	Knows arithmetic, geometry, perspective, and natural magic; makes men invisible, teaches those who serve him how to fly through the air and turn themselves invisible.
Pamachiel	Teaches physics, oneiromancy (dream interpretation), and the properties of animals.
Pommeriel	Makes men bellicose and able to fight fearlessly; gives invisibility and invulnerability.
Sacriel	Chemistry, transmutation of metals, knows the art of lapidairies, sculpture, the properties of stones and images. He pulls the dead from the grave and gives them life, stops the course of the sun, and excites meteors.
Nechariel	Teaches grammar, logic, medicine, all the liberal arts, and the properties of herbs. Imparts admirable virtues to certain plants, makes men healthy, changes old age to youth, and bestows life and death.

Chariel	Teaches the art of love, makes it so women allow themselves to be charmed by men, bestows and removes beauty and genital potency, and excites and extinguishes love.
Pantheriel	Presides over commerce, sailing, and games; prevents shipwreck and breaks the bonds of captives.
Arathon	Presides over amorous undertakings, makes and breaks alliances, presides over births, feeds jealousy, and brings about reconciliations.
Agiaton	Bestows bravery and courage, makes people invulnerable, excites antipathies, presides over duels, and heralds battles.
Begud	Teaches divination and palmistry, works with magic and sorcery, and makes men impotent and women sterile.
Trainor	Arouses tempests, storms, and hail.

One final detail: the *Clavicles* sometimes carry the title of *Legemeton Clavicula Salominis* or *Theosophia pneumatica,* such as the book printed in Duisburg and Frankfurt by Andreas Luppius or even *Clavis solomonis et thesaurus omnium scientiarum regi salomoni per angelum Dei iuxta altare revelatum et per antiquum Rabonem Hama descriptus, jam vero per Balthasar Neydecker translatus, in Germania editus* (1716).

Written in English during the seventeenth city, the *Legemeton*[4] consists of five parts. While the first part (*Theurgia Goetia*) names and establishes the hierarchy of seventy-two spirits, the second part (*Theurgia goetia*) is of the same vein as the *Testament*. In it, in fact, we read the names, properties, and seals of thirty-one air spirits that Solomon is said to have imprisoned as well as the way to protect oneself from them and the rituals necessary to invoke them. The third part (*Ars Paulina*) names the angels of the hours, their relationships with the seven planets, and how to summon them. They are followed by the angels of the zodiac and their connections with the four elements. The fourth part (*Ars Almadel*) lists and details everything necessary for crafting the Almadel, namely a wax tablet that carries apotropaic symbols and four wax candles. The last part (*Ars notoria*) gives us prayers studded with magic words and their connections with the aspects of the moon.

The *Clavicles* were translated into Hebrew under the title *Book of the Key of Solomon (Sepher Maphteah Shelomoh)*,[5] a book that contains twenty-six prayers, some of which consist of the listing of kabbalistic words or names of God. Notably what we find here is the list of instruments necessary for magic operations, the knife and sword, the sickle, the stylus, virgin parchment, and so forth.

The influence of the *Clavicles* can be seen again in a book printed in Rome in 1750 with the title: *The True Black Magic or the Secret of Secrets. Manuscript found in Jerusalem in the Tomb of Solomon, Containing Forty-Five Talismans with their Engravings, as well as the Way to Use Them, and Their Marvelous Properties*. Translated from the Hebrew by Mage Iroe Gregor. In the prologue, Solomon tells his son Roboam:

> I have composed a true and certain work, *The Secrets of Secrets,* in which I have hidden and enclosed all the secrets of the magical art, without which one cannot acquire or fulfill any of these sciences. I have written this *Clavicles* again because, as that one opened the treasure, this one opens the science and intelligence of the magical arts. . . . This is why, my son, I command by the blessing you expect of me, to have crafted an ebony casket in which you shall place my *Clavicles,* and when I have passed from this life to the next, you shall have it placed in my tomb so that it never falls into the hands of the iniquitous. This which was done as Solomon commanded.

During work on the tomb led by Babylonian philosophers, this casket was discovered and Iroe Gregor prayed to God to give him the ability to understand the secrets of the *Clavicles*. An angel appeared to him who demanded of him "to never reveal to any living creature what I am about to show to you, and know to keep them hidden, lest the secrets will be profaned and have no effect."

This version of the *Clavicles* consists of two books. The table of contents are as follows:

1. On the Love of God
2. On the Hours and the Virtue of the Planets

Fig. 15.6. The veritable Black Magic or the secret of secrets

3. Concerning the Times the Arts Should Be Prepared and Perfected Once They Have Been Prepared

4. On All the Tools Necessary to the Art

5. On the Ritual for Theft and What Way It Is to Be Performed

6. On the Ritual of Invisibility

7. On the Love Spell and How It Is Performed

8. On the Ritual of Grace and Impetration

9. Spells of Hatred and Destruction

10. For Preparing Burlesque and Derisory Spells

11. On How to Prepare Extraordinary Spells

12. On How to Be an Exorcist

CONCLUSION

If we compare the content of the book titled *Clavicula Salomonis of Secrets* with the manuscript of the Narodowa Library,[6] their similarities are striking. However, there is one variation that should be pointed out, that of the introduction of "meteorological" chapters for when it rains, snows, thunders, or the absence of cold. . . .

Another work of Solomonic magic, the *Theosophia pneumatica Salomonis,* another name for the *Shehamforas* (*Semiphoras,* fig. 15.7), was published at the same time as *The Clavicles.*[7] This is a grimoire dealing with the inexpressible name of God, formed from seventy-two letters taken from verses 19–21 of the fourteenth book of Exodus and attributed

Fig. 15.7. The *Theosophia pneumatica* (left),
also known as the *Shehamforas* (*Semiphoras*) grimoire,
which deals with the inexpressible name of God.

to Solomon. The name is taken from the Hebrew *Shem ha-mephorash* (שם המפורש). Straight from kaballah, it uses the numerical value of the letters to find all the divine names. These names consist of seventy-two groups of three letters, each being the name of an angel. This grimoire primarily indicates how to address the elements, the spirits, the dead, and so forth, by two series of magical words. In the *Legemeton*, the first book of the *Clavicles of Solomon*, "shehamphoras" designates seventy-two demons.

SIXTEEN

The Other Magic Books

The saying "one lends only to the rich" applies particularly well to Solomon, to whom numerous treatises were attributed. Going from the Middle Ages to the eighteenth century, the list remains fairly stable:

1. *Liber Lamen:* it instructs the reader to acquire all the sciences through prayers to demons.

2. *Le Liber pentaculorum Salomonis* and the *Liber de novem candariis*, for which we have only one manuscript, makes it possible to summon demons.

3. The *De quatuor annulis* (*The Four Rings*), which is sometimes titled *De arte eutonica et ydaica* or even that of *Ydea Salomonis,* describes a complex ritual using magic words like *yrach, boicon, rigor, yehcar* with suffumigations and exorcisms. This crafting recipe for the central system of the Solomonic idea makes it possible to dominate evil spirits. This arrangement consists of a goat hide on which the faces of the four kings of the demons who rule over the four cardinal points have been painted. This operation can be found in the *Liber Almadel* or *De figura Almandel,* as well as the way to craft a gold or white bronze ring under Mercury's patronage. David Pingree has even identified Arabic prayers in the text.[1]

4. *Officium spirituum* or *Liber officiorum spiritum* (*Book of the Functions of Spirits*) is a catalog of demons. Solomon is said to

have concealed it inside of a cave in an Arabian mountain. Then the enchanter Virgil is supposed to have discovered it with a lot of other books during the time of Emperor Augustus and translated it from Arabic into Latin.[2]

5. *De tribus figuris spirituum*
6. *Livre des esperitz*
7. The *De sigillis ad demoniacos* (The Seals for the Possessed) includes the Gandal and Tanchil seals that make it possible to heal people possessed by demons, (fig. 16.1).

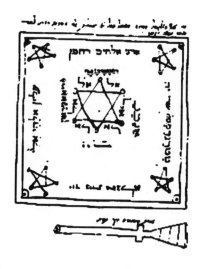

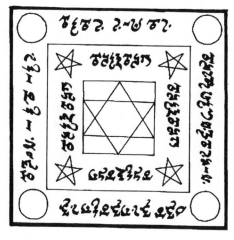

Fig. 16.1. Two depictions of the Almadel

There is a long list of works in Hebrew attributed to Solomon.
The Book of King Solomon (*Sifra di-Shelomoh Malka*) or Book of the
Wisdom of King Solomon (*Sifra de-Hokmeta di-Shelomoh Malka*). The
Book of Ashmedai (*Sifra de-Ashmedai*), which circulated under various
titles, like the *Book of Ashmedai Bequeathed to King Solomon,* is perhaps
identical to the *Kitab al-Uhud* containing magic spells for subjugating
demons and a book on medications (*Sefer ha-Refu'ot*).[3]

Around 1435–1504, Yohanan Allemano listed thirty works attributed to Solomon, such as *The Desire of Solomon* (Heshek Shelomoh),
but researchers have shown that they were drawn from Apollonius of
Tyana and Abu Aflah al-Sarakosti.

Solomon is also credited with writing several scientific works in
Arabic and it is said he invented Syriac script.

Let's return to the *Treatise of the Four Rings*. In Italy it was given
the title *The Necromantic Rings of Solomon King of the Hebrews,* of
which there are fourteen copies in the Leipzig and Rome manuscripts.[4]
It is indicated for each ring how and when to make it, then includes a
conjuration of the spirit by its name, its *charakteres,** its planet, its lunar
house, and invocations of heaven, earth, and sun, and so on. The entire
creation is mobilized, and the function of each ring noted.

Function	Ring Metal and Stone	Name of the Spirit to Engrave (Moreover, its seal should be reproduced)
To be victorious in any kind of game	Golden mercury and chrysoberyl	Daleph
To make yourself invisible to all	Lead and *paragon* (?)	Astaroth
To be loved by any women you desire	Copper and emerald or *celeste* (?)	Surbisach
To obtain any favor from anyone	Tin and sapphire or *celeste* (?)	Methe
To earn the friendship of princes	Tin and sapphire	Fusariel

---

*Ancient ritual symbols found across Mediterranean civilizations.

Function	Ring Metal and Stone	Name of the Spirit to Engrave (Moreover, its seal should be reproduced)
To heal all kinds of illnesses and fevers	Tin and sapphire or *zalla* (?)	Asmodeus
To take the game when hunting	Silver and crystal or diamond	Astafal
To catch fish	Silver and garnet	Emes
To make whoever you wish ill	Lead and black stone	Sonotras
To defeat all your enemies	Iron and garnet	Sichel
To put a person to sleep as often as you wish	Silver and unspecified stone	Biqviel
To not be subject to legal pursuit by your enemies	Copper and emerald	Binas
To be loved by all	Copper and emerald or green stone	Ramiel
To ensure no weapon can wound you	Iron and garnet	Rafan

Numerous manuscripts vouch for the influence and widespread distribution of the Solomonic grimoires, not only in the Middle East but throughout Europe. For example, we find in a sixteenth century Latin manuscript the description of how to make a mirror of Solomon for forcing a spirit to answer the questions posed to it.[5] It is necessary to abstain from all sexual relations for three days, wash one's hands in water, wear clean garments, and draw a complex figure on one's left hand. This figure is then anointed with a blend of olive oil and soot until it shines like a mirror, then one must speak the following conjuration twenty-three times: *hyr hensym caulesym schemin beneim lechelimurietin cellen hierfaucim elfiramhi faraym mynclmensy henycaly huheydem letu metemie ylle calle.* It is then necessary to call each god of the day whose *charakter* is inscribed in the figure, starting with the one of the days on which the work is being done. For example, if the working is on a Saturday, first write "Saday" with its *charakter* above.

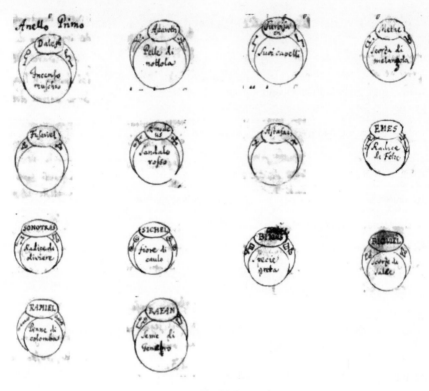

Fig. 16.2.

There is another account in Middle Dutch about this mirror "that sages called the mirror of Solomon because clever things could be seen within it."[6] Although there is no explicit mention of hidden treasures, they are easily counted among "clever things." For when Solomon saw that magicians (*constenaers*) were easily putting the principles of the Book into action he wrote only three words and discovered that, stamped by three magic signs, their power was such that they allowed a human being in less than an hour, or during one hour of the day, to govern a kingdom, which is why the Babylonian sages called it Solomon's mirror, for in it could be seen many secrets (*subtiilheit*) as if in a mirror.

And these are the three words with the ability to bestow such power, that the extremely wise Solomon chose from the old books of the Chaldeans, namely *fennoch, cumbanichel,* and *polidon.* Over *fennoch,* which means "he spoke and thus was done," draw this *charakter* (a);

over *cumbanichel*, which means "accomplished with the signs from On High" draw this design (b); and over *polidon,* which means, "we are compelled to achieve that," draw this *charakter* (c).

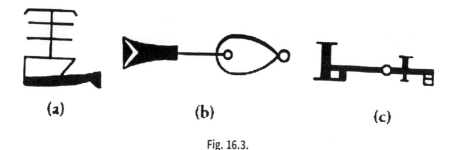

(a) (b) (c)

Fig. 16.3.

The master writes what has been depicted above on virgin wax, then has a human being sit down in a three-legged chair. He then orders this individual to look East. He places *fennoch* with its symbol drawn in virgin wax under the right leg, *cumbanichel* with its symbol beneath the left leg, and under the third chair leg behind the person's back, he places *polidon* with its symbol. It should conform to the figure below:

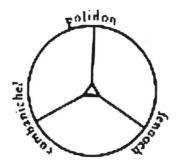

Fig. 16.4.

Sometimes Solomon is summoned by means of a crystal for the purpose of compelling him to reveal where "treasures and hidden money" (*abscondita thesaurorum et absconditam pecuniam*)[7] can be found. There is an *Ars Salomonis* in the same vein that teaches one how to find treasure, make oneself invisible, win the love of a woman, and be able to travel instantaneously from one spot to another.[8] In short, our ancestors were convinced that magic was all powerful, as said in a Latin text of the *Pentaculum Salomonis regis*: "You can do and obtain whatever you like." Of course, it is necessary to begin by collecting some hoopoe blood and keeping it in a phial, going into a secret forest with a shining sword and virgin parchment, and so forth.[9]

SEVENTEEN

The Archaeological Traces of Solomon

Archaeologists have unearthed a good number of seals and talismanic medals connected to King Solomon. The oldest Greek text that mentions the seal of Solomon is an exorcism (Προς δαιμονιξομένους) passed on by means of the great magical papyrus of Paris, which states that when the seal placed on a victim of possession, it would free him or her from the demon.[1]

A talismanic medal, found in Cyzicus and now in the Louvre, depicts the angel Araaph and Solomon on horseback overcoming a demon on the obverse side. This demon can be seen as Onoskelis, who is mentioned in *The Testament of Solomon*.

Fig. 17.1. The engraved words say: "Flee accursed one, Solomon and the angel Araaph pursue you" (ΦΕΥΓΕ ΜΕΜΙΣΙΜΕΝΙ ϹΟΛΟΜΟΝ ϹΕ ΔΙΟΚΙ Ϲ (= ΚΑΙ) Ο ΑΓΓΕΛΟϹ ΑΡΑΑΦ).[2]

Fig. 17.2.

Several other medals carry the same theme. Paul Perdrizet has put together an interesting body of work,[3] including a medal found in Carthage that on one side has the bust of Christ between two angels and a knight slaying a devil on the other side. The inscription reads: "Solomon's Seal" (ΣΦΡΑΓΙΣ ΣΟΛΟΜΩΝΟΣ).

A copper medal purchased in Smyrna by Gustave Schlumberger[4] shows on the obverse side a knight pointing his sword over a demon with its chest laid bear. The legend mentions Solomon and Saint Sisinnios: "Flee, accursed one, Solomon is after you, Sisinnios, Sisinnarios" (ΦΕΥΓΕ ΜΕΜICΙΜΕΝΙ CΟλΟΜΟΝ CΕ ΔΙΟΚΙ CICΙΝΝΙΟC CICΙΝΝΑΡΙΟC). The other side shows the evil eye being attacked by daggers, a lion, an ibis, a snake, and a scorpion; beneath them is a demon or demoness. The text says: "Seal of Solomon; it drives all evils away from its bearer" (ΣΦΡΑΓΙΣ ΣΟΛΟΜΩΝΟΣ ΑΠΟΔΙΟΞΟΝ ΠΑΝ ΚΑΚΟΝ ΑΠΟ ΤΟΥ ΦΟΡΟΥΝΤΟC).

One side of an opal reads: "Seal of Solomon, Lord of Naioth" (ΣΦΡΑΓΕΙΣ ΣΑΟΛΟΜΩΝ(ΟΣ) ΚΥΡΙΟΣ ΝΑΗΘ), Naoith being the city in which David found refuge. This engraving is on the other side:

Fig. 17.3.

ΑΒΑΚΔΑΜΟ
ΖΑΡΡΑΧΙΣΑΜΑΝΣΑ
ΟΝΟΒΑΒΙΑΖΑΛΑΣΑΔ
ΚΑΛΑΙΛΟΥΩΑΓΙΟΝ
ΘΙΕΡΜΑΤΕΛΕΒΑΙΔ
ΔΩΜΔΔΟΚΜΟΥΦ
ΒΕΒΑΛΛΛΩΟΙΒΑ
ΔΒΛΛΒΑΤΒΑΛΛ
ΛΒΕ

Sorin Nemeti[5] notes that this inscription is an attempt to reproduce a folk magic spell called Aianagba-Logos, for which the correct form is:

Aianakba
Aianagba, Amorachthi
Amoraththei, Salamaza
Salamaxa, Bameaza

Bameaxa

In Yemen, Solomon's Seal (the star with five branches) is often depicted on building facades and the doors of houses for protection against the elements and enemies. Coins like this one below can also be found:

Fig. 17.4.

Stone	Engraving	Action
Carbunculus (Garnet)	Dragon	Heals paralysis and trembling
Yopasius (Topaz)	Falcon	Bestows chastity and grace
Smaragdus (Emerald)	Scarab	Increases wealth and provides predictions
Iacinta (Jacinth)	Lion	Protects from gout and preserves health
Crisopasius (Chrysoprase)	Donkey	Allows prophecy of the future
Saphirus (Sapphire)	Ram	Grants honor, peace, harmony, and heals eye disorders
Berillus (Beryl)	Frog	Inspires love between two men
Onyx	Camel's head or two goats between two myrtle trees	Creates terrible dreams, permits coercion of spirits
Sardius (Sard)	Eagle	Procures high honors for its bearer
Crisolitus (Chrysolite)	Vulture	Provides protection against evil spirits
Eliotropia (Bloodstone)	Bat	Gives power over demons and enchantments
Cristallus (Quartz)	Griffin	Increases lactation
Cornelius (Carnelian)	A well-dressed man holding a rod in his hand	Curbs nosebleeds
Jaspis (Jasper)	Aries, Leo, or Sagittarius	Protects from the poison of venomous animals
Iris (Agate)	Armored man holding a bow and arrows	Protects the place where one is
Corallus (Coral)	Man holding a sword in his hand	Protects from lightning, storms, all pestilence and all evil spells
Prasius	Taurus	

Stone	Engraving	Action
Thatel	Something resembling a dragon or a snake	Permits all locks to be opened
Celonites (Selenite)	Swallow	Gives peace and harmony
Calcedonius (Chalcedony)	Man raising his right hand toward heaven	Overcomes all dissent
Ceraunius (Thunderstone)	Carve Rafael, Michael, and Gabriel on one side, Panthaferon, Sapdafen on the other	Protects from lightning and defends its bearer against his enemies
Ametistus (Amethyst)	Bear	Prevents intoxication
Magnes (Magnesium)	Man at Arms	Allows one to work his will on men
Adamas (Diamond)	Five angels	Protects the embryo, bestows honor, grace, and dominance

EIGHTEEN

The Lapidaries of Solomon

Several lapidaries attributed to Solomon have made their way into the present in manuscripts and books coming from the fifteenth up to the eighteenth centuries. The attribution of these works to the son of David is no sure thing because they can also be found under another author's name. They are essentially astrological lapidaries.

In his *Annals* the Byzantine historian Michael Glycas alludes to a *Book of Solomon on Gems and Demons* (*Salomonis libri de gemmis & demonibus*).[1] According to him, this lapidary deals with the uses that stones can be put to, notably as remedies, as well as for repelling "evil spirits" (*malos genios abigere*) and for protecting chastity.

In Spain, the *Libro de las formas et de las ymágenes,* a translation made during the reign of Alphonse X the Wise (1252–1284), includes a lapidary in which each stone is accompanied by its magical property once it has been engraved (see the preceding table, pages 182–83).

Now these engravings correspond to those in the *Livre des secrez de nature* and to the *Liber alarum,* which is to say the second part of the *Liber Razielis,*[2] and crops up again with Camillo Leonardi, whose book we will look at next.

It was at the end of the Middle Ages that Camillo Leonardi (1451–1550), a doctor of Pesaro, compiled several lapidaries in his *Speculum lapidum,*[3] printed in Venice in 1502 and republished in 1516 and 1533. In 1610, the book was inserted into *The Treatise of the Seven Metals* (*Sympathis septem metallorum ac septem selectorum lapidum ad planetas*) by Pietro Arlensis of Scudalupis (1580–1637). *Le Sculptiræ seu imagines Salomonis* includes forty-seven sections presenting the seals of the planets, but only sixteen stones are cited: green jasper appears three times and jacinth twice, followed by such stones as carnelian, quartz, turquoise, pyrite, and paragone. By way of an example, here are the encrypted seals of Mercury and Venus:

> If you hang on your neck a stone depicting a man seated on a plow with a thin neck and a heavy beard who is holding a fox in one hand and a vulture in the other, with, by his neck four men prone, know that it favors all plantings and helps in the finding of treasures. To feel its powers, do the following thing: take pure black wool without any color, wrap the stone inside, put it in the middle of balls of wheat, and when stretching out, stick your head inside. In your sleep you will see all the treasures of your region and how to get them. This stone has an additional power as it can cure all animal diseases if these animals drink water in which this stone has been steeped (chapter 17, 1).
>
> If you find a carnelian with a carving of a seated man and a woman standing before him with her hair unbound and hanging to her knees, know that this stone has the power to bend to your will any man or woman who you touch with this image. It is necessary to set it on a piece of gold equal in weight to the stone and place it on top of betony and amber (chapter 17, 4).

Variants appear over the course of the transmission of the texts, but the engraving remains constant. The most unstable are the virtues attributed to the engraved gems, which can be seen from a comparison of *The Lapidary of Solomon, The Book of Raziel,* and *The Book of the Secrets of Nature.*[4] Detectable in these texts are reading errors (*idolum* for *obulum, virum* for *urnam*), unclear attributions (to Raziel, which Leonardi spells as Ragiel, Chael and Thetel), repetitions because the scribe did not realize that he had already dealt with a stone, confusions on the names of the gems (carnelian for coral), and comically poor spellings (*pangonus* for *peragonus*). This is the kind of tangle that has to be unsnarled. Despite the testimony of Byzantine authors, the paternity of this lapidary remains open to question. Furthermore, Leonardi writes in his chapter "The engravings or Images According to Solomon" (*Sculpture seu imaginaire Salomonis*): "I have discovered a very ancient book on engraved stones, but one in which the author's name does not appear. However, I think it is by Solomon because many of his books appear in this book."

Let's look at an example of these confusions:

A man with a sword in his hand in a carnelian has the power to protect the place it is located from lightning and storms, and to protect its owner from vices and enchantments (Leonardi 15).

[Coral's] virtue is such that it guards the house it is in and the vineyard and the land from storm and lightning and all pestilence and torment and keeps the place healthy of all evil spells and all enchantments and works against the flow of blood from the nostrils. And its figure is a man holding a sword in his hand (*Secrets* III, 15).

Here is an example of a variant. The text of *Secrets* departs from that of Ragiel concerning the powers of the lodestone but the engraving is the same:

An image of a man at arms carved in a lodestone has the power to fight enchantments and bring its possessor victory in war (Raziel 22).

And he who has this with him will be able to work his will over men or other things that are in the house. In this stone there will be pictured a man at arms, luna in ariete coniuncta cum sole (*Secrets* III, 20).

A treatise on magic in three volumes due to Cesar Longuin appeared in 1673 that included a Solomonic lapidary with the title *The Seal of the Stones According to Your Name, Lord, and According to the Course of the Stars.* It was organized in three parts, the Solomonic sculptures, those of the planets, and those of the constellations. While it shares great kinship with that published by Leonardi, it nonetheless contains significant differences:[5] the order of the gems is not the same, and it contains information that is not present in Leonardi.

A curiosity within the evolution of these traditions, Johannes Rhenanus published the *Salomonis Regis liber des lapide minerali, quem philosophorum appellant* in 1625,[6] which has no connection with the one published by Leonardi and discusses the genesis of the philosopher's stone! This coming together was likely engineered because a treatise was attributed to Solomon on the secret of secrets, which for alchemists could only be that of the stone that made it possible to change lead into gold. This book "teaches how to make the stones of Saturn (*facere de saturno lapides*), how to blanch copper, and retain all volatile spirits."[7]

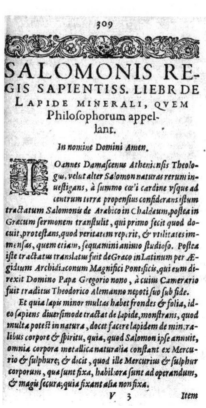

Fig. 18.1.

NINETEEN

The Account of Zosimos of Panopolis

Born in Upper Egypt during the third century, Zosimos of Panopolis left behind a considerable opus that was translated into Syriac. In it we find mention of a book by Solomon that, to the best of my knowledge, is not mentioned anywhere else.

> There is a book of the Egyptians attributed to Solomon that is called *The Seven Heavens,* against demons. But it is not exactly correct that it is by Solomon because these talismans were at one time provided to our priests. Rather it is what the language used to describe them allows to be assumed, for the phrase "talisman of Solomon" is a Hebrew expression. In all times, the high priests of Jerusalem drew them, in the simplest sense of the word, from the lower gulf of Jerusalem [Gehenna]. After these writings had spread widely, as they were still unfinished, they were corrupted.
>
> Solomon is their inventor as I said earlier, but he only ever wrote one lone book on the seven talismans, while commentaries on them were conceived over the various ages to explain what this book contained. However, these commentaries contain fraud. Almost all are in agreement that the work of the talismans targeted demons. These talismans act like the prayer and no demon can resist the nine letters written by Solomon.

But let us examine this particular subject in greater detail. The seven bottles (talismans) in which Solomon imprisoned the demons were made of electrum. It is helpful to put your faith in the Jewish writings on demons in this case. The corrupted book that we have under the title *The Seven Heavens* contains the following in summary. The angel commanded Solomon to make these talismans [bottles]. It goes on to say: "Solomon made the seven talismans [bottles] based on the number of the seven planets, while conforming to the divine prescriptions on the work of the [philosopher's] stone for the blending of gold and copper from Cyprus, with the body named orichalcum and copper of Marrah [. . .].

The sage, Solomon also knew how to summon demons. He provides a conjuration spell that indicates electrum, which is to say the electrum bottles on which this spell was inscribed."[1]

These "bottles" are copper jars or vases in *The Thousand and One Nights,* or even glass flasks, as stated by the author of the *Bibliotheka anecdotorum.*[2]

TWENTY

Solomon's Successors

Solomon's fame as king and magician drew other individuals practicing the arcane arts into his circle. The *Bibliotheka anecdotorum,* a compilation published in Spain during the fourteenth century, and which partially features the enchanter Virgil who follows the example set by the sovereign of Jerusalem, retraces the path of the Solomonic grimoires from Jerusalem into the West in its particular fashion:

> Accompanying Alexander the Great during his conquests and having heard it said that Solomon's library was located in the Temple of Jerusalem, Aristotle secretly pillaged it and gained possession of the son of David's grimoires, which he studied. He then became a great philosopher and teacher thanks to them.[1]

A century later, the *Liber angelicus,* sometimes attributed to Hermes, makes Virgil Solomon's successor;[2] its author mentions the magician Nectanebus, Alexander the Great's father, so it is evident he was acquainted with a tradition reminiscent of the one we can read in the *Bibliotheka anecdotorum.*

During this same period, Thomas of Toledo wrote his *Tractatus artis notorie* about "the holy science with which the holy Solomon compelled demons and obliged them to appear before him."[3] This science is the work of the good angels who placed it in Solomon's hands.[4] In his essay, Julien Véronèse offers the following glimpse of this work:

The abridged version of Thomas consists of two parts: the first is a short prologue in which the teacher quickly explains the conditions under which he wrote his opuscule, what his purposes were, and the methods he implemented. At the end of the prologue, he confirms of having tested and verified the efficacy of this science. The second and longest part of the book explains the ritual procedure to follow, what the author calls the *pars executive.* This is quite succinct. It necessitates the use of only three prayers, a *figura,* and a *notula.* The procedure is extremely simplified: the adept, after fasting for a time, should, in a secret place, inspect the *figura* and *notula* all while reciting the three prayers. He then gains, at the end of the operation, the faculty (*facultas*) that he wished to obtain when starting the spell. The *figura* is a composition that also has no equivalent in the common *ars notoria* tradition. It consists of a kind of flower surrounded by rectangular motifs. As for the *notula,* it is akin to a magical character of the monogram type.[5]

PART THREE

SOLOMON IN FOLKLORE

Depending on the country, we find various elements that have been grafted onto the son of David. In Central Europe, for example, his connection to musical instruments (violin, trumpet, bagpipe) is surprising, as is his encounter with a snake that after being rescued by a man, coiled itself around him and smothered him,[1] as well as what he experienced from a plague,[2] and many other things.

1. THE PRIDE OF SOLOMON (MALAYSIA)

One day, the prophet Solomon was sitting on his royal throne as the wind carried him through the air along with a countless multitude of men and djinns accompanying him. The prophet Solomon was lost in admiration of his royal prowess and, at that very instant, a feeling of pride took possession of his heart, and his crown shrunk into itself. He promptly tried to pull it back out, but it continued to shrink further away from him. Despite three attempts to pull it back into its original shape, he was not able to succeed. He said, "O crown, why will you not resume your former size?" By the will of God on High, the crown answered: "O Solomon, restore your heart first if you wish for me to restore myself."[3]

2. SOLOMON AND ASCHMEDAI (RUSSIA)

In Russia, Aschmedai is known as Kitoras (Китовасъ)* in the legend of Solomon. This fourteenth-century text says:

> Kitovras was a rapid beast that the sage Solomon made prisoner through cunning. His waist was that of a man, his legs, those of a cow, and it is said that he carried his wife in his ear. He was captured by means of a ruse. His wife had told a young man, her lover, to travel day and night through many lands in order to come to a

*Name derived from the Greek χένταυρος, "centaur."

certain place where there stood two wells. He drank the water from both these wells until they were dry. Solomon gave the command to pour wine in one and mead in the other. Kitovras had jumped close to these two wells and then commenced to drink them dry. This was where he was captured in his drunkenness and shackled in strong chains because his strength was great. He was then brought before Solomon. The tsar then asked him: "What is the most beautiful thing (*uzoročne*) in this world?"

"The most splendid thing in the world," Kitovras replied, "is to have one's freedom." While saying this he stretched out, broke his chains, and bound toward his freedom.

It is said that Kitovras was a son of the tsar David.[4]

Kitovras also appears in chapter 30 of the 1966 novel *Cancer Ward* by Aleksandr Solzhenitsyn.

Kitovras lived in a remote desert. He could only walk in a straight line. King Solomon summoned him and by a trick contrived to bind him with a chain. Then they took him away to break stones. But since Kitovras could only walk in a straight line, when they led him through Jerusalem, they had to tear down the houses which happened to be on his way. One of them belonged to a widow. The widow began to weep and implore Kitovras not to break down her poor, pitiful dwelling. Her tears moved him, and he gave in. Kitovras began to twist and turn to left and right until he broke a rib. The house remained intact, but Kitovras said, "Soft words will break your bones; hard words will rouse your anger."

3. SOLOMON CURSED BY HIS MOTHER

When talking with his mother Solomon the Wisest once said that all women allowed him to seduce them. His mother scolded him and replied that it was not true. One day he said he would show her, in one way or another, that she was no different from any other woman. His mother lost her temper and cursed him: he would never be able to find death until he had explored the depths of the sea and the heights of the sky.[5]

When Solomon was quite advanced in age and had had his fill of life on this earth, he gave thought to a way to lift the curse his mother had cast on him. He began by forging an iron chest that was large enough for him to stand inside upright and attached it to the end of a chain whose length he estimated to be equal to the deepest part of the sea. He took his position inside the chest and ordered his wife to shut it and throw it into the water while keeping hold of the other end of the chain in her hand so she could raise him back up and put him back on the shore once he had reached the sea floor. His wife obeyed, but while she was still holding the chain, a man came up to her and tricked her by telling her that the fish had long since eaten her husband and she would never be able to pull him back up. She should therefore let go of the chain and return home. She followed this advice, and the chain fell with its full weight on the chest and carried it to the ocean floor. A short time later, demons found the staff, cap, and chasuble of Saint John and began fighting over them. They then said to each other, "let's go ask the wisest one for a ruling on our dispute." They then learned where he was and went to the bottom of the sea to tell him of their quarrel. "How can I make a ruling if I can't see what this is all about?" he asked them. "Carry me up to the shore and I will arbitrate your dispute." They did just this immediately. Once he stepped out of the chest and learned what all their fuss was about, he grabbed the objects as if he wished to evaluate them and drew a cross with the staff. This sent the demons fleeing. He therefore held on to their booty.

Now that he had seen the bottom of the sea, his thoughts turned toward finding a means to rise into the uppermost reaches of the heavens. He captured two ostriches and did not feed them for several days until they were starving. He then had a basket tied to their feet and took a seat in it while showing the birds a long spit that was holding a roast lamb. Greedy for this food and trying to get it, the birds soared higher and higher in the sky until the spit touched the celestial vault. Solomon then turned the spit down toward the earth and they brought him back to the ground. This was how he was able to die after having measured the height of heaven.[6]

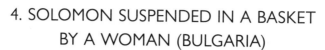

4. SOLOMON SUSPENDED IN A BASKET
BY A WOMAN (BULGARIA)

When Solomon was king, he fell in love with a rich woman one day because she was extremely beautiful and he wished to make her his mistress. He had sent many of his people to plead on his behalf for her to go to him, but the woman was honest above all others. Finally, he threatened to forcibly abduct her from her house. When the woman realized that if it came to a battle of strength that Solomon, being king, would certainly prevail, she sent word to the king to come to her home in the very middle of the night. When he received this message, Solomon rejoiced greatly and went to her house at midnight. She awaited him in a room that was on the third story. She let down a large basket tied to a rope from her window and told him, "Blessed king, enter this basket, which I will hoist up to me, so that my husband, who is sleeping in the stairwell, will not hear a thing."

The king, blinded by his evil desire, without even suspecting that the honest woman sought to fool him, entered the basket and the woman hoisted it halfway up the side of the house and then left it hanging there.[7] He was scared that if he jumped out he might kill himself, and it was not possible to climb higher. Caught in this impasse, he begged the woman to free him, but she told him:

"Solomon the wise, you are so wise that you are not wise! How did it never occur to you that I might play a trick on you? You know how to judge all kinds of tangled affairs and you lose your judgment when it comes to yourself! You must have been completely blinded by your passion to place yourself into that basket like a blind man in the soup. Know that all women are the same, but its your imagination that is disturbing you. So now, tell me, what should I do? Should I let you fall, or should I leave you hanging until it is day so that the great and the common can see you in this position?"

"Honest woman, I have sinned and you have not. Let me down gently, so that I don't get hurt, and I promise to give you a splendid gift and abandon these habits, for what you have told me is to my benefit and I now believe that, as the elders say, 'the wise man and the fool are the same.' I beg you, honest woman, forgive me for sinning against you; I deserved my punishment. I promise you and swear by my crown that I shall cause you no more worries and you will be to me like a sister."

On hearing him swear by his crown, the woman allowed him to go down, and wise Solomon raced back home full of shame. Since this time, he has never gotten involved in these kinds of matters again.[8]

The same story has been told about Aristotle,[9] the great model of wisdom for classical antiquity, and the magician Virgil.[10]

5. SOLOMON'S SISTER (ITALY)

Solomon was so smitten with his wife that he let her ride him and Marcolf* scolded him for it. She then spelled out the following conditions for Solomon: either he send Marcolf away or he abandon conjugal love. Marcolf therefore left the court. When he was on the threshold of death, he asked that someone open his veins in a bath of milk. Seeking to save him, Solomon asked him if there were any remedy, but Marcolf refused to answer. Instead, he said, "What is certain is that I will die, however, if I stay alive, I will manage to make oil out of whey." Solomon had a brother and a sister. His sister's name was Stella.† God sent her two pigeons to make a broth and when she drank the first cup, science came to her. She gave a little to Marcolf who also gained wisdom from it. Solomon had the worst of it because, as there was hardly any broth left, his sister added water to it. So when an exceptional case came his way, Solomon, although quite wise, was forced to rely on his sister's sagacity.

One time when some people with a boat to launch came to Solomon for advice on how to proceed, he told them: "Go see my sister while shouting joyfully, 'The boat has moved on,' and pay attention to what she tells you!" When she heard shouts that the boat had been launched, she said: "It was surely with the help of suet." When these words were reported back to Solomon, he understood what he needed to say, and he instructed the men on how to use suet to launch a boat.[11]

---

*Marcolf is Solomon's brother who is known for being very foolish.
†Depending on the tale, her name is Stella, Sembilya, or Sapienza.

6. SOLOMON'S THREE PIECES OF ADVICE (A) (ISRAEL)

During Solomon's era, three traveling men were caught by surprise on the road by Friday night.* They agreed to place their money in a hiding place. During the middle of the night, one of the three men got up and stole the money, which he buried in another place. When the Sabbath had ended, they went to dig up their fortune, but it had vanished. They each accused the others of larceny, then they went to see Solomon to settle their dispute. The king told him he would hand down his decision on their case the following day.

This case caused Solomon great torment because he told himself: "If I am not able to clear up this matter, people will question my wisdom." He then began to meditate on what he could say to catch the thief out with his words. When they returned the next day, he told them: "You are skilled and intelligent merchants, so I would like to ask your advice on a matter that the King of Edessa brought to my attention. In his lands there lived a young man and a young woman in the same court who fell in love with each other. The young man told the young woman: 'If you wish, we shall agree by oath that if I remain engaged to you for a certain span of time, you will marry me, and if, during this same span of time, another wishes to be your fiancé, you can only wed him with my permission.' She swore this oath. After some time, she was engaged to another man. When her husband wished to assume his marital rights, she refused and told him that he first needed the permission of her former fiancé. They both went to his home carrying gold and silver. The woman said to him:

"'I have kept my oath; if you wish, take this gold and silver, but free me from this promise.'

"'I free you of your promise and you may wed your husband. As for me, I shall take nothing. Go in peace.'

---

*According to the Biblical verse Isaiah 58:13–14, Jews should refrain from traveling over the Sabbath.

"As they were traveling back home, an old brigand waylaid them and took all the gold, silver, and jewelry the young woman was carrying. When he displayed his intention to have his way with her, she told him: 'I beg you, let me tell you my story,' and she told it to him. 'So,' the young woman added, 'this young man whose young age could have served him as a pretext was able to dominate his passion. So shouldn't you, as an old man, be all the more capable of mastering your inclinations and, in obedience to God, refrain from sin?' The old man was moved by these words and allowed her to leave with her fiancé. What's more, he returned everything he had stolen from her.

"Now," said Solomon, "I ask you which of these three individuals is more worthy of praise: the young woman who kept her oath, the young man who gave her permission to marry without taking anything in exchange, or the old brigand who had the capability of taking all they owned and raping the young woman, but was able to tame his passion and take nothing from them? Tell me your opinion, and after I will respond to the subject of your dispute." One of them answered: "I laud the young man who gave permission to the young woman, for he had always loved her." The second man said: "As for me, I praise the young woman, for women are not in the habit of keeping their word, even to their husbands when they sleep together, and this one kept her word." The third one answered: "I praise the old man who had stolen their possessions and could have raped the woman without anyone being able to stop him. However, he refrained from all sin and even returned the money, so I consider him to be perfectly just."

Solomon spoke to the third man: "You have judged well, so hurry up and return their money to your companions, for you are the one that stole it."

The man tried to deny it at first, but Solomon told him: "If you do not return their fortunes, I will throw you in prison for all your life." He immediately left to get the money from his hiding place and return it to his companions. They meanwhile paid homage to Solomon for his decree. This is why it is said that Solomon was the most intelligent of men.[12]

7. SOLOMON'S THREE PIECES OF ADVICE (B) (ISRAEL)

Three brothers had gone to study under King Solomon. He proposed to teach them wisdom if they would consent to serve him, and he made them officers of his court. After thirteen years had passed, they started grumbling to each other: "It has been thirteen years since we left our family to study here, and we have learned nothing. Let's leave and return home." They went to the king and asked it they could take their leave of him. Solomon immediately had three hundred gold pieces brought before him. "Choose," he told them, "I will offer each of you three wise counsels or one hundred pieces of gold." After discussing the matter between them, they opted for the gold, then they left. Shortly thereafter, the youngest brother told his siblings: "What are we doing? We took these gold coins, but are they why we went to spend time with the king for instruction? If you believe me, let's go back to Solomon and heed his advice." His brothers scoffed at his opinion. However, he went back to the king and offered to return the one hundred gold coins in return for his counsel. Solomon then said: "When you travel, make sure you are ready in the morning and that you set up camp by the time night falls, that is my first piece of advice. When you see an overflowing river, don't go into it but wait until it returns to its bed; that is my second counsel. Never entrust a woman with a secret, even if she is your wife; that is my third counsel." The young man then got back upon his horse and returned to join his brothers. When he caught up with them, they asked him: "So, what did you learn?"

"What I learned, I learned," he replied.

They walked together until it was three o'clock in the afternoon and they came across a good place to set up camp. "Here is an excellent place to spend the night," the youngest son said, "There are water, trees, and grass for our horses. If you like, we can stop here and set off again tomorrow at dawn, provided God keeps us alive."

"You're crazy," they replied. "When we saw you giving money to obtain some words, we clearly saw that you had lost your reason. We can easily do another eight miles and here you are advising us to stop here!"

"Do as you please," he responded. "Me, I am not going to budge from this spot."

They left and he stayed behind. He chopped some wood, made a hut for himself and his horse, let his animal graze until evening, then gave him some barley as he ate his own meal in the company of his mount, and spent the night peacefully.

His brothers had continued their journey, but they found neither any grazing place for their animals nor any wood for a fire. The snow fell on them, and they died from the cold. At dawn, their brother, after completing all his preparations, mounted his horse and set off to find them. When he did, they were dead. He threw himself upon them in tears then took their money and buried them. When he left the sun was shining so strongly that it had melted the snow, which caused the river to overflow its banks. When he saw this, he got down from his horse and waited for the water to recede. While walking along the riverbank, he caught sight of some of Solomon's servants, who were leading two animals laden with gold. They asked him: "Why aren't you crossing the river?"

"Because it is too big."

They then tried to cross the river and were drowned. The young man who had waited for the water to return to its normal size crossed over the river, took their money, and peacefully returned home.

When he got back, his sisters-in-law asked for news of their husbands. "They remained to study with the king," he told them. Meanwhile he began to buy up fields and vineyards, build a house, and made many acquisitions. One day his wife told him: "Reveal the source of this fortune." By way of an answer, he grew angry and gave her a good thrashing. "This will teach you to be curious," he told her. But she kept harping on this subject so often that he told her everything. One day when he was quarreling with her, she raised her voice and shouted: "It is not enough that you killed your brothers, you also want to murder me!" When they heard these words, his brothers' widows went to the king to report them and accuse their brother-in-law of murder. The king commanded that the youngest brother be brought there and executed. However, as he was being led to the place of execution, he asked permission to speak to Solomon. He was immediately brought before the king and thrown at his feet. He then told the monarch: "Sire, I am one of the three brothers that came to take lessons from you. I am the youngest one who returned to give back the gold coins in exchange for listening to your advice, and it was your counsel that saved me." The king recognized the truth of his words and replied: "Have no fear. The money that you took from your brothers and my servants belongs to you. The wisdom you learned from me spared you from death and from this woman. So go and rejoice with your companion." This was when Solomon spoke these words: "Better to acquire wisdom than the purest gold."[13]

8. THE THREE PIECES OF ADVICE (ITALY)

One of Solomon's domestic servants wanted to leave his master's service and, having demanded the wages due to him, received three hundred ducats. He set off on his way, but when he recalled all the people that had come to see his former master to seek advice, he retraced his steps to imitate their example.

"Master," he said, "give me some advice!"

"If you give me one hundred ducats like the others."

"I consent to that."

"Never leave the old road for the new one."

The domestic set off again but, feeling unhappy with the advice he had been given, retraced his steps back to the king.

"This advice doesn't please me, give me something better."

"For one hundred ducats."

"Yes."

"Don't put off until tomorrow what you should do today."

Again dissatisfied, he returned, and Solomon, in return for one hundred ducats, told him: "First think carefully about what you should do, and after, do it." He then gave him a piece of bread.

Back on his way, the servant ran into someone who was on his way to buy some oil. Two roads ran before them—one new and the other old.

"We are not going to take the new road?"

"No," said the servant, "this advice cost me one hundred ducats, so I am choosing the old road."

It turned out to be a good thing because he soon heard his companion weeping on the new road because some robbers had stolen all he had.

He reached his home in the evening and found the door closed. He looked through the [key]hole and saw his wife sitting at the table with a priest. He wanted to settle matters with his rifle, but he remembered the advice of his master: "Think first and take action after." He stepped inside his home whereupon he saw that the priest was his son. He took out the piece of bread to eat it but to his surprise he found the three hundred ducats inside of it! His wife then said: "I'm going to give the order to the harvesters to not come tomorrow because I just don't feel like it."

"No," her husband responded. "Don't put off until tomorrow what you should do today."

He did not know how right he was. The day after that, hail devastated all his neighbors' fields.[14]

9. TSAR SOLOMON AND HIS WIFE (UKRAINE)

There was once a wise tsar of the faith named Solomon, and he took a wife from an infidel tsar. His wife heartily detested him and did not wish to obey him. When Solomon went to church, his wife refused until one day he forced her to go there with him. She then told him: "I will go to your church, but when I make the sign of the cross, I will not pray, and when I pray, I will not make the sign of the cross." They got to the church, but his wife did not pray or make the sign of the cross. They returned home and Solomon's wife said to him: "Now let's go to my church!"

"Very well," said Solomon, "But I will remain standing up straight as you did in our church and not bow an inch."

But she was a cunning woman. She ordered that the door be set up so it closed from top to bottom. They came to the infidel church with his wife walking before him. Solomon had barely set foot on the threshold when the door fell on him striking the nape of his neck. "Hey," he thought to himself, "you have shown yourself to be craftier than me, devil worshipper, but I will get the better of you!" He then returned home.

One day, his wife was plotting to flee Solomon's home with an infidel tsarevich.* The wife would pretend to be dead, and once she had been buried, the tsarevich would dig her up and they would flee together. This was exactly what they did. The tsaritsa was bedecked in all her finery and laid upon the table,† and Solomon was summoned. He came in, looked all around, and thought to himself: "No, devil worshipper, you won't trick me a second time, you are not dead." He took an iron spike, heated it until it was glowing red, and, because she was holding her hands clasped, burned them all over with the spike. She was so obstinate she did not even let out a sigh or moan! Solomon did not speak a word. That night, his wife was buried.

She had barely been buried when the infidel tsarevich reached the cemetery, immediately disinterred her, and brought Solomon's wife home with him. But the next day, Solomon visited her father and said: "Come running papa and see if your daughter is in her grave."

"Have fear of God," the father said. "I will not trouble the body of my dead daughter."

But Solomon insisted. They went and looked in the grave and clapped their hands with astonishment: the grave was empty.

Solomon thought and thought, then ordered a wheelbarrow be made and filled with dirt. He brought with him a black army, a red army, and a white army. He ordered that he be carried in the wheelbarrow to the infidel tsarevich's house where he was taking tea with Solomon's wife. He also brought three chalumeaus (small wind instruments) with him. He was brought to the house of the tsarevich and then wheeled inside. The tsarevich and Solomon's wife began laughing and asked: "What do you want here?"

---

*A tsarevich is the son of the tsar, or in other words, a prince.
†The body was displayed on the dining room table where the funeral feast would be held next.

"I have come to see you," he said.

"Then at least take some tea with us."

"I don't want to get off my dirt," he said, "give it to me here."

And his wife said: "Here's a true simpleton! And it was with such a fool that I was supposed to spend my life, but now we have him in our hands." She gave Solomon some tea. The tsarevich went out and ordered that a gallows be built for Solomon.

After they had drunk their tea, the tsarevich said: "Solomon, come out onto the balcony with us."

"No," he said, "I don't want to get off my dirt. I will not budge an inch unless you carry me."

The tsarevich ordered that Solomon be carried to the balcony.

The tsarevich and Solomon's wife sat on chairs while Solomon sat on his wheelbarrow. The tsarevich showed the gallows to Solomon.

"Who is this house being built for?"

"Either for me or for you, but I rather think its for you," said Solomon.

The other two began laughing and said: "He is in our hands and he still says that the gallows is more likely for me than him!" At this point Solomon was led to the gallows and he asked the tsarevich: "Before I die, I would like to play a little." The moment he began playing one of the chalumeaus, then the white army came racing in and charging about. The tsarevich asked: "What is that?"

"That," he said, "is my death."

When he began to play another chalumeau, the red army began racing about to the best of its ability. The tsarevich again asked: "And what is that?"

"That," he said, "is my innocent blood that is rushing."

When he played the third chalumeau, the black army began racing toward them at a swift gallop. "And what are these?"

"These are the devils that have come for your soul, and although I am on the dirt, I shall hang you."

He summoned his army and the tsarevich was soon swinging on the gallows. The tsaritsa then cast herself at Solomon's feet. "Forgive me," she said, "my little pigeon."

"No," said Solomon, "devil worshipper! Henceforth I can no longer live with you."

He ordered that she be tied to the tail of her horse by the tresses of her hair and then had the beast set loose in the country. Such was the wise Solomon.[15]

There are numerous variants of this story in the Slavic countries.

10. SOLOMON'S SON (MIDDLE EAST)

One night Solomon decided to have sexual congress with each of his wives so that each of them would give birth to a son, and all these sons, once grown to manhood, would go slaughter one thousand infidels, and all the glory would go to him. God was not pleased by these thoughts, and one of these women gave birth to a child whose body was completely deformed. After his birth, the archangel Gabriel placed him on the throne. God sent Solomon a vision while telling him: "You have had prideful thoughts. Go take a look at your son who has been sat upon the throne." Solomon went and saw a body that had no arms or legs. He was terrified and repented his earlier thoughts. After this event, he lived another twenty years. He ruled for forty years in all.[16]

11. THE TSAR VASSILI OKULOVICH AND THE TSARINA SOLOMONIDA (KARELIA)

In Karelia alone, the Sokolov brothers[17] collected eleven versions of this tale. It offers some interesting variations that will appear in a footnote. This legend, which is quite similar to the German *Solomon and Morolf*[18] in many aspects, traveled from Jerusalem to Constantinople (Tsarigrad), no doubt due to the orthodox clergy. In fact, Solomon is depicted as a follower of the Orthodox faith.

Beyond the blue sea in the imperial city of Constantinople, the Tsar Vassili Okulovich had organized a magnificent party for many noble princes and knights errant, as well as for powerful heroes, bold warriors, Tartars, bodyguards, and foreign merchants. The party was a huge success and the very satisfied tsar asked for silence with a shake of his blonde curls. "Listen to me my princes, my boyars, my valiant heroes, my wandering maidens, Tartars, and bodyguards! In Constantinople, everyone is married, the hand of every girl and every widow has been given in marriage, and I, Vassili Okulovich, your prince, am not. Do you know of a wife for me? She must be well made and of my rank, with eyes as light as those of a falcon, eyebrows the color of Siberian sands, and she must speak graciously. Her face must be as white as snow, her cheeks as red as poppies, and her walk be that of a stag in a golden wood. She must have no other like her in the world." The entire assembly remained silent.

Then, from one side of the table, Takarashko,* a guest from overseas, stood up from his seat made of precious fish teeth. He approached the tsar, made a deep bow before him, and softly told him: "Blessed, Sire, are the words you just spoke. I have traveled a great distance. Beyond the blue sea in the royal city of Jerusalem there lives the tsarina Solomonida and I have never seen any woman like her on this earth. She dwells in a noble castle, the red sun does not burn her, and the drizzle does not make her wet."

"Are you mad, Takarashko, my guest from overseas? How can we steal a wife from her living husband?"

"I know how! Build me three ships. Their prows should look like dragons, with a fox in the place of the eyes, and the eyebrows should be Siberian black. Erect two cypresses in which two birds of paradise singing imperious songs are perched, and prepare a bed made of ivory with a small guzla (a kind of violin) at its head. This instrument will produce delicate sounds by itself and play all the melodies of Constantinople[19] so that they might be a consolation to her for Jerusalem and inspire on her reason and understanding of the turbulent minds that are those of human beings. My dear lord, laden the boats with foodstuffs, noble vodka, and the potion of forgetting all things. Give me helmsmen and sailors and I will bring back Solomonida for you."

---

*Another version calls him Ivan the chewer.

The tsar did as Takarashko asked, and equipped as requested, he set sail over the blue sea toward Jerusalem.

Solomon told his wife: "My dear Solomonida, I am leaving now to travel the vast plains."

"Most wise tsar Davirovich, I could hardly sleep last night and had many dreams. I dreamt that the gold ring you wear on your right hand melted and that the inhabitants of Novgorod were scattered."

"It was only a dream," replied Solomon.

"No, sire, I hardly slept a wink and had many visions. It seemed to me that your white swan was carried off far from my green garden."

Solomon interpreted that and said, "My dearest Solomonida, don't call up so many wild visions." He left her and traveled twelve years over the vast plains to collect tributes.

Takarashko entered the port, lowered his sails, dropped anchor, and paid the duties. He next took valuable gifts and set off to find the tsarina Solomonida in her noble palace, crossed himself and bowed on command, then said: "Most beautiful queen, here are some presents.[20] Find me some officials to assess the value of the merchandise on my ships so I may receive what they are truly worth, and give me permission to leave Jerusalem." She did as he asked. Takarashko brought her onto the first ship and gave her some royal vodka to drink. He then took her to the second and served her the potion of forgetting. All the officials drank vodka and began wandering around distracted on the bridge. Takarashko bemoaned their state and complained to the queen. "Genteel Solomonida, you have not brought me assessors but bar flies. It seems to be they could not hold the green wine they drank, here they are lolling about the deck." She arose, took five hundred men, and went back to the first ship to see for herself. Takarashko brought her some vodka that had been spiked with the potion of forgetting* like those on the other boat, and they all drank it. Takarashko was cunning and had, by design, the queen transported from the first two boats to the third

---

*She drained the glass of vodka in one swallow; her legs collapsed beneath her, and she fell asleep.

in which the ivory bed had been made. Solomoninda lay down on it, the little guzla produced its sweet sounds, the birds of paradise sang, and she fell into a deep sleep. Then Takarashko shouted in a shrill voice: "Sailors and helmsmen, hoist these linen sails and let's set off on the blue sea!"

When Solomonida awoke from her deep sleep as the sailors were hastily raising the sails, she said: "Takarashko, if you bring me far away, I shall not follow you,"* but he was astute and discerned the meaning of what she said immediately. "If I have abducted you," he replied, "it was not for me but for the tsar Vassili Okulovich. In truth, our faith is better than yours. Friday and Saturday are just days like any other, and we eat meat." She thought that this religion sounded good and no longer put up any resistance.

They quickly returned to Constantinople and dropped anchor at the port. The tsar Vassili Okulovich came to meet them, took Solomonida's white hand, kissed her sugary mouth, and led her to the cathedral where they were immediately crowned. From that time, they lived together and spent their days in joy.[21]

When he returned from the vast plains, Solomon could find no trace of his wife. The very wise tsar assembled an army of forty thousand men,[22] all clad in mail, and crossed over the blue sea with them. Upon reaching a green forest, he stopped, led his men beneath the trees and ordered: "My dear army, I am going to go to Constantinople alone and leave you here. If I do not find a quick death, I will sound my auroch horn. You must then saddle your good steeds in all haste. When I sound it a second time, jump into your saddles, and if I sound it a third time, gallop to the oak gallows and rescue me." He left them and made his way to the city on foot. Once he reached the royal palace, he shouted in a thunderous voice: "Most beautiful tsarina Solomonida, give alms to a wandering psalm singer!" The trellis window opened wide and the tsarina, the white swan, observed: "I see that this is no wandering singer,

---

*In other words, she is saying that since Takarashko has taken her away, her fate is out of her own hands.

but it is Solomon the most wise," and she replied. "I beg you, enter my beautiful palace, what has happened was done against my will." Solomon entered and crossed himself, as commanded, on all sides. Solomonida sat him down at her white oak table, and gave him savory meats and precious wines,[23] then paid him great honors. But the tsar Vassili Okulovich then came back from the vast plains and banged the silver ring [of the door knocker]. Solomon said: "Dear Solomonida, is there somewhere I can hide?"

"Slip into this iron chest."

She opened the double lock and, once Solomon had gotten inside, locked it again. She then bid Vassili Okulovich to enter but she remained sitting on the chest and said to him: "Dear Vassili Okulovich, Solomon is renowned for his wisdom, but in truth, no one is more insane than he because a woman is currently sitting on top of him."

"Show him to me, dear Solomonida."

She opened the chest and begged Vassili: "Put him to death quickly, cut off his unruly head because, by my faith, he is wise and powerful!" Solomon leapt to his agile feet, seized Vassili's white hand and said:

"It is not customary to decapitate a tsar. Have a gallows erected with three nooses: one made of simple rope, one of hemp, and another of silk."

"Tsar Vassili," cried Solomonida, "it is high time to execute the sentence. Part his head from his body, otherwise he will escape thanks to his wisdom and power."

The tsar ceded to Solomon's desire, and they all went to the white oak gallows:[24] Solomon the wise sovereign, Solomonida, the beautiful tsarina, and Takarashko, the guest from overseas. Once they were gathered around the foot of the gallows, Solomon said: "Tsar Vassili Okulovich, the horse pulls the front wheels, so why the devil doesn't it concern itself with the back wheels?" No one could answer this riddle.

Solomon mounted the first step and said: "Most noble tsar Vassili Okulovich, in my childhood and youth, I took care of a flock of sheep.[25] Grant me my wish to blow my auroch horn."

"Blow it as much as you please," the tsar replied, but Solomonida urged him to put him to death quickly. "I have him in my hands," responded Vassili Okulovich.

Solomon blew his horn with all his strength the first time. His men immediately saddled their chargers. Vassili became nervous and scared:

"What marvels accompany you, Solomon?" he asked. "I can hear the clanking of metal and the stamping of horses in the vast plain."

"Fear nothing, tsar Vassili, don't worry. My horses have fled their stables in Jerualem to go frolic in the dark forest,"[26] replied Solomon as he climbed the second step.

With Vassili's consent and against the will of Solomonida, he sounded his horn a second time, and his entire army leaped into their saddles. Vassili trembled in fright:

"What is happening in the vast plains? I can hear the drumming of horse hooves."

"Have no fear, tsar Vasilli! My birds have left my garden in Jerusalem for a dusty grove where they are striking the trees with their wings."[27]

Solomon climbed the final step and asked the tsar Vassili to let him blow his auroch horn one last time. He sounded the charge and his entire army launched forth like light falcons or grey wolves. They flew at top speed to the white oak gallows and freed the most wise Solomon. Around the neck of the tsar Vassili Okulovich he slipped a silken knot; the beautiful Solomonida got a simple rope,[28] and Tarakashko got a hempen rope.

After leaving Constantinople, Solomon and his men returned to Jerusalem by way of the blue sea, where they resumed their joyful lives.

The infidelity of Solomon's wife became almost proverbial and enjoyed wide distribution not only in Eastern Europe but Spain and Portugal as well.[29] The *Livros de Linhagens* (fourteenth century), which deals with the genealogies of noble families, offers the same narrative scheme: false death, abduction, punishment.

In *Élie de Saint Gille,* a chanson de geste (Old French epic poem) composed in the second half of the thirteenth century,[30] we find the following verses:

> *Solomon did take a wife, I think of this often*
> *For four days she feigned death in their palace*
> *When she never moved a hand nor foot, nor limb,*
> *Then a knight did his will with her*
> *By the allegiance I owe you, a woman is a mad thing:*
> *Truly the more you watch over her, the sooner you'll*
> *   lose her.*

This matches an opinion voiced in *Le Blasme des fames* [The Vices of Women]:

> *Wisdom has not he who believes a woman*
> *alive or dead, whoever she be*
> *For the wise King Solomon*
> *Whose wisdom enjoyed such great renown*
> *that none wiser than he could be found*
> *Was deceived by his wife.*[31]

In Romania, it is said that a mythical emperor named Por tried to hang Solomon but, while en route to his execution, the latter smiled because he knew that his army was coming to his rescue.[32]

12. SOLOMON THE SAGE (UKRAINE)

Solomon's mother was pregnant when a lady came to her and begged her to hide her from her husband. The tsaritsa hid her, just as the husband arrived and asked her: "Didn't my wife come in to the serenissimus tsaritsa's place?"

"She didn't come, lord," said the tsaritsa. But from inside her stomach, Solomon said: "Don't listen to my mother, for she is just the same as your wife."

Thus was Solomon when he was still God knows where. And he was not even three years old when he had already weighed the mind of a woman. He made a scale,[33] hung it from the door, then placed his mother's cap in one pan and a handful of wood shavings in the other. He burst out laughing when he saw that the shavings were heavier. His mother then came in.

"Why are you laughing this way, my son?" she asked.

"And how could I not laugh," said Solomon, "when the mind of a woman weighs no more than a handful of wood shavings?"

His mother lost her temper. "Just wait, cursed dog," she said, "I will fix you!" She immediately ordered her servants to bring him into the forest and kill him. For proof they had done as she asked, they were told to bring back his heart and his little finger.

The servants took him to the forest to kill him, but Solomon told them: "Don't kill me, good servants. Let me keep my life a little longer, even if it is only a short while in the white [perpetual] world. Cut off one of my fingers—I can do without it—but take the heart of a dog and bring it to my mother; she will not be able to tell." The servants obeyed Solomon. They cut off his little finger, took the heart of a dog, and brought them to his mother, leaving Solomon alive.

But what was the good of all this, given the fact that he had only lived three years of this life? Poor Solomon sat down and wept, and when they saw this, the saints in heaven also wept. How could a child so intelligent not be granted more years of life? So they begged God to let him live longer, be it only a little while. And God allowed himself to be swayed and told the saints: "Because you desire so strongly for Solomon to go on living in the world, go down there and ask people if they will share their years with him."

So, the saints came down to the earth and traveled about with their request, but no one would yield to their pleas. They finally came to the home of an old woman who had already lived one hundred years and had another hundred left to live. "Woman," they said, "take pity on Solomon and give him your years, even if just half of them." The woman heeded their request and gave them what they asked, and Solomon began living the old woman's years.

Solomon had grown quite a bit and he was thinking of paying the tsaritsa a visit. He picked a time when the tsar would not be home, disguised himself as a merchant, and came to the tsaritsa's place.

When he arrived, he displayed his merchandise, but it must be said that the tsaritsa found him quite pleasing because everything he showed her was very much to her taste. "What would you like for this merchandise, young merchant?" she asked.

"But nothing, tsaritsa, except, possibly, for a girl for the night."

"That's fine, little merchant," she responded. "So, stay for the night."

So here we have the merchant sleeping on the royal cushions and the tsaritsa sent him a girl. The merchant looked her over, sent her back, and said: "Too big!" The tsaritsa then sent in another one, but he also rejected her, saying: "Too small!" So, then the queen herself went in and slept with him. Solomon needed nothing more and once his mother had fallen asleep, he got up and wrote on the wall: "It is quite true that a woman's mind is not equal to a handful of wood shavings, as a mother has slept with her own son!"

The tsar arrived just at this moment. He read it, realized that this was the work of Solomon, and thought to question him. He then had a golden plow crafted and sent it to be paraded in front of everyone with an order to write down how much each person offered for it. The servants transported the plow so it could be seen everywhere, and no one placed its value at less than a thousand gold coins. They were on their return journey when they came across a shepherd who was sitting down, chewing on a piece of bread. "Hey little guy, how much do you think this plow is worth?" they asked him. The shepherd stood up, looked at the plow, and said, "Whether or not you get angry about it, I will tell you the truth. The truth is that if there isn't a drop of rain in May, it is worth no more than this piece of bread I'm eating." They also write this down, and on their return, the tsar asked them: "So, how much was the estimate on the plow's value down there?"

"But always a good price, God be praised! No one offered less than a thousand gold coins. Only one person," they said, "a poor shepherd, said it was not even worth a piece of bread if it didn't rain in May."

"He spoke the truth," said David, "and that is no shepherd. That is my son Solomon. Go fetch him!"

The servants began looking for him; they searched and searched but could not find him. David thought up another trick: he gave a ball to which he invited people from all over the world. All the guests gathered at the ball and took a seat at the tables, and all the food was so good that all they wanted was to eat it, but it was impossible because each guest had been given a spoon two cubits long. All the guests were sitting in front of this feast and looking sorry for themselves. The tsar had already grown bored with watching it and he had left for a moment to see the tsaritsa. Suddenly, Solomon then showed up. "And why aren't you eating, people?"

"How can we eat," they replied, "with these cursed spoons?"

"So feed each other with these spoons across the table as if you were children."

The people heeded his words and began feeding each other. The tsar came in. He was told that everyone was eating and how that had been brought about. He looked for Solomon, but he was gone without a trace.

This is how it came about that David died before ever getting the chance to question Solomon. After his death, Solomon ruled in his place and once he was tsar, he thought to measure the heavens. He made himself a kind of circle and, by holding it above him, he rose toward the sky. And when he had reached the clouds, Saint Peter walking over the clouds told him: "Stop Solomon! This is the border. If you go any farther, you shall never return. Go back the way you came and look carefully. Beneath you, Tsar, there is a blue field and a black spot. Climb down over the black and not the blue because the black is the earth and the blue is the sea!"

As Solomon descended, he thought to himself: "Though I have not measured the heavens, I shall at least measure the sea." He built a glass house, took a seat inside it, and commanded that he be lowered into the sea with a chain to measure it. So, he was going down, down, when a lobster, so large that it could carry two men, came toward him and said, "Solomon, Solomon, you shall never take the measure of the sea!

Twenty years I have searched for the bottom and never found it. And you, Solomon, are not given the right to see it. Retrace your journey to the surface, for it is possible that some young crawfish will sever the chain with its pincers. Solomon obeyed and came out of the sea, and then not much more time remained for him to live.

This inspired him to start thinking of how to escape death. He learned that there was an immortal mountain in the white world, and he headed toward it. It so happened that some monks were building a monastery at the foot of this mountain. This is what the Lord told these monks: "Quickly drop your work and make a coffin and a tomb. The sage Solomon is coming your way to die." They obeyed. Solomon arrived and asked them what they were doing. They replied: "Building a coffin for Solomon!" Solomon realized then that no matter what, he had to die.

"But do you have his measurements?" he asked them.

"No, we don't have them," replied the monks.

"Very well, measure me. He is like me," said Solomon.

The monks measured him. They built a tomb, and in the tomb, they placed the coffin. "Now wait!" Solomon said. "I will try out the tomb." He lay down in the tomb. "Very good, it is the right measurements; now lower me into the grave." They lowered him into the grave. "Now fill the grave!" he commanded. "You have no need to wait for Solomon, for I am Solomon."[34]

13. SOLOMON'S JUDGMENT (UKRAINE)

Once upon a time there were three brothers. The eldest of them had the misfortune to not be able to taste anything he ate. The youngest brother was never able to harvest anything he tried to grow, and the third one— it is laughable to say—was married to a terribly mean woman. This was the lot of the three brothers—misery! But when suffering misfortune, man is not without counsel. They then told themselves: "Let's go find Solomon, he will advise us."

They came into the presence of the tsar. The first brother introduced to him was the eldest. The tsar heard him out and said: "To the forest." The youngest brother entered, and the tsar told him: "Wake up early!" Then the brother with the mean wife came in. He told his story to Solomon. "To the forge!" shouted the tsar.

Two of the brothers got together and questioned each other. They could not believe that Solomon had given them such advice. They did not wish to do anything they had heard Solomon say. "Just look at how he mocks the world! This is how he harps on and on to such unfortunate fellows as us!" But they then agreed that what he advised was not hard: "We can try what he said."

The eldest brother went into the forest where he saw some people who had chopped down a tree unsuccessfully trying to lift it into a cart. He began helping these folk and bustled about quite a bit. He returned home, ate some bread, and the bread was so tasty that he swore he had never had such tasty bread ever before. He told this to his brothers, and they decided to also follow Solomon's advice. They got down to work. The youngest rose early and his crops began to improve. From the time he began rising before everyone else and going to bed later than everyone, work began going swiftly for him and order reigned. Once he saw how things were going for his brothers, the middle brother went to the forge. What did he see there? Nothing other than this: iron becomes softer in fire and under the hammer. "The smiths," he thought, "heat iron to make it softer. I should try to heat my wife up a bit." And in truth, his wife softened a little.[35]

In the church Saint-Jean of Troyes, a stained-glass window from 1512 depicts the judgment of Solomon recorded in the scriptures on the lower panes. But above it there is another judgment. At the top of the tympanum, the king is sitting on his throne with his scepter in his hand. His name is written on the left in uncial script. In the left trilobe there is a young child holding a lemon-yellow ball that Louis Morin[36] has identified as an apple. Another piece of fruit, which is gray, sits on the floor of the throne room. Four elderly individuals behind the child watch what is taking place. An incomplete phylactery tells us that Solomon was called upon to settle a dispute. The trilobe on the right depicts a second child holding a similar ball that is more orange in color. He seems to be about to toss it at the three gray apples beneath him. However, we don't know which legend the stained glass refers to.

14. THE CHILDREN OF DAVID (UKRAINE)

The tsar David had made himself so pleasing to God that God said to him: "David, ask me for whatever you like, I will give you everything!" So, David asked God for three sons: one that was the most handsome, one that was the strongest, and one that was the wisest. And God gave him Joseph, Samson, and Solomon.

The handsome Joseph was responsible for dreams. Even today if we have some terrifying dream, we say before getting up, "May Saint Joseph turn this all to the good!"

The strong Samson fought all over the world and even contemplated waging war against us. He swam over the Dniepr, but as he was getting out of the water, a lion pounced on him. Samson grabbed his jaw, but barely had he set foot on dry ground when all at once, he and the lion were petrified. He is still in Kiev this way.

The wise Solomon remained sitting at home only reading books, or so it was said, when one day a rumor sprang up that he wished to give a sermon. People gathered from the whole world to hear this sermon. He came out and simply said: "If you have something to sew, you must first knot the end." Since that time, people have only talked and joked about Solomon.[37]

15. SOLOMON AND HIS WICKED MOTHER (UKRAINE)

Once upon a time there was a bogatyr* who had a son named Solomon. A time came when the tsar summoned the bogatyr to service and his son told him: "I will also go with you." His father replied, "You are little, remain at home!" The son stayed and began playing. He took a scale and began weighing dog crap and woman crap. His mother asked him: "What are you doing, son?"

"I am weighing the crap of a dog and that of a woman, and the crap of a woman is heavier, which means that she is that much more intelligent."

---

*Russian богатыр; this is a hero and knight errant of the tales and stories.

And his mother said: "Oh, you son of a bitch! Just wait! I will give you what for!" And she went to a cooper and ordered him: "Make me a barrel with iron rings because I need one." The cooper made her one, which she brought back home. She had small loaves of bread baked, sewed a caftan for her son, and placed him in the barrel. She then hired a man to take the barrel out to sea. This man obeyed her command and threw this barrel into the water.

The son sailed on the sea for quite some time—seven years in fact. However, in the meantime his father had returned home and asked: "My son, where is he?"

"He is dead," his wife answered.

"Did you have a funeral service performed for him?"

"I did that," she replied.

The bogatyr then had a gold plow crafted and hired some men to travel the world with it while saying: "Bring to me anyone who can guess the price." These men set off. They looked and looked but found no one who could guess the price.

However, the sea cast the bogatyr's son onto the shore. There were two buffalo passing near by who had come to drink. Solomon heard something moving on the shore and shouted from his barrel: "Hey, who is out there? Please, I beg you, break this barrel!" The buffalo came close and one of them struck it with one of his horns, which caused the bottom to fall out. Solomon then emerged from the barrel, made the sign of the cross, and looked around him. He spotted a cart on the mountain and a man sitting next to it. He approached him and said: "Hello."

"Hello," the old man replied.

"What are you doing?"

"I am grazing my lambs."

"Take me into your service!"

"But I have no money."

"Give me the chalumeau that you are playing, and I will work for you at that price."

"Very well, since you wish it, pasture my lambs in return for this chalumeau!" and he hired him straightaway. Solomon took off his clothes and stuffed them into a bag, put on a shepherd's garment, picked up a staff and the chalumeau, and went out to graze the lambs.

Just then the men carrying the golden plow came through. They saw the shepherd's cart and said: "Let's go to that cart, perhaps someone there will be able to guess." When they got there, they said: "Hello."

"Hello!" replied the old man.

They asked him: "What is the price of this plow?"

"Who could know what it is worth?" said the old man. "Go find my assistant, perhaps he can guess."

They did as he suggested. When he saw them headed his way with the plow, the assistant shepherd squatted down to answer nature's call, ate his bread, and killed his lice. And the men asked him: "What are you doing there?"

"I am discharging the old," he told them, "loading the new, and killing the enemy." The men told themselves: "It is not worth the trouble to show this to him," and they returned home. When they got there, they told the bogatyr, "no one could guess the price of this plow." The bogatyr then said: "At least tell me what you have seen."

"What we saw?" they asked. "Well, we saw a lad . . . but how to tell you about this. It's quite a story. Listen, we came upon a shepherd, we showed him the plow and he told us that he couldn't guess the price but to show it to his helper. We saw not far from there a lad sitting on the grass and headed his way, when, excuse us for saying so, he squatted to do his business, ate his bread, and killed his lice, so we decided he was not worth showing the plow to!"

"Run back there fast as you can," said the bogatyr, "he is the very one that will guess it!"

They returned to the young shepherd with the gold plow and three horses to bring him back to the house. When they reached him, he was again doing the same things: squatting, eating bread, and killing his lice. They said: "You see this plow, tell us its price."

"That plow has no value," he replied.

They then helped him mount a horse and started bringing him back to the house. He began playing his chalumeau, and the horses as well as the lambs began immediately to dance and fled toward the hill.

The men grew scared and let go of the horse he had mounted. He then went up to the hill, took his clothes and the caftan his mother had sewn for him when she imprisoned him in the barrel, and then went to his home. When he got there his father looked at him and said: "Good day, my son!"

"Good day," he replied. Then the bogatyr told his wife: "Look, you told me he was dead. So were you lying?" And he began yelling at her and punching her.

The son did not live with his father very long. His father's services were once again required, and he left his son with the mother. One day, she tried to get her son to sleep with her. He did not want to. His mother closed the doors so he couldn't flee, but he simply said: "Open up!" and the doors opened. No matter how hard she tried to keep them closed, they kept reopening. "Very well, just you wait," his mother said. "I'll give you what for!" She got along well with someone who made brandy, the distiller, as gentlemen called him, and told him: "I'm going to send him to you and you can toss him into the brandy." The distiller consented.

The next day, the mother sent him her son, but it was her son who tossed the distiller into his brandy. He then kept forging straight ahead. He walked and walked. All at once he saw a forge before him. He entered and spoke to the smith: "Hello. May God aid you!"

"Thank you!" the smith replied.

"Hire me!" he requested, and he hired him.

They then got down to forging. The smith ordered him to strike with the hammer. When the bogatyr's son took the hammer and struck, the anvil was noisily forced deep into the ground,[38] and the forge collapsed. The smith grew scared and the bogatyr's son told him: "Stay, don't be scared, it is only because I haven't yet figured out the strength of my own blow."

They then built a new forge and the bogatyr's son said: "Forge a long chain, then build a glass house. After that, attach the chain to the house and I will go inside. You will lower it down to the bottom of the sea and I will see what there is to see there." They forged the chain, built the house, and made their way to the ocean. There the bogatyr's son said this: "Pay attention, when I pull on the chain, pull me back up."

"Fine, fine," the smith replied, and he lowered the glass house with the bogatyr's son inside into the sea. When he was in the sea, he saw a whale who spoke to him:

"Why have you come here? Is it by or against your will?"

"Rather by my will, than against my will."

The bogatyr's son did not remain there for a long time—seven years. At the end of the seventh year, he tugged on the chain and the smith pulled him back up [out of the water].

"Very well," said the bogatyr's son, "now that we have reached the bottom of the sea, lets try to reach the heights." They made an iron ladder. The son of Solomon climbed until he reached heaven, and there he could go no higher. God, when he saw this, asked his angels to open the heavens. The angels obeyed and God asked: "Why have you come here? Is it by or against your will?" The bogatyr's son answered: "Rather by my will than against it."

"Do you have any relatives?"

"I have a brother on earth."

God spoke to the angels: "Go down to earth and take this man's brother." The angels soared off and brought back his brother, the smith, and both became blessed.[39]

16. THE CHILDREN OF THE OTTER (INDIA)

One day the Otter said to the Elk: "Friend, would you like to look after my children until my return? I am going to go fishing, and when I return, we will share the fish I caught." The Elk agreed to this request, and the Otter set off for the river.

All at once, the Green Woodpecker sounded the war gong. Immediately the Elk, who was the lead dancer of the dance, started dancing, and in his growing excitement, trampled the Otter's children with his hooves. They were literally flattened. At that very moment, the Otter returned carrying a net filled with fish, and he saw the remains of his poor children and began to shout: "How were my children flattened?" The Elk answered: "The Green Woodpecker rang the war gong and I, as leader of the war dance, began dancing. Unfortunately, I forgot all about your children and trampled them underfoot."

Overwhelmed by this confession, the Otter went to Solomon and bowing before him, said: "Your servant humbly asks pardon for presenting himself before you, but the Elk murdered my children and I wish to know if, in accordance with the laws of men, he is guilty or not of this murder." Solomon replied, "The Elk is surely responsible for the murder if he killed your children intentionally," and he asked for the Elk to be brought before him.

When the Elk was in Solomon's presence, the king asked the Otter: "What is the accusation you are bringing against him?"

"I accuse him of killing my children."

The Solomon spoke to the Elk: "Is it true that you slew the children of the Otter?"

"It is true," the Elk confessed, "but I am very sorry and ask that I might be forgiven."

"Then," said the king, "how was it that you killed them?"

The Elk told how the Green Woodpecker had rung the war gong, and that naturally, forgetting all about the Otter's children, he had begun to dance.

The king then sent someone to fetch the Green Woodpecker, and the bird came before him. "Was it truly you that sounded the war gong, Green Woodpecker?" asked Solomon.

"Definitely," the bird replied, "because the great Lizard was coming toward me carrying his sword and I quickly rang the gong."

The king then asked for the great Lizard to be brought before him, and as soon as he arrived, asked him: "Is it true that you drew your sword?"

"It is quite true, O king," the Lizard replied.

"And why?"

"Because I saw that the Turtle had put on his coat of mail."

Summoned in turn, the Turtle was questioned:

"Why had you put on your coat of mail?"

"Because the King of the Crabs was pulling his triple-edged claws along."

The King of the Crabs was then called in and Solomon asked him:

"Why were you dragging along your triple-edged claws?"

"Because the Crawfish was coming toward me with his spear on his shoulder."

The Crawfish was called in and interrogated:

"Is it true that you were carrying your spear?"

"Completely true, O king."

"And why?"

"Because I saw the Otter had come down to the river and was getting ready to devour my children."

On hearing these words, Solomon turned to the Otter and said: "If this is the way it is, O Otter, it is you who are guilty, and you cannot support your complaint."[40]

17. THE KANTJIL AND THE ROYAL TIGER (INDONESIA)

While the kantjil* was enjoying peace and quiet in the jungle, he heard a royal tiger (*matjan*). He then began thrashing the air with his arms and the tiger asked him what he was doing. "On the orders of the Nabi Solomon, I am stirring his broth," and he went on to say, "I am scared of Solomon, the king of all living beings."[41]

This story enjoyed great success, and there is an Indonesian restaurant in Amsterdam—Kantjil & de Tijger—that bears the very name of this story.

18. ADULTERY AND DEFAMATION (FRANCE)

A wife and her husband were accusing each other of infidelity. Solomon, who had listened to them attentively, took each of them aside personally and understood each of their commitments to kill their spouse. The husband took a dagger and went into the sleeping chamber, but when he saw his wife asleep, the idea of the crime repulsed him, and he tossed the cursed weapon away.

---

*This word refers to a dwarf deer.

The next day, the wife entered the room with her sleeping husband and the unfortunate man would not have escaped the knife already close to his throat were it not for the intervention by the guards posted there by Solomon.

"The person who has no hesitation about killing her spouse will have even less hesitation about deceiving me," the king said.[42]

19. DAVID AND SOLOMON (ARMENIA)

A man that planned to undertake a long journey concealed all his gold in seven pots, taking pains to cover them with a layer of honey four fingers thick. He asked his banker, deemed by all to be an honorable man, to keep these honey pots in his home until he returned, adding that he would leave them to him as an inheritance in the event that he died during his travels. The banker accepted, and the traveler set off on his journey.

One night when the banker was entertaining several visitors, he wished to offer them some confections with honey. He ordered his servant to open one of the traveler's pots and take some honey from it on the condition that the honey was replaced the next day. The servant found the gold and informed his master of his discovery. The banker then took possession of the traveler's entire fortune and filled the pots back up with honey.

After some time had passed, the traveler returned to his land, retrieved his pots, and realized that he had been robbed. He demanded the banker return his gold coins, but the banker denied their existence. He therefore filed a lawsuit against him. This was during the reign of the prophet David. The king listened more than once to the contending parties but, discomfited by the statement of the traveler and the banker's denial, he dared not issue a judgment. Little Solomon, who had attended the last of these sessions, secretly went to both parties and told them: "Ask my father the king to hand your problem over to me and I will settle it in a minute." On their insistence, David consented. Solomon had the pots brought in and emptied completely. On the bottom of each pot there remained several gold coins that had become stuck there. From this he deduced that the banker was guilty as charged.[43]

20. SOLOMON (ARMENIA)

Solomon understood and spoke the language of all animals. One day the king of the ants came and told him: "Your elephant crushes thousands of ants beneath his feet. Prevent him from doing this as we are unable to prevent him ourselves." Solomon gazed scornfully at the puny creature and answered him with a smile: "Do whatever you like." The king of the ants went off, boiling with rage. He convoked his people and made a resolution to dig a deep pit on the road where the elephant walked every day and hide the hole beneath a thin layer of dirt. No sooner said than done, the elephant fell into the hole and was not able to get out. The ants dug out his eyes and gnawed on his body.

The King of the Hebrews, who had been waiting for the elephant in vain for three days and three nights, sent his servants to go fetch him. They discovered the trap set by the ants and returned to tell their master what had happened. Solomon took hold of his beard and said: "Even if you are a giant, avoid having even an ant as your enemy."

Solomon had a favorite concubine who forced him to comply with all her whims. "If you love me," she said one day, "build me a palace from bird bones." Solomon had countless birds slain to build the palace in question. Only the sparrows, a very cunning race, escaped the carnage. Their king even had the idea to go speak to the King of the Hebrews directly as he knew the language of the birds. Perched in a tree facing the royal palace, he shouted to Solomon:

"Come to the window and hear me out. Who do you think are more numerous in the world? Men or women?"

"Men most likely," replied Solomon.

"You are wrong," replied the king of the sparrows, "for we should count among the number of women those men who are effeminate and possess the brain of a woman. You are one of this number, you who follow the counsel of a woman and put innocent birds to death."

Solomon grabbed his beard in his hands and ordered his people to halt construction. The bone palace remained unfinished.[44]

21. PREMINTE SOLOMON (ROMANIA)

One day a princess gave birth to a son. To avoid dishonor, she hid him
in a small chest that she entrusted to the water. The casket floated until
it came to a mill where it became stuck beneath the wheel. The miller
came down to unblock the wheel and discovered the small chest, which
he opened. In it he found a small boy, and as his wife had given birth to
a son the night before, he kept him and raised him as his own. He gave
him the name of Preminte Solomon.

He put the money that had been placed in the chest with the child
aside. This foundling was a better student than his own son and so
clever that he loved him like his own.

When the boy was seventeen, he got into a quarrel with the miller's
son who he had always believed to be his brother. Because his "brother"
called him a foreign bastard, he raced to his adoptive father to ask about
his origins. He was given back the money that had been set aside for
him and he left.

After he had gone a good distance, he met an angel who told him:
"Don't enter the city or, if you do, avoid showing yourself to the princess
for she will want to marry you, although she is your mother." Preminte
Solomon did not wish to believe him and entered the city where the
princess saw him and fell immediately so much in love with him that
she wanted to take him as her husband. He accepted but refused to
share her bed. She then cursed him and drove him out of the city.
Preminte Solomon did not put up any resistance and nourished no ill
feelings toward her, for he knew that she was his mother.

Tormented by remorse for marrying her, he wandered for many
years before going to Hell,[45] from which he freed his grandfather and
grandmother.[46]

22. THE WILD HUNT (BASQUE COUNTRY)

Solomon was attending mass on the day of Easter. His dogs remained
at the church door. At the moment the benediction was being given, a
hare crossed the road and the dogs set off in pursuit, baying at the top

of their lungs. The king grabbed his gun and left the church to join his dogs. He was therefore damned to hunt every day with his pack, and he could be heard traveling through the air on stormy nights.[47]

23. THE ELDERBERRY AND SOLOMON'S SISTER

Saint Šembilja [Sibylla], the sister of Solomon, commanded that she be buried beneath a grapevine after her death, but evil men buried her beneath an elderberry bush, which is why this plant bears such an abundance of fruit each year, but not the vine.[48]

24. SOLOMON AND ADAM'S SKULL (SERBIA)

Adam's head was so large that thirty men could stand inside it as if it were a cave. One day, one of Solomon's servants took shelter in it with his greyhound and his falcon. He told Solomon about it who went to the cave and recognized it as Adam's skull. He ordered all his men, large and small, to gather together and he then commanded them to do as he did. He picked up a stone, bowed before the skull, and said: "I pay you homage as God's first creation," and he threw the stone at the skull while adding: "I strike you for having disobeyed God." All the people lapidated the skull, then built the Lithostraton, which the Hebrews call Golgotha.[49]

25. THE NOMAD AND KING SOLOMON'S PRISON (MOROCCO)

Once upon a time lived four sultans, two of whom were believers and two of whom were infidels. Sidam ben Daoud (Sulayman ibn Dawud) and Sidna Duül Karnaïn were the two sultans of the faithful. Nemrod and Chadad ben A'ad were the two infidel sultans. When he was young Sulayman ibn Dawud had one hundred nomad shepherds who guarded his camels. One day, one of his nomads glanced at the child Sulayman and the latter asked him what he thought of him. The shepherd responded: "Your eyes are those of royalty. Stay at my house to guard my camels and I guarantee that you will become king on condition that you rid me of all my rival animal breeders." Sidam Sulayman ibn Dawud lived with this nomad until he reached maturity, and all this time the shepherd treated him as his own son, as he had no children of his own. When he became king, Sulayman captured the nomad's rivals and put them three by three on camels to be transported across the Sahara to be left in Soussa. Among these nomads there were—Ouled Ali, Ouled Kerum, Ouled Teyma, Ouled Rehou, Ouled Ouled—all our ancestors. He filled the Haoura region where he left the children of Badrahoneyn with the Cananyoun.[50]

26. SOLOMON IN ROMANIA

In Romania, Solomon is associated with the herb white swallowwort (*Iarba Fiarelor, Vincetoxicum hirundinaria*) that makes it possible to open all locks and break chains. It is said that he had incestuous relations with his mother, that he was the son of Adam and Eve, that he was the son of the Tsar Constantine, and so forth. Solomon allegedly survived the great flood by hanging onto the ears of heaven, but God sent some insects to sting him. When he was forced to use one of his hands to drive them away, he fell into the water.[51]

Tales are told of his voyage to the bottom of the sea thanks to a wondrous fish and his flight into the heavens on the wings of a royal eagle. It is also said that he imprisoned the plague for seventy years in a jar made from a rabbit bone lattice, and no one has died of this illness since then. Once this period of time had elapsed, the plague told Solomon that no one could die as long as he did not permit it to carry his soul into paradise.[52]

When he was young, Solomon was scared of his mother and fled in disguise with three horses: one blind, one fat, and the last, weak. When the emperor asked him what the meaning of this was, he told him that the fat horse represented the wealthy, the weak horse, the poor, and the blind horse, the emperor himself.

One day, Solomon went down into hell with Joseph and Mary, who left him there. He was in danger of never being able to leave, so he built a church.[53] Another tale tells us that he pretended he wanted to build a church in hell, and in order to make him abandon his plan, the devils freed many souls.[54]

According to another legend, Solomon wanted to be born a second time. His dismembered body was placed in the protection of a jar that had to be opened after a specific period of time had passed. But it was broken before that deadline and the son of David could not be reborn.[55]

Romanian folktales also depict Solomon as an inventor. We owe him for the invention of the trumpet (*Legenda trâmbiței*), the violin (*Legenda ciorii*), the bagpipes (*Legenda cimpoiului cu carabü simplü*), and even the scales, which he used for measuring the minds of women.[56]

He is also the presumed inventor of the chalumeau (*Legenda trisiței*) that shepherds play. The mother of Solomon acted as if no man could touch her. One night, Solomon slept in her bed and grazed her breast while saying: "This is the breast on which I was suckled with my mother's milk." His mother cursed him and refused to forgive him this sin until she heard a voice coming out of the woods. A longtime after, he obtained a chalumeau and when his mother heard the "voice of the woods," she forgave him.

Conclusion

Over the course of this investigation, we have been able to extract the various facets of the legend of Solomon, master of the djinns, magician, and exorcist. We have shown the extent of his extraordinary popularity across the world, his enduring presence in tales and legends, all of which we have based on a very large body of texts. We have pursued the traces of this legendary king on paths that have been forgotten by all except a few specialists.

Six details of the legend speak in favor of a shamanic component in the portrait of the son of David: spirits, dreams, the bronze tree, flying, the descent to the bottom of the sea, and his conflict with Asmodeus.[1]

Mircea Eliade has noted that the "shaman is a man who has immediate concrete experiences with gods and spirits; he sees them face to face, he talks with them."[2] We first have Solomon's relationships with the spirits, djinns, and others. The *Testament* shows us that he held power over them—he could summon them, master them, and impose his will on them. It so happens that these spirits came in the form of half human, half animal hybrids, something detected and underscored by Eliade.[3]

Dreams play an important role in the legend of Solomon. A dream is initiatory in Gabaon, and God allows the king of Jerusalem to acquire wisdom.[4] His relationships with animals also make Solomon a master of Nature. Was it not said that he "understood the language of mortal men, the roaring of wild animals in the forests, the cry of the four-legged creatures, the chirping of birds, the buzzing of insects, and also what the trees of the forests and the small flowers of the paths were saying?"⁵

Solomon went down to the bottom of the sea, which is a common exploit for shamans,⁶ and he came back with a new way to organize his army. As for flying, it had been rationalized quite a bit as he was able to do so with the help of a carpet.

There remains the gilded bronze tree that stood next to his throne and whose branches were full of all kinds of birds. Liutprand of Cremona speaks of it and explicitly says that the one he saw in Byzantium was an imitation of Solomon's. This tree is a symbol of the *axis mundi,* the World Pillar that can be seen in numerous civilizations.⁷ There is also the placement of Jerusalem, which ancient cartographers located at the center of the earth. This is exactly where the king sits on his throne, and it could well be a depiction of this *axis mundi* around which every-thing revolves, but in the current state of research this can only be a hypothesis.

A rivalry of a shamanic nature can be seen in the opposition between Solomon and Asmodeus. Both climb to heaven and the *Emek Hamelach,* written at the end of the third century, says that Solomon flies every day to the firmament where the demons Asa and Asaël initiated him into the secrets of celestial wisdom.⁸ If Solomon does not descend into the hell regions, he can make the demons come out of them thanks to his ring, which can be interpreted as a reversed katabasis. Lastly, Asmodeus stole Solomon's ring and passed himself off as the king, usurping his duties and his throne, which speaks to a rivalry between two individuals of equal power.

Solomon has also been seen as a Jewish Orpheus who, in addition to the virtue of the poet, also possessed that of thaumaturgy, endowed with magic powers over both the beings and the objects of nature. It is very commonly believed today that Orpheus was a shaman.⁹

The legend of Solomon follows a logic specific to it and empha-sizes its hero, exalts his actions, not the least of which is his power over the djinns and demons, which some say is due to the divine aid of God or Allah who procured wisdom for him. But in parallel, Solomon remained for centuries the great master of magic, the inventor of the *Ars Notoria* and, most importantly, the author of the *Clavicula* that can even today be easily found in esoteric bookstores. Alas, most often these are counterfeits, reworkings with vague sources that are far removed from the texts of the manuscripts and only capable of giving their readers a pale idea of the tradition. But wouldn't plagiarism, rewriting, and imitation be the ransom of the posthumous glory of the son of David who remains alive in memory certainly as the builder of the Temple of Jerusalem but above all as a second Hermes Trismegistus and a master of the arcane arts? This allows us to realize that the longevity of his memory is due to his extraordinary destiny as simultaneously builder, scholar, poet, sage, judge, magician, and a major figure in human history but also an individual blameworthy for his propensity for lust, although this judgment is essentially that of the Medieval West. It is understandable that Solomon left his mark on human history, and he deserves all the study given to his extraordinary handiwork.

The sum of the dreams and fears of a vanished world, his memory defies the centuries, for he takes us into an era in which the supernatural and the marvelous form part of everyday life, one in which demons—djinns, shaytans, and divs—were on the lookout, catching men in their snares and leading them on the left-hand paths, a world that was still enchanted in the magical sense of the word. The history of this king has never lost its power to fascinate.

Notes

INTRODUCTION. THE LEGEND OF KING SOLOMON

1. Cf. Särkiö, "Salomo und die Dämonen," 305–22.
2. Bokhâri de Djohôre, *Makota radja-radja* (La Couronne des rois).

ONE. THE SOURCE TEXTS

1. 1 Kings 1:11; 2:35; 3:1–15; *La Sainte Bible* vol. 2.
2. 1 Kings 4:22–23.
3. Flavius Josephus, *Antiquités judaïques* VIII, 2.
4. Cf. R. Basset, "Solaiman dans les légendes musulmanes VI," 145.
5. Cf. Ispas, *Legenda populară românească între canonic și apocrif,* 231–33.
6. Litmann, *Die Erzählungen aus den Tausendundein Nächten,* vol. 2, 684.
7. Litmann, *Die Erzählungen aus den Tausendundein Nächten,* vol. 6, 191.
8. Litmann, *Die Erzählungen aus den Tausendundein Nächten,* vol. 3, 91*ff.*
9. Litmann, *Die Erzählungen aus den Tausendundein Nächten,* vol. 4, 203*ff.*
10. Litmann, *Die Erzählungen aus den Tausendundein Nächten,* 14*ff.*
11. Litmann, *Die Erzählungen aus den Tausendundein Nächten,* vol. 3, 684.
12. Litmann, *Die Erzählungen aus den Tausendundein Nächten,* vol. 4, 18; 76.
13. Litmann, *Die Erzählungen aus den Tausendundein Nächten,* 190.
14. Litmann, *Die Erzählungen aus den Tausendundein Nächten,* 102.
15. Litmann, *Die Erzählungen aus den Tausendundein Nächten,* vol. 5, 296; 470; vol. 6, 554.
16. Litmann, *Die Erzählungen aus den Tausendundein Nächten,* vol. 3, 262; 629; vol. 5, 348, 558; vol. 6, 454.

TWO. SOLOMON AND THE ANIMALS

1. Nicolaïdes and Carnoy, "L'hirondelle et le serpent, légende circassienne," 80–82. Collected in Lesbos in 1883 from the mouth of a young Circassian.

2. G. Weil, *Biblische Legenden der Muselmänner, aus arabischen Quellen zusammengetragen und mit jüdischen Sagen verglichen,* 237*ff.*

3. Fabricius, *Codex pseudepigraphus veteris Testamenti,* vol. 1, 1041*ff.*; *Salomonis colloquium cum Regulo formicarum, Persarum de Salomone fabulae.*

4. Basset, *Contes populaires berbères,* no. 13.

5. Basset, *Contes populaires berbères,* no. 76.

6. al-Muqaddasī (Elmocaddessi) died in 1279; Garcin de Tassy, *Les oiseaux et les fleurs,* 94–97.

7. Dähnart, *Natursagen. eine Sammlung naturdeutender Sagen, Märchen, Fabeln und Legenden,* vol. 1, 335.

8. Dähnart, *Natursagen. eine Sammlung naturdeutender Sagen, Märchen, Fabeln und Legenden,* "Syria," vol. 1, 326.

9. Dähnart, *Natursagen. eine Sammlung naturdeutender Sagen, Märchen, Fabeln und Legenden,* "Georgia," vol. 4, 190.

10. Büttner, *Lieder und Geschichten der Suaheli,* 126*ff.* Swahili legend (East Africa).

THREE. SOLOMON'S CONSTRUCTIONS

1. Ma'ûdî, *les Prairies d'or,* vol. 2, 541. This author adds: "The wind held there day and night made a noise like thunder; this is why the Muslims of the area say that Solomon imprisoned the winds in this place."

2. Berthelot, *Les Origines de l'alchimie,* 171.

3. For more details, cf. Basset, "Salomon (Salaiman) dans les légendes musulmanes, VII: les constructions de Salomon," 190–94.

4. Battûta, *Voyages; 1: De l'afrique du Nord à la mecque,* 155*ff.*

5. Ansbacher, *Die abschnitte über die Geister und wunderbaren Geschöpfe aus Qazwînî's Kosmographie,* Dissertation, 22.

6. Cf. Lecouteux, "La mer et ses îles au moyen âge: un voyage dans le merveilleux," 11–24.

7. Wüstenfeld, ed., *Mu'djam al-buldān* [Geographical Dictionary], vol. 4, 375*ff.*

8. Guilielmus de Pastrengo, *De originibus rerum libellus, in quo agitur de*

scripturis virorum illustrum, de fundatoribus Vrbium, 90, 92, 98*ff.*

9. Estaban, "Altos son y relucian. Tradicion oriental de los Palacios relucientes," 301–14.

10. Variant: he broke his bonds. They then bound him with goat hair that resisted all his efforts and brought him to Solomon, who questioned him about the tribes of the djinns. There are fifty-eight with the Greeks and twelve in Islam. Sakhr named them, described their members, their habitats, their food, the way they took possession of human beings, how they can be summoned, and how they can be exorcised; cf. *The Book of the Spells of Union of Solomon (Kitab al-mandal al-Sulaymani).*

11. G. Weil, *Biblische legenden der muselmänner,* 234–37.

12. Nabigha al-Dhubiyani (end of sixth century) is famous for two verses in which he recalls that God gave the djinns permission to build Tadmor/Palmyra and gave Solomon the power to imprison them. The great historian Tabari (died 923) indicates that Solomon made this city the depository of all the treasures and books in his possession.

13. Blunt, *Voyage en Arabie; pèlerinage au Nedjed,* 355–57. It should be compared with "Solomon and Dragon."

14. See also Ruth 3:3; Daniel 13:17; 2 Kings 5:10.

15. Mornand, *La vie arabe,* 25*ff.;* Certeux, "Les eaux thermales et minérales," 258.

16. Cf. Jean V, 2–3; The name of the pool was Bethsheba, the evangelist added.

17. Geyer, ed., *Itinerarium Burdigalense,* in *Itinera Hierosolymitana Saeculi III–VIII,* 1–33. *"Sunt in Hierusalem piscinae magnae duae ad latus templi, id es una ad dexteram, alia ad sinistram, quas Solomon fecit, interius uero ciuitati sunt piscinae gemellares, quinque porticus habentes, quae appelantur Bethsaïda. Ibi aegri multorum annorum sanabantur. Aquam autem habent hae piscinae in modum coccini turbatam. est ibi crepta, uni Salomon daemones torquebat."*

18. Qu'ran, Sura Saba (أبس), verse 11.

19. *Al-mu'rib 'an ba'd 'adja'ib al-maghrib* (A clear presentation of several wonders of the West), cited from Weber, "La Ville de cuivre, une ville d'al-Andalus," 51–54.

20. *Glaive-des-Couronnes (Seif el-tidjan),* 276–78.

21. Massé, *Ibn al-Faqih al-Hamadani, Abrégé du livre des pays,* 78, 103–8.

22. Ruska, *Das Steinbuch des Aristoteles,* 9*ff.*

23. Mehren, *Manuel de la cosmographie du Moyen Âge,* 88.

24. Littmann, *Die erzählungen aus den tausendundein Nächten,* vol. 4, 208–18.

25. Singer and von Neustadt, "*Apollonius von Tyrland*" *nach der Gothaer handschrift,* "*Gottes Zukunft*" *und* "*Visio Philiberti*" *nach der Heidelberger Handschrift,* v. 14705–14773.

26. Bacher, *Nîzamîs Leben und Werke und der zweite Teil des Alexanderbuches,* 98*ff.*

27. Bockhoff and Singer, *Heinrichs von Neustadt Apollonius von Tyrland und seine Quellen,* 73–74.

FOUR. THE JUDGMENTS OF SOLOMON

1. III, Kings 1:11; 2:35; 3:1–15. *La Sainte Bible* . . .

2. Ispas, *Legenda populară românească între canonic și apocri,* 198–200; 211–14; 225–28; 231–33; 246–47.

3. Tabari, *Chronique,* vol. 1, chap. XV, 58–60.

4. Coulon, *La Magie islamique et le Corpus bunianum au Moyen Âge,* vol. I, 936*ff.* Mîm (م), hâ' (ه) et wâw (و) are consonants of the Arab alphabet.

5. Saif, "Magic in the Thirteenth Century."

6. Montgomery, *Aramaic Incantation Texts from Nippur,* 232.

7. Montgomery, *Aramaic Incantation Texts from Nippur,* 46*ff.*

8. Cf. C. Lecouteux, *Dictionnaire des formules magiques,* Paris, Imago, 2014, p. 36*ff.*

9. G. Weil, *Biblische Legenden der Muselmänner,* op. cit., pp. 217–219. Chez les Juifs, Salomon est le plus sage de tous les hommes ('*hakham mikol haadam*).

10. Glycas, *Annales,* 340.

11. Basset, *Contes populaires berbères,* no. 15; Shilha text collected in Oran in 1883. The Persians told the story to Khosrow Anushiravān.

12. G. Weil, *Biblische legenden der muselmänner,* 215.

13. Saintyves, *Les cinquante jugements de Salomon,* 80–83.

FIVE. SOLOMON'S POSSESSIONS

1. G. Weil, *Biblische legenden der muselmänner,* 225–32.

2. What we have here is a variant of Polycrate's ring; cf. P. Saintyves, *Revue de l'histoire des religions,* 49–80.

3. Tabari, *Chronicle,* 96, 450–54.

4. Reinaud, *Description des monuments musulmans du cabinet de M. le duc de Blacas,* vol. 1, 164*ff.*

5. Coulon, *La Magie islamique*, vol. 1, 928.

6. Euringer, "Das Netz Salomos," 76–100.

7. Feer, trans., *Les trente-deux récits du trône (Batris-Sinhasan) ou les Merveilleux exploits de Vikramaditya*; Julg, *Mongolische Märchen-Sammlung.*; Iafrate, *The Wandering Throne of Solomon.*, chap. 2; Liut-prand, *Antapodosis*, 488.

8. Balbir, *Somadeva*, 1260*ff.*

9. Gaulmin, *De vita et morte mosis libri tres*, II, chap. 9, "*Est apud magos incantationis species vinculum Deorum seu Daemonum dicta, cujus auctorem Salomonis, sive Æthiopicam fabulam; quam his diebus in venatione latinam fecimus.*"

10. *Tractatus de throno Salomonis*, Codex Cus. folio 65, vol. 1–vol. 8; prologue: "*Opusculum de throno Salomonis dictavi, dictatumque, quamquam ob meritum non satis dignum memoria, stili offcio commendavi.*" Texte (folio 2r): "*Igitur sicut in regum gestis legimus, rex Salomon fecit sibi thronum ex ebore grandem et vestivit eum auro fulvo nimis.*"

11. Tabari, *Chronicle*, chap. 96, 449*ff.*

12. Ansbacher, *Die abschnitte ü ber die Geister*, 21*ff.* For a similar tradition Basset in *Revue des Traditions populaires* 1 (1892): 165; cf. also Canova, "La Tâsat al-ism: note su alcune coppe magiche Yemenite," 73–92.

13. Brélian-Djahanshahi, *Histoire légendaire des rois de Perse d'après le* Livre des Rois *de Ferdowsi*, 32.

14. Ispas, *legenda populară românească între canonic și apocrif*, 201–3.

15. Bornemann, *Das testament des Salomo, aus dem Griechischen übersetzt, zeitschrift für die historische theologie*, 55–56.

16. Ibrâhim ibn Waçîf Châh, *L'Abrégé des merveilles*, 119*ff.*

17. Bonaventure des Périers, *Récréation et Joyeux devis* in *Conteurs français du XVIe siècle*, 397–400.

18. *Écrits gnostiques chrétiens*, 1424*ff.*

19. *Placides et Timeo, les secrez aus philosophes*, 28*ff.*

20. *Bibliotheca anecdotorum seu veterum monumentorum ecclsiast*, Coll. Noviss., ed. Johann Jacobus Moser, Nuremberg: In officina Hoffmanniana, 1722.

SIX. SOLOMON'S LITERARY AND SCIENTIFIC WORKS

1. Cf. Bovon and Geoltrain, *Écrits apocryphes chrétiens*, 681–743.

2. Erman, "Eine ägyptische Quelle der Sprüche Salomos," 86–89.

3. Benary, *Salomon et Marcolfus,* 8.

4. Kemble, *The Dialogue of Salomon and Saturnus.*

5. Paris, BnF, French manuscript 19152, folio 116r a–117r c

6. Cf. Kemble, *The Poetry of the Codex Vercellensis with an English Translation,* 78–80.

7. Paris, BnF, French manuscript 24432, folio 420r a–436r b

8. Allen and Fisher, *The Complete Poetry and Prose of Geoffrey Chaucer,* 269–80.

9. Rabelais, *Œuvres,* 4 vol., Vol. 1, chap. 33, 101.

10. Vogt, *Die Deutschen Dichtungen von Salomon und markolf,* XLI–LVI.

11. Kemble, ed., *Swylce ðu miht / mid beorhtan gebede / blod onhætan, / ðæs deofles dreor* (var. *drý*), *136ff.*

12. Kemble, *His leóma he is hlutra and beorhtra ſtonne ealra heofona tunglu,* 150.

13. Kemble, *Forðon nænig man / scile oft orðances / útábredan / wænes ecgge,* 145.

14. Kemble, *The Poetry of the Codex Vercellensis with an English Translation,* 178*ff.*

15. Viteau, *Les Psaumes de Salomon;* Wright, *The Psalms of Solomon.*

16. Viteau, *Les Psaumes de Salomon,* 371–75.

17. Denis, *Introduction aux pseudépigraphes grecs d'Ancien Testament,* 66–69; Starcky, "Pseudo apocryphe de la grotte 4 de Qumrân," 353–71; Sanders, *The Psalms Scroll of Qumran cave 11,* 151, 154*ff*; Strugnell, "Notes on the Text and Transmission of the Apocryphal Psalms 151, 154 (= syr. II) and 155 (= syr. III)," 257–81.

18. Leroy, "Instruction de David à Salomon," 329–31.

19. Morhof, *Polyhistor litterarius, philosophicus et practicus cum accessionibus Joan. Fickii et Joh. Molleri,* chap. 6, 49.

20. Dalechamp, *Histoire générale des plantes,* chap. 35, 489.

21. Regourd, "Le *Kitâb al-mandal al-Sulaymânî,* un ouvrage d'exorcisme yéménite postérieur au Ve-XIe siècle," 133–36.

22. Zwinger, *Tractatus theologicus de rege Salomonis peccante,* 199; "*Sermones de arboribus a cedro qua est in Lebanon, ad hyssopum, qua egreditur de pariete.*"

23. Suidas, *Suidae lexikon,* 5 vol. s. v. Ezechias. "*Fuit Salomonis liber remediorum cuiusvis morbi, vertibilo templum incisus. Eum revellit ezechias, quod populus, neglecto Deo, nec invocato sanationem malorum inde peteret.*"

24. Preisendanz, "Salomo," suppl. 8, col. 660–704.

25. Pseudo-Justinian, *Responsiones ad orthodoxos,* quaestio 55; Migne, *Patrologia græca,* 6, col. 1249–1400.

26. Author of a monumental *Thérapeutique des maladies helléniques* in twelve volumes. Cf. P. Särkö, "Salomon und die Dämonen," 305–22, 306.

27. Cf. Toledano, *La médecine du Talmud. Au commencement des sciences modernes,* 59–62.

28. Braekman, *Der vrouwen nature ende complexie. Een volksboek, naar de Utrechtse druk van Jan van Berntsz, van omstreeks 1538.*

29. Cocles, *Chyromantie anastasis,* folio 3r b.

SEVEN. SOLOMON'S EXPLORATIONS

1. Schischmanova, *Légendes religieuses bulgares,* 84–87.

2. Rambaud, *La Russie épique,* 399.

3. Delpech, "Salomon et le jeune homme à la coupole de verre," 483–84; original text 485*ff.* See also P. Roisse, "L'Histoire du sceau de Salomon, ou de la *coincidentia Oppositorum* in the "Livres de Plomb," 360–407.

4. Cf. *La Bordah du cheikh el Bousiri, poème en l'honneur de Mohammed,* 75.

5. Bokhâri de Djohôre, *Makota radja-radja,* 89.

6. Rambaud, *La Russie épique, étude sur les chansons héroïques de la Russie,* 398*ff.*

7. Brélian-Djahanshahi, trans., *Histoire légendaire des rois de Perse d'après le Livre des Rois de Ferdowsi,* 32.

EIGHT. SOLOMON AND THE DJINNS

1. *Kitab al-'uhud alladi ahadaha Sulayman ben Dawud 'laa gami al-ginn wa-al-shayatin.* Cf. Fahd, T. "Anges, démons et djinns en Islam," 155–214, 201.

2. *Revue des Traditions populaires,* 9 (1913), 354. The last phrase of the text refers to the building of the Temple of Jerusalem.

3. *Revue des Traditions populaires,* 9 (1913), 356*ff.*

4. Qu'ran, Sura Saba 2, 11.

5. Qu'ran, Sura Sad 38, 37–39.

6. We find this motif again in one of the versions of "Solomon and Kitovras," cf. A. Mazon, "Le centaure de la légende vieux-russe de Salomon et Kitovras," 4262.

7. Mazon, "Le centaure de la légende vieux-russe de Salomon et Kitovras," 42–62.

8. Mazon, "Le centaure de la légende vieux-russe de Salomon et Kitovras," 42–62.

9. Cf. *Talmud de Jérusalem,* vol. 6.

10. See Tendlau, *Das Buch der Sagen und legenden jüdischer Vorzeit,* no. 39, 195–217.

11. Gervais de Tilbury, *Otia imperialia* III, 104, in *Scriptores rerum Brunsvicensium I.*

12. A. Weil, *Contes et Légendes d'Israël,* based on the midrash.

13. *Sippurim,* Eine Sammlung jüdischer Volkssagen, Erzählungen, Mythen, Chroniken, Denkwürdigkeiten und Biographen berühmter Juden, 5 Sammlungen in zwei Bänden, Prague: Wolf Pascheles Verlag, 1847–1867, 19*ff.* See also Berdyczewski, *Die Sagen der Frankfurter Juden,* vol. 5, 159.

14. Jeremiah 9:23.

15. *The Nameless Scripture* from the Nag Hammadi codex provides an explanation of this letter that is also one of the names of the divinity, cf. *Écrits gnostiques chrétiens,* 488.

16. Cf. 2 Samuel 8:18.

17. Warnhagen, *Ein indisches Märchen auf seiner Wanderung,* 16–18.

18. Cf. Kaminka, "The Origin of the Ashmedai Legend in the Babylonian Talmud," 221–24.

19. Numbers 24:8.

20. Warnhagen, *Ein indische Märchen,* 16–19; Eisenmenger, *Entdecktes Judentum oder gründlicher und wahrhaffter Bericht,* 356*ff.*

21. This is most likely a book by Flavius Josephus that Saint Jerome often cites in his works; he even devotes an article to Flavius Josephus in his *De viris illustribus;* cf. Scherer, "Salomo und der Drache," 19–24.

22. Waag, *Kleinere deutsche Gedichte des XI. und XII. Jahrhunderts,* 26–34.

23. Basset, *Contes populaires berbères,* 29*ff.*

24. We are using the edition and translation found in Regourd, "Images de djinns et exorcisme dans le *Mandal al-Sulaymânî,*" 253–94.

NINE. THE SINS OF SOLOMON

1. Wünsche, *Midrasch Bemidbar rabba, die allegorische Auslegung des vierten Buches Mose,* 340.

2. Zwinger, *Tractatus theologicus,* 53–135, 173–231, 281*ff.*

3. See the Babylonian Talmud, *Gittin* 68b; Cf. Lévi, "L'orgueil de Salomon," 59*ff.*

4. Mahé and Poirier, *Écrits gnostiques: la bibliothèque de Nag Hammadi,* 1132.

5. Ispas, *Legenda populară românească între canonic și apocrif,* 207–10.

6. Ibrâhim ibn Waçîf Châh, *l'abrégé des merveilles,* 69–72.

7. Tabari, *Chronique,* chap. 96, 450–54.

8. Véronèse, *l'Almandal et l'almadel latins au moyen Âge.*

9. *Écrits gnostiques chrétiens,* 1424.

10. Sprenger and Institoris, *Malleus Maleficarum,* 1487, folio 37r and 92 vol.: *"Praeterea sicut Salomon dijs suarum uxorum reuerentia exhibuit propter complatientiam, nec tamen propterea postasiam perdifie incurrebat, quia mente fidelis et veram fidem semper retinuit."*

11. Zwinger, *Tractatus theologicus,* chap. 3: "De conjugio & pellicatum Regis Salomonis cum mulieribus alienigenis & idolatricis," 53–135; chap. 4: "De excessivo numero Vxorum & Pellicum Regis salomonis," 136–173; chap. 5: "De intemperanti Amore, quo salomon vxores & pellices suas fuit complexus," 173–231; chap. 6: "De idolatria Regis Salomonis," 231*ff.*

12. Glycas, *Annales,* I, 183–85.

13. *Écrits gnostiques chrétiens,* 799.

14. Zwinger, *Tractatus theologicus,* chap. 4, 136–73; chap. 5, 173–231.

TEN. SOLOMON AND THE QUEEN OF SHEBA

1. Glycas, *Annales,* 342.

2. Littmann, *The Legend of the Queen of Sheba in the Tradition of Axum,* 1*ff.*

3. Cf. Venzlaff, *Al-Hudhud: eine Untersuchung zur kulturgeschichtlichen Bedeutung des Wiedehopfs im Islam.* In the work of Aristophanes, for example, it guards the celestial gates of the city of Birds.

4. Qu'ran, Sura 27, 22–24.

5. Cf. Pennacchietti, "La reine de saba, le pavé de cristal et le tronc flottant," 8.

6. Tabari, *Chronicle,* chap. 95, 437–42.

7. Cf. Hetzel, "La reine de saba dans les légendes médiévales," 154–58.

8. Ruska, "Ein dem Châlid ibn Jazîd zugeschriebenes Verzeichnis der Propheten, Philosophen und Frauen, die sich mit Alchemie befaßten," 296.

9. Halévy, *"La Légende de la reine de Saba.* École pratique des hautes études, section des sciences historiques et philologiques," 5–24; Pennacchietti, "La reine de saba," 1–26.

10. McCown, *The Testament of Solomon,* 60.

11. Caquot, "La reine de saba et le bois de la Croix selon une tradition éthiopienne," 143.

12. Maillet, G. "Sur les différents types de Pédauques," 189.

13. Gervais de Tilbury, *Otia imperialia*, III, 54.

14. Boureau, de Voragine, et al. *La Légende dorée*, chap. 64, 364*ff*. See also Köhler, "Zur Legende von der Königin von Saba oder der Sibylla und dem Kreuzholze," 87–94.

ELEVEN. SOLOMON AND DEATH

1. The Qu'ran, Sura 83, 18*ff*; Al Mutaffifin (the Cheats) says that the soul is raised to 'Iliyyûn, the highest degrees of paradise; that of infidels descends to Sijjîn, the abyss.

2. Cf. G. Brecher, *l'Immortalité de l'âme chez les juifs*.

3. Cf. *Le Livre de la création et de l'histoire d'Abou-Zéïd Ahmed ben Sahl el-Bakhî*, 160–61.

4. Cf. Qu'ran 83, 18*ff*.

5. Qu'ran 83, 7*ff*.

6. Cf. Qu'ran 18, 93*ff*. (sura Al Kahf [the cave]): "Until, when he reached a place between the Two Barriers [mountains], he found beside them a people who could hardly understand any form of speech. They said: 'O Dhul-Qarnayn, the Yajuj and the Majuj sow disorder across the land. So may we offer you a tribute so that you might make a barrier between us and them?' He said: 'What my Lord has endowed me with is better [than what you offer] but assist me with your strength and I will build an embankment between you and them. Bring me sheets of iron,' then, once he had filled the space between the two mountains with them, he said, 'Blow' until he had made it [created a furnace], then he said, 'Bring me molten copper that I may pour over it.'" In this way they were not able to scale it or penetrate it at all anymore.

7. G. Weil, *Biblische legenden der Muselmänner*, 275–79; cf. also Ispas, *Legenda populară românească între canonic şi apocrif*, 176*ff*.

8. Ibrâhim ibn Waçîf Châh, *L'Abrégé*, 57.

9. Cf. Ferrand, *Relations de voyages et textes géographiques arabes, persans et turks relatifs à l'Extrême-Orient du VIIIe au XVIIIe siècle*, 584*ff*.

10. Tabari, *Chronicle*, chap. XVI, 60–61.

11. Cf. J.C. Garcin, *Pour une lecture historique des Mille et une Nuits*, 249–54. I would like to thank my colleague who so kindly sent me his study.

12. Tertullien, *Contra Marcion*, II, 23, III, 20; Cyprien, *Epistola 6 ad rogatianum*; Augustine, *Contra Faustum*, cap. 71 & 88; *De doctrina christiana*, cap. 21; Gregory the Great, *Moralia in Job*, cap. 2.
13. Bloch, "La vie d'outre-tombe du roi Salomon," 349–77.
14. Jean Juvénal des Ursins, *Histoire de Charles Vi roy de France*, 1403.

TWELVE. SOLOMON AMONG THE SABAEANS

1. Cf. Green, *The City of the Moon God: Religious Traditions of Harran*.
2. Caiozzo, *Images du ciel d'Orient au Moyen Âge*, 136.
3. Siouffi, *Sur la religion Soubbas ou des Sabéens*, 150–57.
4. For more on this figure, cf. Bencheikh, "Iram ou la clameur de Dieu. Le mythe et le verset," 70–81.
5. See Bencheikh, "Iram ou la clameur de Dieu," 70–81.
6. *La Bordah du Cheikh El Bousiri*, 101.

PART TWO. THE MAGICIAN

1. Cf. Filippi, "Légendes et croyances de la Corse," 8.
2. Flavius Josephus, *Antiquités judaïques*, VIII, 2.
3. Glycas, *Annales*, 341.
4. Cf. Abumalham, "Salomón y los genios," 42.
5. Gervais de Tilbury, *Otia imperialia*, III, 28.
6. Véronèse, *L'Ars notoria au Moyen Âge. Introduction et édition critique*.
7. Cf. Lecouteux, *Dictionnaire des formules magiques*, 75–77.

THIRTEEN. *THE TESTAMENT OF SOLOMON*

1. McCown, *The Testament of Solomon*.
2. Véronèse, "La transmission groupée des textes de 'magie salomonienne' de l'Antiquité au moyen âge," vol. 405, 193–223.
3. McCown, *The Testament of Solomon*, 51–90.
4. Glycas, *Annales* I, 341.
5. Mahé and Poirier, *Écrits gnostiques: la bibliothèque de Nag hammadi*, 434.
6. Ibn al-nadîm, *al Fihrist*, cited by Coulon, *La Magie islamique et le corpus burianum au Moyen Âge*, 354.

7. *Kitab tafsir ma qalat-hu l-shayatin li-Sulayman b. Dawud wa-ma ahada 'alay-him min al-'uhud.*

8. Gundel, *Dekane und Dekansternbilder, ein Beitrag zur Geschichte der Sternbilder der Kulturvölker,* 49–62.

9. McCown, *The Testament of Solomon,* XV, 5, XVIII, 40.

10. For more on this demon, cf. Delpech, "Salomon tempestaire et les démons embouteillés: maîtrise magique des vents et stratégie eschatologique," 68.

11. Bornemann, "Das Testament des Salomo," 9–56; Rießler, *Altjüdisches Schrifttum außerhalb der Bibel;* McCown, *The Testament of Solomon,* 1251*ff.*

12. *Les Clavicules de Salomon,* manuscript 25314; *The Key of Solomon the King.*

13. Salzberger, *Die Salomo-Sage in der semitischen literatur,* 108–111.

14. Cf. Ansbacher, *Die abschnitte über die Geister,* 19–21.

15. Cf. Horovitz, "Wahb b. munabbih," *Encyclopédie de l'Islam,* vol. IV, 1142–1144.

16. Cf. Ansbacher, *Die abschnitte über die Geister,* 23*ff.*

FOURTEEN. SOLOMON'S *HYGROMANCY*

1. A symbol; cf. Bardon, *Die Praxis der magischen evokation,* chap. I, 11. 3.

2. Paris, BnF, cod. Grec. 2419, folio 243v–246r.

3. Cf. Marathakis, ed., *The Magical Treatise of Solomon* or *Hygromanteia.*

4. Cf. Torijano, *Solomon the Esoteric King,* 202.

FIFTEEN. THE KEYS OF SOLOMON

1. London, British Library, Ms. Harleian 5596 (fifteenth century).

2. Mathiesen, "The Key of Solomon: Towards a Typology of the Manuscripts."

3. National Library of Poland, Warsaw, Manuscript Rps. 3352 II.

4. Mathers, Liddell, and Crowley, *The Goetia. The Lesser Key of Solomon the King.*

5. Gollancz, *Sepher maphteah Shelomoh.*

6. Cote Rps 3352 II.

7. *Claviculae Salomonis et Theosophia pneumatica, das ist die warhafftige Erkänntnüß Gottes, und seiner sichtigen und unsichtigen Geschöpffen, die Heil. Geist - Kunst genannt.*

SIXTEEN. THE OTHER MAGIC BOOKS

1. Pingree, "Learned Magic in the Time of Frederic II," 45.

2. "[. . .] quem librum cum multis aliis per Salomonem in arabia in certis montium cavernis absconditum reperit Virgilius tempore Octaviani imperatoris et de arabica lingua in nostram latinam prolationem transtulit . . . ," F. Hemmerlin, Varie oblectationis opuscula et tractatus, Bâle, 1497, folio 108v–109r.

3. Singer, ed., Jewish Encyclopedia, vol. 11, 444–48.

4. Les Anneaux nécromantiques de Salomon roi des Hébreux, Leipzig, Universitätsbibliothek, Cod. Mag. 35; Vatican Library, num. 75, a.

5. Gand, Universiteitsbibliotheek, Ms. 1021 A, folio 109r–110v.

6. London, British Library, Ms. Sloane 3002, folio 67v–68r.

7. Gand, Universiteitsbibliotheek, Ms. 1021 A, folio 110v–112v.

8. London, Wellcome Historical Medical Library, Ms. 517, folio 223r–224r.

9. Hälsig, Der zauberspruch bei den Germanen bis in die mitte des 6. jahrhunderts, 55–56; "Pentaculum Salomonis regis. . . . Potest quidlibet operari vi vult, et habeat quidquid voluerit. Primo quere sanguinem upupe et custodi bene in vitro, et cum operari volueris, tunc vade ad nemus secretum cum ense lucido, cum quo facies circulum, et habeas pergamentum virgineum."

SEVENTEEN. THE ARCHAEOLOGICAL TRACES OF SOLOMON

1. Wessely, Zauberpapyri von Paris und London, 27ff.

2. Cf. Goodenough, Jewish Symbols in the Greco-Roman Period, 227–35.

3. Perdrizet, "ΣΦΡΑΓΙΣ ΣΟΛΟΜΩΝΟΣ," 42–61.

4. Schlumberger, Mélanges d'archéologie byzantine, I, 117; Baum, "Die Goldbrakteaten von Attlens und La Copelenaz," 21–39.

5. Nemeti, "Magical practices in Dacia and Moesia inferior," 148.

EIGHTEEN. THE LAPIDARIES OF SOLOMON

1. Glycas, Annales, I, 183–185.

2. For more on this book, cf. Vescovini, Le Moyen Âge magique, 135–144.

3. Leonardi, Les Pierres talismaniques (Speculum lapidum, livre III).

4. Delatte, Textes latins et vieux français relatifs aux Cyranides. With the edition of the Livre des secrez de nature, 297–352.

5. Caesar Longinus, ed., *Trinum magicum; sive, Secretorum magicorum opus. Continens I. De magia naturali, artificiosa & superstitiosa diquisitiones axiomaticas. II. theatrum naturae praeter curam magneticam, & veterum sophorum sigilla et imagines magicas . . .* III. *Oracula Zorastris, & mysteria mysticae philosophiae, Hebraeorum, Chaldaeorum, Aegyptiorum, Persarum, Orphicorum, & Pythagoricorum. Acessere nonnulla secretorum & mirabilia mundi et Tractatus de proprii cujusque nati daemonis inquisition.*

6. Rhenanus, *harmoniae chymico-philosophicae, sive philosophorum antiquorum consentientium,* 309–23.

7. Caesar Longinus, ed., *Trinum magicum.*

NINETEEN. THE ACCOUNT OF ZOSIMOS OF PANOPOLIS

1. Zosime de Panopolis, *La Chimie au Moyen Âge*, vol. 2: L'alchimie syriaque, 264–66.

2. *Tunc sanctus Salomon conjuravit eos omnes, et alligavit eos in quadam phiola vitrea et demergit eos in profundum maris, Bibliotheca anecdotorum,* 242.

TWENTY. SOLOMON'S SUCCESSORS

1. "*[. . .] intravit in templum Salomonis et vidit ibi multa mirabilia et stetit ibi aliquamtulum temporis et habebat secum quendam hominem, qui erat custos suus et magister suus et vocabatur Aristotiles, et iste Aristotiles scivit secrete quod Salomon habuerat multos libros de omnibus scientiis et ibit occulte ad illum locum et extraxit inde omnes illos libros Salomonis et coepit studere per eos efficaciter, ita quod post paucum temporis fuit inde philosophus maximus et magister, et sic aristotiles habuit scientiam magnam cum illis libris, Salomonis, quod ante parum sciebat, et a natura sua nimis rudis erat, et ideo per illos libros regis Salomonis Aristoteles illuminatus est et magnus philosophus factus est, ideo bona est scientia adquisita.*"

2. Cf. Véronèse, "Virgilius Hispanus, philosophe et magicien," 305.

3. *Per istam scientiam sanctam sanctus Salomon daemones constringebat et ad se venire faciebat;* cf. Véronèse, *L'Ars* notoria *au Moyen Âge et à l'époque moderne. Étude d'une tradition de magie théurgique (XIIᵉ–XVIIᵉ siècle),* 317–319; Delpech, "Virgilio, Aristóteles, salomón y otros sabios del montón. Nigromancia y Arte notoria en la *Filosofía de Virgilio Cordobés,*" 99–137.

4. "[. . .] *angeli boni et sancti composuerunt eam et fecerunt, et postea sancto regi Salomoni angeli boni et sancti dederunt," Bibliotheca anecdotorum,* 242.

5. Véronèse, *L'Ars* notoria *au Moyen Âge,* 318*ff.*

PART THREE. SOLOMON IN FOLKLORE

1. Dan, "Preminte solomon și șerpele," 49–51

2. Cf. Ispas, *Legenda populară românească între canonic și apocrif.*

3. Anecdote from the Malaysian writer Bukhari of Johore (Bokhâri de Djohôre) in *Makota radja-radja,* 208*ff.*

4. Lur'e, "Une légende inconnue de salomon et Kitovras dans un manuscrit du XVe siècle," 7-11. The kinship of this text with the story of Aschmedai can be easily seen. See also Mazon, "Le centaure de la légende vieux-russe de Salomon et Kitovras," 42–62.

5. Cf. Ispas, *Legenda populară românească între canonic și apocrif,* 199, 214, 225*ff.*

6. Karadžić, *Volksmärchen der Serben,* 236*ff.*

7. Variant of motif K 1211. *Virgil in the Basket.*

8. Schischmanova, *Légendes religieuses bulgares,* 82–84.

9. Cf. Schmitt, "Der gerittene Aristoteles. Ein Motiv misogyner Dichtung bei Matheus von Boulogne."

10. Cf. Comparetti, *Virgilio nel medioevo;* Berlioz, "Virgile dans la littérature des *exempla* (XIIIe–XVe siècle)," 65–120.

11. *Mélusine, recueil de mythologie, littérature populaire, traditions et croyances* 4 (1888): col. 269–270.

12. *Midrasch du Décalogue* (eighth commandment), anonymous tenth century work; *Mélusine, recueil de mythologie, littérature populaire, traditions et croyances,* (1884): col. 543*ff.*

13. Lévi, "Les trois conseils de Salomon," col. 514*ff.* Solomon's last advice is citing Proverbs 16:16.

14. Palumbo, "Les trois conseils du roi Salomon," 555–560; this concerns a Greco-Salentin folk tale written in the dialect spoken in the Pouilles region with Greek letters.

15. *Revue des Traditions populaires* 11 (1887): 518–20. This Ukrainian story is directly inspired by the German Solomon and Morolf; cf. Lecouteux and Lecouteux, *Voyages dans l'au-delà et aventures extraordinaires. Contes et récits du Moyen Âge,* 125–168. English translation: *Travels to the Other World and other Fantastic Realms: Medieval Journeys into the Beyond.*

16. Tabari, *Chronique,* chap. 96, 454.

17. Sokolov and Jurij, "La recherche des bylines," 202–15.

18. Lecouteux and Lecouteux, *Voyages dans l'au-delà et aventures extraordinaires.*

19. Variant: "We will equip a purple ship with a vermillion cabin, a bed made from precious wood with a quilt of swan eiderdown and a Damascus pillowcase. On the bed's canopy support we shall place a bird of paradise that will sing royal songs. We will take forty times forty barrels of beer, a cup that will hold one and a half measures, and many sweetmeats."

20. Variant: he displayed before her precious stones, rich clothes, royal garments, and seduced Solomonida this way.

21. Variant: they lived three quiet years.

22. Variant: winged knights and winged chargers were part of his troop.

23. Variant: she made him empty a mug of beer that was one measure and a half. He rolled over the ground, got up, and put himself in the chest.

24. Variant: Solomon was brought there on a cart. He leaned over to look at the wheels and started to smile. Vassili asked him the reason and he answered: "I am laughing to see half of the wheel buried in the muck."

25. Variant: "I took the cows to pasture."

26. Variant: Then all the wild beasts could be seen gathering and all the birds racing thither. Because Vassili expressed his surprise, Solomon replied: "When I was still just a lad, I was a great hunter, this is why all the animals come together and the birds race to watch my death."

27. Variant: "Then all the mountains and forests were shaken, the blue seas churned, and a huge noise raced over the waves."

28. Variant: Solomonida begs his forgiveness, and he answers: "If you had been a wise woman, you would not have boarded the red ship, you would not have drunk the intoxicating liquor, but this transgression that God does not forgive you. If you had been a wise woman, you would not have locked a tsar inside a forged chest, but this transgression, may God forgive you! If you had been a wise woman, you would not have arranged silken ropes to hand the King Solomon, and this transgression I cannot forgive you."

29. Ferreira, "Entre la terre et la guerre: Salomon, Tristan et les mythes d'alternance en Espagne de la Reconquête," *E-Spania,* 16 (2013), http://journals.openedition.org/e-spania/22657.

30. Raynaud, *Élie de Saint Gilles,* v. 1793 *ff.*

31. *Le Blasme des fames,* 81 *ff.*

32. Gaster, *Literatura populară Ediție, prefață și note de Mircea Anghelescu,*

78–80, 103–4, 216–26; Ispas, "Ciclul narativ despre regale Solomon în literatura română," 221–22.

33. We see this "women's mind scales" again in a Romanian folktale in which the mother demands the heart and little finger of her son, but the executioner takes a dog's heart and brings it back with Solomon's little finger; cf. Ispas, *legenda populară românească între canonic și apocrif,* 204 *ff.*

34. "Légendes chrétiennes d'Ukraine," 511–14; Ispas, *legenda populară românească între canonic și apocrif,* 186–95.

35. "Légendes chrétiennes d'Ukraine," 520–521.

36. *Revue des Traditions populaires,* 4 (1898), 212*ff.*

37. "Légendes chrétiennes d'Ukraine," 510.

38. The same narrative sequence can be seen in the legend de Siegfried/Sigurðr. Cf. C. Lecouteux, *La Légende de Siegfried d'après le Seyfrid à la peau de corne et la Thidrekssaga.*

39. "Légendes chrétiennes d'Ukraine," 514–18.

40. Saintyves, *Les Cinquante jugements de Salomon ou les arrêts des bons juges d'après la tradition populaire,* 90–93.

41. Bezemer, *Volksdichtung aus indonesien,* 87*ff.*

42. Saintyves, *Les Cinquante jugements de Salomon,* 27*ff.*

43. Tchéraz, *L'Orient inédit. Légendes et traditions arméniennes, grecques et turques,* 16–17.

44. Tchéraz, *L'Orient inédit. Légendes et traditions arméniennes, grecques et turques,* 18–19.

45. Obert, *Magazin für Geschichte, Literatur und alle Denk- und merkwürdigkeiten* 1, 112–21, refers to *jaad,* meaning *iad,* "hell," but he uses *unterwelt* as a synonym, which corresponds to Romanian *lumea de jos,* "the world below, the subterranean world, hell."

46. In Romania, Ispas has collected two tales of this type, cf. *Legenda populară românească între canonic și apocrif,* 225–28.

47. Cerquand, *Légendes et Récits populaires du Pays basque,* vol. IV, 132.

48. Dähnhardt, *Natursagen. eine Deutung naturdeutender Sagen, märchen, Fabeln und legenden,* vol. 1, 335.

49. Dähnhardt, *Natursagen,* vol. 1, 245.

50. Simenel, *L'origine est aux frontierres,* 64.

51. Taloș, *Gândirea magico-religioasă la români,* 172 (s.v. Toartele cerului).

52. Scurtu, "Cercetări folclorice în Ugocea românească (jud. satu mare)," 105*ff.*

53. Ispas, *legenda populară românească între canonic și apocrif,* 175.

54. Ispas, *legenda populară românească între canonic și apocrif,* 229.

55. Taloș, *Gândirea magico-religioasă,* s.v. Solomon. This is strangely reminiscent of the legend of Virgil the magician in the chapbook literature, cf. Lecouteux, "La Légende de Virgile dans les Volksbücher: variations et continuité," 333–42.

56. Ispas, *Legenda populară românească între canonic și apocrif,* 215, 218*ff,* 220; the scales: 211, 223, 227*ff,* 233.

CONCLUSION

1. It was Ronald Grambo who drew my attention to this aspect of the sovereign in a personal communication.

2. Eliade, *Shamanism: Archaic Techniques of Ecstasy,* 88.

3. Eliade, *Shamanism: Archaic Techniques of Ecstasy,* 89.

4. Eliade, *Shamanism: Archaic Techniques of Ecstasy,* 38*ff.*

5. Eliade, *Shamanism: Archaic Techniques of Ecstasy,* 214 s.

6. Eliade, *Shamanism: Archaic Techniques of Ecstasy,* 218*ff.*

7. Eliade, *Shamanism: Archaic Techniques of Ecstasy,* 206*ff.*

8. Cf. Eisenmenger, *Entdecktes judentum oder gründlicher und wahrhaffter Bericht,* vol. I, 318.

9. Martin, "Le matin des hommes-dieux: Étude sur le chamanisme grec."

Bibliography

Abumalham, Montserrat. "Salomón y los genios." *Anaquel de Estudios Árabes* 3 (1992): 37–46.

Allen, Mark, and John H. Fisher. *The Complete Poetry and Prose of Geoffrey Chaucer.* Boston: Wadsworth, 1848.

Anonymous. *Elye of Saint-Gilles: A Chanson de Geste.* Translated and Edited by A. Richard Hartman and Sandra C. Malicote. New York: Italica Press, 2010.

Ansbacher, J. *Die abschnitte über die Geister und wunderbaren Geschöpfe aus Qazwînî's Kosmographie.* Dissertation, Erlangen, Kirchhain N. L., Max Schmersow, 1906.

Bacher, W. *Nîzamîs Leben und Werke und der zweite Teil des Alexanderbuches.* Leipzig: Engelmann, 1871.

Bacon, Roger. *Epistola de secretis operibus naturae et artis et de nullitate magiae (Lettre sur les prodiges de la nature et sur la nullité de la magie)* (circa 1260). In *Fr. Rogeri Bacon Opera quaedam hactenus inedita,* vol. 1, edited by J.S. Brewer, 523*ff.* London: Longman, 1859.

Balbir, Nalini. *Somadeva.* Paris: NRF, 1963.

Bardon, F. *Die Praxis der magischen evokation.* Wuppertal: Hermann Bauer, 1990.

Basset, René. *Contes populaires berbères.* Paris: E. Leroux, 1887.

———. "Salomon (Solaiman) dans les légendes musulmanes: VI: Les objets merveilleux de Salomon." *Revue des Traditions populaires* 4 (1889): 231–34; 10 (1891): 610–612; 6 (1892): 377–79.

———. "Salomon (Solaiman) dans les légendes musulmanes: VII les constructions de Salomon." *Revue des Traditions populaires* 3 (1894): 190–94.

———. "Salomon (Solaiman) dans les légendes musulmanes." *Revue des Traditions populaires* 3 (1888): 353*ff*; 6 (1891): 145.

———. "Solaiman (Salomon) dans les légendes musulmanes." *Revue des Traditions populaires* 7 (1888): 190*ff*; 353*ff*.

———. "Un recueil des contes de l'Australasie." *Revue des Traditions populaires* 2 (1905): 3–11.

Battûta, Ibn. *Voyages; 1: De l'afrique du Nord à la mecque.* Translated by C. Defremery and B. R. Sanguinetti. Paris: Maspero, 1982.

Baum, Julius. "Die Goldbrakteaten von Attalens und La Coppelenaz." *Revue suisse de Numismatique* 27 (1939): 21–39.

Benary, Walter, ed. *Salomon et Marcolfus: Kritischer Text mit Einleitung, Anmerkungen, Übersicht über die Sprüche, Namen-und Wörterverzeichnis.* Heidelberg: Winter, 1914.

Bencheikh, Jamel Eddine. "Iram ou la clameur de Dieu. Le mythe et le verset." *Revue du monde musulman et de la Méditerranée* 58 (1990): 70–81.

Berdyczewski, M. Y. *Die Sagen der Frankfurter Juden,* vol. 5. Frankfurt a/Main: Rütten & Loening, 1913–1922.

Berlioz, Jacques. "Virgile dans la littérature des *exempla* (XIIIᵉ–XVᵉ siècles)." In *Lectures médiévales de Virgile,* 65–120. Rome: Collection de l'École française de Rome, 1985.

Berthelot, M. *Les Origines de l'alchimie.* Paris: Georges Steinheil, 1885.

Bezemer, Tammo Jacob. *Volksdichtung aus Indonesien.* Den Haag: Nijhoff, 1904.

Biblia sacra juxta vulgatam Clementinam. Rome, Tornaci, Paris: Desclée et socii, 1947.

Bibliotheca anecdotorum seu veterum monumentorum ecclsiast. Coll. Noviss. Edited by Johann Jacobus Moser. Nuremberg: In officina Hoffmanniana, 1722.

Bloch, Marc. "La vie d'outre-tombe du roi Salomon." *Revue belge de Philologie et d'Histoire* 4 (1925): 349–77.

Blunt, Lady. *Voyage en Arabie; pèlerinage au Nedjed.* Translated by Léopold Derôme. Paris: Hachette, 1882.

Bockhoff, A., and S. Singer. *Heinrichs von Neustadt Apollonius von Tyrland und seine Quellen.* Tübingen: J. C. B. Mohr, 1911.

Bokhâri de Djohôre. *Makota radja-radja (La Couronne des rois).* French translation by Aristide Marre. Paris: Maisonneuve & Co, 1878.

Bonaventure des Périers. *Récréation et Joyeux devis* in *Conteurs français du XVIᵉ siècle.* Paris: NRF, 1965.

Bordah du Cheikh El Bousiri, poème en l'honneur de Mohammed (La). Translated and commented by René Basset. Paris: Ernest Leroux, 1894.

Bornemann, Friedrich August. "Das Testament des Salomo." *Zeitschrift für die historische Theologie* 3 (1844): 9–56.

Boudet, Jean-Patrice. *Entre science et nigromance. Astrologie, divination et magie dans l'Occident médiéval (XIIe–XVe siècle)*. Paris: Publications de la Sorbonne, 2006.

———. "Le modèle du roi sage aux XIII et XIVe siècle: Salomon, Alphonse X et Charles V." *Revue historique* 3 (2008): 545–66.

Boureau, A., Jacques de Voragine, et al. *La Légende dorée*. Paris: Gallimard, 2004.

Bovon, François, and Pierre Geoltrain, eds. *Écrits apocryphes chrétiens*. Paris: NRF, 1997.

Braekman W. L., ed. *Der vrouwen nature ende complexie. Een volksboek, naar de Utrechtse druk van Jan van Berntsz, van omstreeks 1538*. Sint-Niklaas: Zeldzame Volksboeken uit de Nederlanden, 1980.

Brecher, Gidéon. *L'immortalité de l'âme chez les Juifs*. FV Éditions, 2017.

Brett, Gerard. "The Automata in the Byzantine Throne of Salomon." *Speculum* 29 (1954): 477–87.

Brélian-Djahanshahi, Frouzandéh, trans. *Histoire légendaire des rois de Perse d'après le Livre des Rois de Ferdowsi*. Paris: Imago, 2001.

Burkhardt, Evelyn, and Dorothea Salzer, eds. *Sefer Ha-Razim I und II-Das Buch der Geheimnisse I und II: Einleitung, Übersetzung und Kommentar*. Heidelberg: Mohr Siebrek, 2009.

Büttner, Carl Gotthilf. *Lieder und Geschichten der Suaheli*. Berlin: Emil Felber, 1894.

Caesar Longinus, ed. *Trinum magicum; sive, Secretorum magicorum opus. Continens I. De magia naturali, artificiosa & superstitiosa diquisitiones axiomaticas. II. theatrum naturae praeter curam magneticam, & veterum sophorum sigilla et imagines magicas ... III. Oracula Zorastris, & mysteria mysticae philosophiae, Hebraeorum, Chaldaeorum, Aegyptiorum, Persarum, Orphicorum, & Pythagoricorum. Acessere nonnulla secretorum & mirabilia mundi et Tractatus de proprii cujusque nati daemonis inquisition*. Frankfurt: Jacobi Gothofredi, 1673.

Caiozzo, A. *Images du ciel d'Orient au Moyen Âge*. Paris: P.U.P.S., 2003.

Canova, G. "La Tâsat al-ism: note su alcune coppe magiche Yemenite." *Quaderni di Studi Arabi* 13 (1995): 73–92.

Caquot, André. "La reine de Saba et le Bois de la Croix selon une tradition éthiopienne." *Annales d'Éthiopie* 1 (1955): 137–47.

Cartwright, Christoph. *Mellificium Hebraicum seu observationes diversimodae ex Hebraeorum, praesertim antiquorum, monumentis desumptse, unde plurimi cum Veteri cum Novi Testamenti loci vel explicantur vel illustrantur.* In Critica Sacri, vol. 8, edited by John Pearson. Amsterdam: 1698.

Cerquand, Jean-François. *Légendes et récits populaires du Pays basque*, vol. IV. Pau: Léon Ribaut, 1880.

Certeux, A. "Les eaux thermales et minérales: l'origine des sources chaudes et des bains maures." *Revue des Traditions populaires* 6 (1887).

Chitimia, Silvia. "Les traces de l'occulte ans le folklore roumain." In *Le défi magique II: satanisme, sorcellerie*, edited by Jean Baptiste Martin and Massimo Introvigne, 135–48. Lyon: Presses universitaires, 1994.

Choniatès, Nicétas, and B. G. Niebuhr, eds. *Corpus scriptorum Byzantinae, Nicetas Choniata.* Bonn: Ed. Weber, 1835.

Cizek, Alexandre. "La rencontre de deux sages: Salomon le Pacifique et Alexandre le Grand dans la légende hellénistique et médiévale." *Senefiance* 11 (1982): 75–99.

Claviculae Salomonis et Theosophia pneumatica, das ist die warhafftige Erkänntnüß Gottes, und seiner sichtigen und unsichtigen Geschöpffen, die Heil. Geist-Kunst genannt. Frankfurt: Andreas Luppius, 1686.

Cocles, Barthélémy. *Chyromantie anastasis.* Bologna: 1517.

Comparetti, Domenico. *Virgilio nel Medioevo.* Florence: Nuova edizioni a cura di G. Pasquali, 1937.

Conybeare, F. C. "The Testament of Solomon." *Jewish Quarterly Review* 20 (1898): 15–45.

Cottonianus Vitelius A. XV. British Library, London.

Coulon, Jean-Charles. *La Magie islamique et le Corpus burianum au Moyen Âge.* Thesis of Paris–Sorbonne, 2013.

Dähnhardt, Oskar. *Natursagen. Eine Sammlung naturdeutender Sagen, Märchen, Fabeln und Legenden*, 4 vol. Leipzig & Berlin: Teubner, 1907–1912.

Dalechamp, J. *Histoire générale des plantes.* Lyon: Borde, Arnaud & Rigaud, 1653.

Dan, D. "Preminte solomon și șerpele." *Șezătoarea* 5 (1899): 49–51.

Dawkins, J. McG. "The Seal of Solomon." *Journal of the Royal Asiatic Society* 76 (1944): 145–150.

Delatte, A., ed. *Textes latins et vieux français relatifs aux Cyranides.* Liège and Paris:

Bibliothèque de philosophie et lettres de l'Université de Liège, XCIII, 1942.

Delpech, François. "Salomon et le jeune homme à la coupole de verre. Remarques sur un conte sapiential morisque." *Revue de l'histoire des religions* 4 (2006): 483–84.

———. "Salomon tempestaire et les démons embouteillés: maîtrise magique des vents et Stratégie eschatologique." In *Tempus et Tempestas*, edited by Pierre Sylvain Filliozat and Michel Zink, 66–99. Paris: Académie des Inscriptions et Belles-Lettres, 2016.

———. "Virgilio, Aristóteles, Salomón y otros sabios del montón. Nigromancia y Arte notoria en la *Filosofía de Virgilio Cordobés*." In *Cien años de Julio Caro Baroja (Anejos de la Revista de Historiografía, no 1)*, edited by J.I. Ruiz Rodriguez and F.J. Gonzalez, 99–137. Madrid: Instituto de Historiografía Julio Caro Baroja, Univ. Carlos III, 2014.

Denis, Albert-Marie. *Introduction aux pseudépigraphes grecs d'Ancien Testament*. Leyden: J. Brill, 1970.

Dictz de Salomon avecques les Responces de Marcoul fort joyeuses, translate du latin. (Salomonis et Marcolphi dialogus, Antuerpiae, Gerard Leeu, 1488). Translated into French rhyme by Jehan Divery. Paris: Guillaume Eustace, 1509.

Ducros, Alexandre, trans. *La légende du ver-à-soie*. Paris: E. Dentu, 1876.

Duling, Dennis C. "Solomon, Exorcism, and the Son of David." *The Harvard Theological Review* 68 (1975): 235–52.

Écrits gnostiques chrétiens. Paris: NRF, 1997.

Eisenmenger, Johann Andras. *Entdecktes Judentum oder gründlicher und wahrhaffter Bericht*. Königsberg: 1711.

Eliade, M. *Shamanism: Archaic Techniques of Ecstasy*. Princeton: Bollingen, 1972.

Erman, Adolf. "Eine ägyptische Quelle der Sprüche Salomos." *Sitzungsberichte der Preussischen akademie der Wissenschaften zu Berlin* (1924): 86–89.

Estaban, Fernando Díaz. "Altos son y relucian. Tradicion oriental de los Palacios relucientes." *Revista de Filología Española* 49, no. 1/4 (1966): 301–14.

Euringer, Sebastian. "Das Netz Salomos." *Zeitschrift für Semistik und verwandte Gebiete* 6 (1928): 76–100, 178–99, 300–14.

Eymeric, Nicolas. *Directorium inquisitorium cum commenariis Francisci Pegñae*. Rome: Georg Ferrari, 1587.

Fabricius, Johannes Albertus. *Codex pseudepigraphus veteris Testamenti*, vol. 1. Hamburg: Christian Liebezeit, 1713.

Faerber, R. *König Salomon in der Tradition. Ein historisch-kritischer Beitrag zur Geschichte der Haggada, der Tannaiten und Amoräer*, Teil 1. Wien: Jos. Schlesinger, 1902.

Fahd, T. "Anges, démons et djinns en Islam." In *Génies, Anges et Démons*. Paris: Le Seuil, 1971.

Feer, Léon, trans. *Les trente-deux récits du trône (Batris-Sinhasan) ou les merveilleux exploits de Vikramaditya*. Paris: Ernest Leroux, 1884.

Ferrand, Gabriel. *Relations de voyages et textes géographiques arabes, persans et turks relatifs à l'Extrême-Orient du VIIIe au XVIIIe siècles*, vol. 1. Paris: Ernest Leroux, 1913.

Ferreira, Maria do Rosário. "Entre la terre et la guerre: Salomon, Tristan et les mythes d'alternance en Espagne de la Reconquête." *E-Spania* 16 (2013). http://journals.openedition.org/e-spania/22657.

Firdousi. *Le livre des rois*, vol. 1. Translated by Jules Mohl. Paris: Imprimerie nationale, 1876.

Filippi, Julie. "Légendes et croyances de la corse." *Revue des Traditions populaires* 8 (1894).

Flavius Josephus. *Antiquités judaïques*. Translated by Julien Weil. Paris: Ernest Leroux, 1926.

Garcin de Tassy, M. *Les oiseaux et les fleurs (Kitāb kashf al-asrār àn ḥukm al-ṭuyūr wa-'l-azhār), allégories morales d'Azz-Eddin Elmocaddessi*. Paris: Imprimerie royale, 1821.

Garcin, J. C. *Pour une lecture historique des Mille et une Nuits*. Arles: Actes Sud, 2013.

Gaster. *Literatura populară Ediție, prefață și note de Mircea Anghelescu*. Bucarest: 1983.

Gaulmin, G. *De vita et morte mosis libri tres*. Paris: 1629.

Genequand, Charles. "Autour de la Ville de Bronze: d'Alexandre à Salomon." *Arabica* 39 (1992): 328–45.

Gervais de Tilbury. *Otia imperialia* III. In *Scriptores rerum Brunsvicensium I*, edited by G.W. von Leibniz. Hanover: 1707.

Geyer, Paul, ed. *Itinerarium Burdigalense*. In *Itinera Hierosolymitana Saeculi III–VIII*. Vienna: F. Tempsky and Leipzig: G. Freytag, 1898.

Glaive-des-Couronnes (Seif el-Tîdjân). Translated from Arabic by Dr. Perron. Paris: Benjamin Duprat, 1862.

Glycas, Michael. *Annales*. Edited by Immanuel Bekker. Bonn: Weber, 1836.

Gollancz, Hermann. *Mafteah Shelomoh, Clavicula Salomonis*. Frankfurt and Main: J. Kauffmann, 1903.

———. *Sepher maphteah Shelomoh, an exact Facsimile of an original Book of Magic in Hebrew*. London and Edinburg: Oxford University Press, 1914.

Goodenough, Erwin R. *Jewish symbols in the Greco-Roman Period*. Princeton: Bollingen Foundation, 1953.

Green, T. M. *The City of the Moon God: Religious Traditions of Harran*. Leyden: E. J. Brill, 1992.

Gretser, Jacob. *De ivre et more prohibendi, expurgandi et abolendi libros hæreticos et noxios*. Ingolstadt: Abdrea Angermar, 1603.

Guilielmus de Pastrengo. *De originibus rerum libellus, in quo agitur de scripturis virorum illustrum, de fundatoribus Vrbium*. Venice: 1547.

Gundel, Wilhelm. *Dekane und Dekansternbilder, ein Beitrag zur Geschichte der Sternbilder der Kulturvölker*. Glückstadt & Hambourg: J. J. Augustin, 1936.

Halévy, Joseph. "*La légende de la reine de Saba*. École pratique des hautes études, Section des sciences historiques et philologiques." *Annuaire* (1904): 5–24.

Hälsig, F. *Der zauberspruch bei den Germanen bis in die mitte des 6. jahr-Hunderts*. Leipzig: 1910.

Hapgood, Isabel Florence. *The Epic Songs of Russia*. New York: Charles Scribner's Sons, 1916.

Haquette, J-L, and K. Ueltschi, eds. *Les métamorphoses de Virgile*. Paris: Champion, 2018.

Hetzel, A. "La reine de saba dans les légendes médiévales." In *Magie et Divination dans les cultures de l'Orient*, edited by J.M. Durand and A. Jacquet, 154–58. Paris: Jean Maisonneuve, 2010.

Horovitz, Josef. "Wahb b. Munabbih." *Encyclopédie de l'Islam* vol. IV, 1142–4. Leyden and Paris: E. J. Brill & Klincksieck, 1934.

Iafrate, Allegra. *The Wandering Throne of Solomon: Objects and Tales of Kingship in the Medieval Mediterranean*. Leiden-Boston: Brill, 2016.

Ibrâhim ibn Waçîf Châh. *L'Abrégé des merveilles*. Translated by Carra de Vaux. Paris: Sindbad, 1984.

Ispas, Sabina. "Ciclul narativ despre regale Solomon în literatura română." *Anuarul Institutului de Etnografie și Folclor Constantin Brăiloiu* 3 (1992): 221–22.

———. *Legenda populară românească între canonic și apocrif*. Bucharest: Saeculum, 2006.

Jean Juvénal des Ursins. *Histoire de Charles VI, roy de France*. n.p., 1403.

———. *The Genuine Works of Flavius Josephus the Jewish Historian*. Translated by William Whiston. London: 1737.

Julg, Bernard. *Mongolische Märchen-Sammlung. Die neun Märchen des Siddhi-Kür nach der ausführlichen Redaction und die Geschichte des Ardschi-Bordschi Chan*. Innsbruck: Wagnersche Universitätsbuchhandlung, 1868.

Junglas, Johann Peter. *Leontius von Byzanz. Studien zu seinen Schriften, Quellen und Anschauungen*. Paderborn: Schöningh, 1908.

Kaminka, Armand. "The Origin of the Ashmedai Legend in the Babylonian Talmud." *The Jewish Quarterly Review* 13, no. 2 (1922): 221–24.

Karadžić, Vuk Stefanović. *Volksmärchen der Serben*. Berlin: Georg Reimer, 1854.

Kemble, John M., ed. *The Dialogue of Salomon and Saturnus*. London: Ælfric Society, 1868.

———. *The Poetry of the Codex Vercellensis with an English Translation*. London: Ælfric Society, 1843.

Köhler, R. "Zur Legende von der Königin von Saba oder der Sibylla und dem Kreuzholze." In *Kleinere Schriften zur erzählenden Dichtung des mittelalters* II. Berlin: Emil Felber, 1900.

La Bordah du cheikh el Bousiri, poème en l'honneur de Mohammed. Translated and analyzed by R. Basset. Paris: E. Leroux, 1894.

La sainte Bible, traduction de l'Ancien Testament d'après les Septante et du nouveau Testament d'après le texte grec par P. Giguet, vol. 2. Paris: Poussielgue & Fils, 1865.

Lapidary of King Philip, 1784. Sloane Collection. British Museum.

Lansdowne 1202 4to. British Library, London.

Le Blasme des fames. Edited by A. Jubinal. Paris: Albert Merklein, 1835.

Le livre de la création et de l'histoire d'Abou-Zëïd Ahmed ben Sahl el-Bakhî, vol. 1. Paris: Ernest Leroux, 1899.

Les Anneaux nécromantiques de Salomon roi des Hébreux. Leipzig: Universitätsbibliothek, Cod. Mag. 35; Bibliothèque du Vatican, Num. 75, a.

Les Clavicules de Salomon. Traduit de l'hébreux en langue latine par le Rabin Abognazar et mis en langue vulgaire par monseigneur Barault archevêque d'Arles. English translation by S. L. MacGregor Mathers. Paris: BnF, manuscrit français 25314, 1634.

Liut-prand. "Antapodosis, VI. 233–589." In *Quellen zur sächsischen Kaiserzeit*, edited by A. Bauer and R.D. Rau, 233–589.

Livre des secrez de nature. In *Textes latins et vieux français relatifs aux Cyranides*, edited by A. Delatte, 297-352. Liège, Paris: 1942.

Lecouteux, Claude. *Dictionnaire des formules magiques*. Paris: Imago, 2014.

———. *Dictionary of Ancient Magic Words and Spells*. Rochester, Vt.: Inner Traditions, 2015.

———. *La Légende de Siegfried d'après le Seyfrid à la peau de corne et la Thidrekssaga*. Besançon: La Völva, 2015.

———."La Légende de Virgile dans les Volksbücher: variations et continuité." In *Les métamorphoses de Virgile*, edited by J.L. Haquette and K. Ueltschi.

———. "La mer et ses îles au moyen âge: un voyage dans le merveilleux." In *Démons et merveilles, le surnaturel dans l'océan indien*, edited by V. Magdeleine Andrianjafitrimo, et. al. La Réunion: Océan Éditions, 2005.

Lecouteux, Claude, and Corinne Lecouteux. *Travels to the Other World and other Fantastic Realms: Medieval Journeys into the Beyond*. Rochester, Vt.: Inner Traditions, 2018.

———. *Voyages dans l'au-delà et aventures extraordinaires. Contes et récits du Moyen Âge*. Paris: Imago, 2018.

"Légendes chrétiennes d'Ukraine." *Revue des Traditions populaires* 11 (1887): 509–25.

Leon the Grammarian. *Leonis Grammatici Chronographia*. Edited by Immanuel Bekker. Bonn: Weber, 1842.

Leonardi, Camillo. *Les pierres talismaniques (Speculum lapidum, livre III)*. Translated and edited by C. Lecouteux and A. Montfort. Paris: P.U.P.S., 2002.

Leroy, L. "Instruction de David à Salomon." *Revue de l'Orient chrétien* 20 (1915–1917): 329–31.

Lévi, Israël. "L'orgueil de Salomon." *Revue des Études juives* 17 (1888): 59*ff.*

———. "Les trois conseils de Salomon." *Mélusine, recueil de mythologie, littérature populaire, traditions et croyances* 4 (1888): col. 269*ff.*; 514*ff.*

Littmann, Enno, trans. *Die Erzählungen aus den Tausendundein Nächten*, vol. 4. Wiesbaden: Insel Verlag, 1953.

———. *The Legend of the Queen of Sheba in the Tradition of Axum*. Leyden: Brill, Princeton, University Library, 1904.

Lur'e, Ja. S. "Une légende inconnue de Salomon et Kitovras dans un manuscrit du XVᵉ siècle." *Revue des Études slaves* 43 (1964): 7–11.

McCown, Chester Charlton. *The Testament of Solomon*. Edited from manuscript. Leipzig: J. C. Hinrich, 1922.

Mahé, Jean-Pierre, and Paul-Hubert Poirier, eds. *Écrits gnostiques: la bibliothèque de Nag Hammadi*. Paris: NRF, 1997.

Maillet, G. "Sur les différents types de Pédauques." In *Mélanges de mythologie française offerts à Henri Dontenville.* Paris: Maisonneuve et Larose, 1980.

Mandonnet, Pierre. "Roger Bacon et le *Speculum Astronomiae* (1277)." *Revue Philosophique de Louvain* 67 (1910): 313–35.

Marathakis, Ioannis. *The Magical Treatise of Solomon Hygromanteia.* Singapore: Golden Hoard Press, 2011.

Martin, Michaël. "Le matin des hommes-dieux: Étude sur le chamanisme grec." *Folia electronica Classica* 8 (2004).

Massé, H. *Ibn al-Faqîh al-Hamadanî, Abrégé du livre des pays.* Damascus: IFPO, 1973.

Mathers, MacGregor, Samuel Liddell, and Aleister Crowley. *The Goetia. The Lesser Key of Solomon the King.* London: Trubner & Co, 1904.

Mathiesen, Robert. "The Key of Solomon: Toward a Typology of the Manuscripts." *Societas Magicas Newsletter* 17 (2007).

Ma'ûdî. *Les Prairies d'or* vol. 2. Translated by Barbier de Meynard and Pavet de Courteille. Paris: Société asiatique, 1965.

Mazon, André. "Le centaure de la légende vieux-russe de Salomon et Kitovras." *Revue des Études slaves* 7 (1927): 42–62.

Mehren, A. F., trans. *Manuel de la cosmographie du Moyen Âge.* Translated from the Arabic *Nokhbet ed-dahr Fi 'Adjaib-il-Birr wal-Bah'r de Dim de Sheikh Shams al-Din al-Ansari al-Dimashqî.* Paris: Leroux; Copenhagen: Bianco Luno; Leipzig: Brockhaus, 1874.

Mélusine, recueil de mythologie, littérature populaire, traditions et croyances 4 (1888): col. 269–270.

Menner, Robert J. "The *Vasa Mortis* Passage in the Old English *Solomon and Saturn.*" In *Studies in English Philology,* edited by Kemp Malone and Martin B. Ruud, 240–53). University of Minnesota Press: Minneapolis, 1929.

Midrasch Bemidbar rabba. Translated by Karl August Wünsche. Leipzig: Otto Schulze, 1885.

Migne, *Patrologia græca,* 6, col. 1249–1400.

Moland, A. G. "Roger Bacon as Magician." *Traditio* 30 (1974): 445–60.

Montgomery, James A. *Aramaic Incantations Texts from Nippur.* Philadelphia: University Museum, 1913.

Morhof, D. G. *Polyhistor litterarius, philosophicus et practicus cum accessionibus Joan. Fickii et Joh. Molleri.* Lubeck: Boeckmann, 1747.

Mornand, Félix. *La vie arabe.* Paris: Michel Lévy, 1858.

Nemeti, S. "Magical practices in Dacia and Moesia inferior." In *Jupiter on Your Side. Gods and Humans in Antiquity in the Lower Danube Area,* edited by C.G. Alexandrescu. Bucarest: 2013.

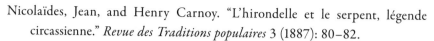

Nicolaïdes, Jean, and Henry Carnoy. "L'hirondelle et le serpent, légende circassienne." *Revue des Traditions populaires* 3 (1887): 80–82.

Nünlist, Tobias. *Dämonenglaube im Islam. Eine Untersuchung unter besonderer Berücksichtigung schriftlicher Quellen aus der vormodernen Zeit (600–1500).* Berlin and Boston: De Gruyter, 2015.

Obert, F. *Magazin für Geschichte, Literatur und alle Denk- und merkwürdigkeiten* 1 (1859): 112–21.

Palumbo, Vito D. "Les trois conseils du roi Salomon." *Le Muséon, Revue internationale* 3 (1884): 555–60.

Pennacchietti, F. A. "La reine de saba, le pavé de cristal et le tronc flottant." *Arabica* 49, no. 1 (2002): 8.

Perdrizet, Paul. ΣΦΡΑΓΙΣ ΣΟΛΟΜΩΝΟΣ, *Revue des Études Grecques* 16 (1903): 42–61.

———. *Negotium perambulans in tenebris: Études de démonologie gréco-orientale.* Strasbourg, Paris, & London: Publications de la Faculté des Lettres de l'Université de Strasbourg, 1922.

Pingree, David. "Learned Magic in the Time of Frederic II." *Micrologus* 2 (1994): 39–56.

Placides et Timeo, les secrez aus philosophes. Critical edition with introduction and notes by C. A. Thomasset. Geneva and Paris: Droz, 1980.

Preisendanz, K. "Salomo." In *Realenzyklopädie des classischen Altertumswissenchaft,* edited by Pauly-Wissowa, suppl. 8, col. 660–704.

Procope de Gaza. *Procopii Gazaei in libros regum et paralipomenon schola.* Edited by Joannes Meursius. Leyden: Lugduni batavorum, Elsevier, 1620.

Pseudo-Justinian. *Responsiones ad orthodoxos.* Edited by Migne. *Patrologia græca* 6, col. 1249–1400.

Rabelais, François. *Œuvres,* 4 vol. Paris: Jean de Bonnot, 1995.

Rainbow, Jesse. "The Song of Songs and the Testament of Solomon: Solomon's Love Poetry and Christian Magic." *The Harvard Theological Review* 100 (2007): 249–74.

Rambaud, Alfred. *La Russie épique, étude sur les chansons héroïques de la Russie.* Paris: Maisonneuve & Cie, 1876.

Raynaud, G., ed. *Élie de Saint Gilles.* Paris: Firmin-Didot, 1879.

Regourd, Anne. "Images de djinns et exorcisme dans le Mandal al-sulaymani." In *Autour de Picatrix: Images et magie, Proceedings of the International Congress, Institut national d'histoire de l'art,* edited by A. Caiozzo, J.-P. Boudet, and N. Weill-Parot, 253–94. Paris: Champion, 2011.

——. "Le *Kitâb al-mandal al-Sulaymânî,* un ouvrage d'exorcisme yéménite postérieur au Ve-VIe siècle ?" *Res Orientales* 13 (2001): 309–45.

Reinaud, Joseph Toussaint. *Description des monuments musulmans du cabinet de M le duc de Blacas,* vol. 1. Paris: Imprimerie nationale, 1822.

Revue des Traditions populaires, 11 (1887): 514–20.

Rhenanus, Johannes. *Harmoniae chymico-philosophicae, sive philosophorum antiquorum consentientium.* Frankfurt: Conrad Eifrid, 1625.

Ribémont, Bernard. "Le sage et juste roi Salomon dans la littérature médiévale." In *Le roi fontaine de justice: pouvoir justicier et pouvoir royal au Moyen Âge et à la Renaissance* 3, edited by Silvère Menegaldo and Bernard Ribémont, 29–54. Paris: Klincksieck, 2012.

Richard and Giraud. *Bibliothèque sacrée ou dictionnaire universel, historique, dogmatique, canonique, géographique et chronologique des sciences ecclésiastiques,* vol. 21. Paris: Boiste fils aîné, 1825.

Rießler, Paul. *Altjüdisches Schrifttum außerhalb der Bibel übersetzt und erläutert.* Augsburg: Benno Filser, 1928.

Rodriguez, Lorente and Juan Jose. "El sello de Salomón en un dirhem indedio de 'Abd al-Rahmân." *Al-Qantara* 12 (1991): 277–79.

Roisse, Philippe. "L'Histoire du Sceau de Salomon, ou de la *Coincidentia Oppositorum* dans les 'Livres de Plomb.'" *Al-Qantara* 24, no. 2 (2003): 360–407.

Ruska, Julius, ed. *Das Steinbuch des Aristoteles.* Heidelberg: Carl Winter, 1912.

——. "Ein dem Châlid ibn Jazîd zugeschriebene Verzeichnis der Propheten, Philosophen und Frauen, die sich mit Alchemie befaßten." *Der Islam* 18 (1929): 293–99.

Saif, Liana. "Magic in the Thirteenth Century: Albertus Magnus, Thomas Aquinas and Roger Bacon." In *The Arabic Influences on Early Modern Occult Philosophy.* London: Palgrave Macmillan, 2015.

Saintyves, Paul. *Les cinquante jugements de Salomon ou les arrêts des bons juges d'après la tradition populaire.* Paris: Domat–Montchrestien, n. d.

——. "Salomon, son pouvoir et ses livres magiques." *Revue des Traditions populaires* 9 (1913): 410–25.

Salzberger, Georg. *Die Salomo-Sage in der semitischen Literatur, ein Beitrag zur vergleichenden Sagenkunde.* Berlin-Nikolassee: Max Harrwitz, 1907.

Salomonis colloquium cum Regulo formicarum, Persarum de Salomone fabulae. Codex Pseudepigraphus Veteris Testamenti / Collectus, Castigatus,

Testimoniisque, Censuris et animadversionibus illustratus a Johan. Alberto Fabricio, SS. Theol. D. and Professore Publ. In *Gymnasio Hamburgensi*, vol. 1. Hamburg: Felginer, 1722.

Sanders, J. A. *The Psalms Scroll of Qumrân cave 11*. Oxford: Clarendon Press, 1965.

Särkö, Pekka. "Salomo und die Dämonen." *Studia Orientalia* 99 (2004): 305–22.

Scherer, Wilhelm. "Salomo und der Drache." *Zeitschrift für deutsches Altertum* 22 (1878): 19–24.

Schischmanova, L. *Légendes religieuses bulgares*. Paris: E. Leroux, 1896.

Schlumberger, G. *Mélanges d'archéologie byzantine,* I. Paris: E. Leroux, 1895.

Schmitt, Alfred. "Der gerittene Aristoteles. Ein Motiv misogyner Dichtung bei Matheus von Boulogne." In *Arbor amoena locis*, edited by Ewald Könsgen. Stuttgart: Franz Steiner, 1990.

Scurtu, V. "Cercetări folclorice în Ugocea românească (jud. satu mare)." *Anuarul Arhivei de Folklor* 6 (1942): 105*ff.*

Secret, François. "Gilbert Gaulmin et l'histoire comparée des religions." *Revue de l'histoire des religions* 177 (1970): 35–63.

Seymour, J. D. *Tales of King Solomon*. London: Oxford University Press, 1924.

Shah, Idries. *Oriental Magic*. London: Octagon Press, 1988.

Simenel, Romain. *L'origine est aux frontiers: les Aït Ba'amran, un exil en terre d'arganiers (Sud Maroc)*. Paris: CNRS éditions, 2014.

Singer, Isidore, ed. *The Jewish Encyclopedia*, vol 11. New York and London: Funk and Wagnalls Company, 1905.

Singer, Samuel, and Heinrichs von Neustadt. *Apollonius von Tyrland nach der Gothaer Handschrift, "Gottes Zukunft" und "Visio Philiberti" nach der Heidelberger Handschrift*. Berlin: Weidmannsche Buchhandlung, 1906.

Siouffi, Nicolas. "Les traditions des Yézidis." *Revue de l'Orient chrétien* 20 (1915–1917): 243–56.

———. *Sur la religion Soubbas ou des Sabéens*. Paris: Imprimerie nationale, 1880.

Sloane 3826, folio 2r–57. British Library, London.

Sokolov, Boris, and Jurij. "La recherche des bylines." *Revue des Études slaves* 12 (1932): 202–15.

Solzhenitsyn, Aleksandr. *Cancer Ward*.

Somnia Salomonis. Venice: M. Sessam and P. de Ravenis, 1516.

Sprenger, Jacques, and Henry Institoris. *Malleus maleficarum*. Spire: Peter Drach, 1487.

———. *The Malleus Maleficarum of Heinrich Kramer and James Sprenger*. New York: Dover, 1971.

Starcky, J. "Pseudo apocryphe de la grotte 4 de Qumrân." *Revue biblique* 23 (1966): 353–71.

Strugnell, J. "Notes on the Text and Transmission of the Apocryphal Psalms 151, 154 (= syr. II) and 155 (= syr. III)." *The Harvard Theological Review* 59, no. 3 (1966): 257–81.

Suidas. *Suidae lexicon,* 5 vol. Edited by Ada Adler. Leipzig: Teubner, 1928–1938.

Tabari. *Chronique,* vol. 1. Translated by Hermann Zotenberg. Paris: Imprimerie impériale, 1867.

Talmud de Jérusalem, vol. 6. Translated by Moïse Schwab. Paris: Maisonneuve & Cie, 1883.

Taloş, I. *Gândirea magico-religioasă la români*. Bucarest: 2001.

Tchéraz, M. *L'Orient inédit. Légendes et traditions arméniennes, grecques et turques*. Paris: E. Leroux, 1912.

Tendlau, A. M. *Das Buch der Sagen und legenden jüdischer Vorzeit*. Stuttgart: Cast'schen Buchhandlung, 1845.

Toledano, A. *La médecine du Talmud. Au commencement des sciences modernes*. Paris: In Press, 2014.

Torijano, Pablo A. *Solomo the Esoteric King: from King to Magus: Development of a Tradition*. Leiden: Brill, 2002.

Tractatus de throno Salomonis. Codex Cusanus 65, folio 1 vol. 8, manuscrit de l'hôpital de Cues.

Venzlaff, Helga. *Al-Hudhud: Eine Untersuchung zur kulturgeschichtlichen Bedeutung des Wiedehopfs im Islam*. Frankfurt: M. Peter Lang, 1994.

Véronèse, Julien. *L'Almandal et l'Almadel latins au Moyen Âge*. Florence and Sismel: Edizioni del Galluzo, 2012.

———. *L'Ars notoria au Moyen Âge et à l'époque moderne. Étude d'une tradition de magie théurgique (XIIᵉ–XVIIᵉ siècle),* 2 vol. Edited by Colette Beaune. Université Paris X – Nanterre, 2004. www.univ-orleans.fr/polen/cesfima /julien-veronese.

———. "La transmission groupée des textes de 'magie salomonienne' de l'Antiquité au Moyen Âge. Bilan historiographique, inconnues et pistes de recherché." In *L'Antiquité tardive dans les collections médiévales: textes et représentations, VIᵉ-XIVᵉ siècle,* edited by S. Gioanni and B. Grévin, 193–223. Rome: EFR, 2008.

———. "Virgilius Hispanus, philosophe et magicien." In *Les métamorphoses de Virgile. Réception de la figure de l'Auctor: Antiquité, Moyen Âge, Temps modernes,* edited by J. L. Haquette and K. Ueltschi. Paris: Champion, 2018.

Vescovini, Graziela Federici. *Le Moyen Âge magique. La magie entre religion et science aux XIIIᵉ et XIVᵉ siècles.* Paris: Vrin, 2011.

Viteau, Joseph, ed. *Les Psaumes de Salomon, introduction, texte grec et traduction, avec les principales variantes de la version syriaque par François Martin.* Paris: Letouzey et Ané, 1911.

Vogt, Friedrich. *Die Deutschen Dichtungen von Salomon und markolf.* Halle: Niemeyer, 1880.

Waag, A. *Kleinere deutsche Gedichte des XI. und XII. Jahrhunderts.* Halle a. Saale: Niemeyer, 1890.

Wagenseil, Johann Christoph. *Tela ignea Satanae, noc est: arcani, & horribiles Judæorum adversus Christvm Devm & Christianam religione Libri.* Altdorf: Schönerstædt, 1681.

Warnhagen, Hermann. *Ein indisches Märchen auf seiner Wanderung.* Berlin: Weidmann, 1882.

Weber, E. "La Ville de cuivre, une ville d'al-Andalus." *Al-andalus* 6 (1989): 43*ff.,* 51–54.

Weil, Arthur. *Contes et légendes d'Israël.* Paris: Nathan, 1927.

Weil, G. *Biblische Legenden der Muselmänner, aus arabischen Quellen zusammengetragen und mit jüdischen Sagen verglichen.* Frankfurt am Main: Literarische Anstalt, 1845.

Wessely, Karl. *Zauberpapyri von Paris und London.*Vienna: Tempsky, 1888.

Winkler, Hans A. *Salomo und die Karīna eine orientalische Legende von der Bezwingung einer Kindbettdämonin durch einen heiligen Helden.* Stuttgart: W. Kohlhammer, 1931.

Wright, Robert B. *The Psalms of Solomon: A Critical Edition of the Greek Text.* New York: T&T Clark, 2007.

Wünsche, K. A. *Midrasch Bemidbar rabba, die allegorische Auslegung des vierten Buches Mose.* Leipzig: Otto Schulze, 1885.

Wüstenfeld, F., ed. *Muʿdjam al-buldān* [Geographical Dictionary], 6 vol. Leipzig: Brockhaus, 1866–1873.

Zauberpapyri von Paris und London. Vienna: Tempsky, 1888.

Zonaras, Jean. *Chroniqves ov Annales de Iean Zonare.* Translated by Millet de Saint-Amour. Lyon: Macé Bonhome, 1560.

Zosime de Panopolis. *La Chimie au Moyen Âge,* vol. 2. L'alchimie syriaque. Translated by M. Berthelot. París: 1893.

Zwinger, Johann. *Tractatus theologicus de rege Salomonis peccante.* Basel: Joh. Philipp Richter, 1696.

Index

Page numbers referring to illustrations are in *italic* type.

BOOKS OF RELATED INTEREST

Dictionary of Ancient Magic Words and Spells
From Abraxas to Zoar
by Claude Lecouteux

**Encyclopedia of Norse and Germanic Folklore,
Mythology, and Magic**
by Claude Lecouteux

Tales of Witchcraft and Wonder
The Venomous Maiden and Other Stories of the Supernatural
by Claude Lecouteux and Corinne Lecouteux

Mysteries of the Werewolf
Shapeshifting, Magic, and Protection
by Claude Lecouteux

Traditional Magic Spells for Protection and Healing
by Claude Lecouteux

The Tradition of Household Spirits
Ancestral Lore and Practices
by Claude Lecouteux

The Pagan Book of the Dead
Ancestral Visions of the Afterlife and Other Worlds
by Claude Lecouteux

Dictionary of Gypsy Mythology
Charms, Rites, and Magical Traditions of the Roma
by Claude Lecouteux

INNER TRADITIONS • BEAR & COMPANY
P.O. Box 388
Rochester, VT 05767
1-800-246-8648
www.InnerTraditions.com

Or contact your local bookseller